T0137269

Agent-Based Business Process Simulation

Emilio Sulis • Kuldar Taveter

Agent-Based Business Process Simulation

A Primer with Applications and Examples

 Springer

Emilio Sulis
Department of Computer Science
University of Torino
Torino, Italy

Kuldar Taveter
Institute of Computer Science
University of Tartu
Tartu, Estonia

ISBN 978-3-030-98818-0   ISBN 978-3-030-98816-6   (eBook)
https://doi.org/10.1007/978-3-030-98816-6

This Springer imprint is published by the registered company Springer Nature Switzerland AG
The registered company address is: Gewerbestrasse 11, 6330 Cham, Switzerland

to Manuela, Beatrice, Giorgia, Jacopo - Emilio

to my family - Kuldar

Foreword by Pietro Terna

Through my research, I pioneered the development of agent-based modeling (ABM) in the 1990s, my first article in the field being in 1993. Consequently, I follow with great interest the development of applications of agent-based techniques in new fields, as is the case with this significant book linking these techniques to business process modeling.

A solid analysis in business process modeling requires, first of all, the ability to understand the world to which the analysis applies: the surest way to understand a world is to reconstruct it artificially. Let me report here as a pillar the phrase of the famous Feynman last blackboard:[1] "What I cannot create I do not understand." With the simulation agent-based, we create worlds and create them in a very realistic way, with all their imperfections and inconsistencies.

In similar environments, we can experiment with the effects of the reengineering choices typical of business process modeling (BPM) solutions, considering that if the new sequences and adaptations work in the simulation, they could work in reality. On the contrary, if they fail to succeed in the simulation, it is wise to change or abandon them.

Joining BPM and ABM is the primary goal of this book. I highly appreciate the choice of NetLogo as the tool for that operation. NetLogo is both a rigorous and highly popular tool for agent-based simulation. On the home page, we read that: "It is used by many hundreds of thousands of students, teachers, and researchers worldwide." Its language has roots in Lisp, with the capability of prefixed operators to know perfectly the position and number of the operands, without the need of the annoying parentheses of Lisp. Effectively, parentheses in NetLogo are required only when the number of the operands is unknown.

This volume is a primer (with detailed introductory pages to BPM, ABM, and NetLogo) but also moves toward real-life applications and opens a path to advanced techniques like genetic algorithms. We can consider genetic algorithms as tools for the advanced search of complex solutions in artificial intelligence problems

---

[1] https://blackboardlist.com/feynman/.

when the space of the solutions is enormous. We can also view them to explore the innovative and challenging territories of the inverse generative social science, where we look for models to produce the structures under investigation.

With theoretical insights and practical examples, the book of Emilio Sulis and Kuldar Taveter represents both a manual and a research book, which deserves great attention and success.

Torino, Italy   Pietro Terna
February 2022

Foreword by Marlon Dumas

Business process management (BPM) is a well-established discipline to analyze and improve the way work is performed in an organization. BPM is supported by a rich set of methods and tools, including process modeling, process simulation, and process mining, among others.

Among this rich set of methods and tools, process simulation stands out as a versatile approach to analyze business processes in order to answer what-if questions. In the field of process simulation, a process is seen as a discrete event system, which evolves according to a set of mechanisms. A crucial question is: How to capture these mechanisms? The agent-oriented approach proposed in this book provides a vision toward the application of agent-oriented concepts in the field of BPM in general and process simulation in particular. This vision is centered on the behaviors, interactions, and knowledge of autonomous proactive, reactive, and social entities, called agents.

Throughout this book, Sulis and Taveter thoroughly describe the process analysis capabilities offered by agent-based modeling and simulation approaches. The authors describe the agent-oriented paradigm and its multiple interpretations in different research communities, including the multi-agent systems (MAS) community and the agent-based modeling (ABM) community. The practical value of the book is further enhanced by putting ABM in the context of modeling organizational goals and providing explicit support for decision-making activities.

This exploratory book is full of practical examples that the reader can try out by using freely accessible ABM tools, particularly NetLogo. These examples enable an avid reader to get a full grasp of the key concepts in the book by running agent-based simulations, performing scenario analysis, and applying AI techniques. The book also makes a considerable effort to introduce relevant formalisms and notations, such as Petri nets and BPMN, in order to facilitate communication between different stakeholders. The book also discusses case studies as well as directions for further research and development such as integration with georeferencing technologies, machine learning methods, algorithmic search, and reinforcement learning.

In conclusion, I am happy to see this new attempt of merging ABM with goal modeling and decision support to analyze organizations. The book helps raise awareness about the importance of process analysis, facilitates the understanding of the BPM discipline, and explores it in a wide spectrum of application areas starting from the what-if analysis and digital twins and concluding with advanced topics such as process mining and AI-driven process optimization techniques.

Tartu, Estonia   Marlon Dumas
February 2022

Preface

The main subject of the book is "agent-based business process simulation," a topic that brings together three different perspectives. First of all, the book is concerned with organizational management by means of business process modeling. This entails modeling and analyzing the goals of an organization and the activities to be performed to achieve the goals. Another important aspect of analyzing business processes is supporting decisions to be made by stakeholders within the processes. This aspect is concerned with supporting decisions to be made by organizations of different kinds: from governments to companies, corporations, and nongovernmental organizations.

The second perspective addressed by this book is simulation as a way of investigating the behavior of current and future activities of a business process mainly by means of scenario analysis. The book discusses both a running example and different other models to help the readers understand how the evolution of a business process can be supported by simulation so that the daily work of the stakeholders would be improved.

Third, we exploit the conceptual modeling metaphor of *agents* to address interactions within complex sociotechnical systems and improve their understandability for stakeholders. We also utilize the notion of *agent* from artificial intelligence as a concept on which are based many useful algorithms and techniques of business process simulation and management.

In our view, agent-based modeling and simulation is a way to capture the behavior of complex institutions and sociotechnical systems. Agent-based simulation captures the behavior of a system in a bottom-up manner. The behavioral rules of individual component "agents" are defined and then used to create an agent-based model. The purpose of the model is to reproduce the behavior of the complete system as a whole. The result is a bottom-up approach to modeling and simulation that allows organizations to convert their knowledge of individual behaviors into an understanding of the overall system-level behavior. Our book combines this kind of bottom-up modeling with a top-down approach of agent-oriented modeling that proceeds from modeling the goals, quality goals, and key performance indicators of an organization for decision support. Organizations rendered by complementary bottom-up and top-down models can discover which combinations of individual-level actions and influences bring about positive results and which ones have negative consequences. Organizations can utilize such models as laboratories for exploring the range of outcomes that can be expected from systems in case of different decisions to be made.

The models described in the book are publicly available on the companion website at the following address: http://www.bpmagents.org. Further in this book, we simply refer to this website as "the web repository." All supplementary material is provided under the Creative Commons CC-BY license. You may copy, distribute, display, and perform this work and make derivative works and remixes based on it, provided that you give the book authors credits for their work.

Torino, Italy   Emilio Sulis
Tartu, Estonia   Kuldar Taveter
February 2022

Acknowledgments

This book draws from the work of many researchers who provided suggestions, inspiration, moments of confrontation, and in-depth analysis with respect to the specific parts of their competence. The actual contents of the book are entirely our responsibility, but we must thank all the people who, consciously or unconsciously, have been essential, and without whom a book like this would never exist.

A special thanks goes to Pietro Terna, who has pushed forward a non-mainstream vision of scientific research, in favor of interdisciplinarity and dissemination of knowledge. An important role was also played by the projects carried out by the Computer Science Department of the University of Turin. First of all, thanks to Guido Boella with his strength and design capacity, and to Antonio Di Leva, with his experience in the field of process analysis and simulations. Thanks also to several colleagues from the University of Turin, including Luigi Di Caro, Matteo Baldoni, Roberto Micalizio, Sara Capecchi, Lavinia Tagliabue, Barbara Demo, Stefano Tedeschi, Ilaria Angela Amantea, and master students Eugenio Liso and Alessandro Marino.

Profitable hints were also derived from the discussions with the researchers Chiara Di Francescomarino, Chiara Ghidini, Fabrizio Maria Maggi, Carlos Fernandez-Llatas, and Niels Martin. Valuable suggestions for the direction of the work also come from the discussions during a visiting period at the School of Computing and Information Systems, Faculty of Engineering and Information Technology, at the University of Melbourne. Thanks to Marcello La Rosa, Adriano Augusto, Farbod Taymouri, Abel Armas Cervantes, Artem Polyvyanyy, and Anna Kalenkova.

Last but not least, the authors of the book have special thanks for the valuable contribution of Leon Sterling with his suggestions in the early stages of the work.

Emilio Sulis's research work in this publication has been partially funded by the "Circular Health for Industry" project under the call "Artificial Intelligence, man and society" of "Compagnia di San Paolo" of Torino, by the research grant "Call for the Internationalization of Research" from Ateneo di Torino and "Compagnia di San Paolo" of Torino, by the "CANP - CAsa Nel Parco" project of Regione Piemonte – POR FESR-PIEMONTE 2014–2020.

Kuldar Taveter's research work has been partially funded by the IT Academy program of the European Social Fund.

Contents

Acronyms

ABBPS	Agent-based business process simulation
ABM	Agent-based modeling
ABMS	Agent-based modeling and simulation
ABOS	Agent-based organizational simulation
ACE	Agent-based computational economic
AI	Artificial intelligence
AOM	Agent-oriented modeling
AOSE	Agent-oriented software engineering
BDI	Belief-desire-intention
BIM	Business information modeling
BPM	Business process management
BPMN	Business Process Modeling Notation
BPMS	Business process management system
BPR	Business process re-engineering
BSC	Balanced scorecard
CAS	Complex adaptive system
CAS	Clustering coefficient
CC	Conformance checking
CMMN	Case Management Model and Notation
CRMS	Customer relationship management systems
CSV	Comma-separated value
DES	Discrete-event simulation
DFG	Direct follower graph
DMN	Decision Model and Notation
DTDT	Door-to-doctor time
EBM	Equation-based modeling
ED	Emergency department
EDPC	Event-driven process chain
EIS	Enterprise Information System
ERP	Enterprise resource planning
ESRI	Environmental Systems Research Institute

FAD	Functional allocation diagram
FOSS	Free and open-source software
GIS	Geographic information system
GUI	Graphical user interface
HIS	Hospital information system
HS	Human resources
IBM	Individual-based modeling
ICT	Information and communication technology
IDE	Integrated development environment
IDEF3	Integrated DEFinition for Process Description Capture Method
IS	Information system
IoMT	Internet of Medical Things
IoT	Internet of things
IT	Information technology
KISS	Keep It Simple, Stupid
MAS	Multi-agent system
ML	Machine learning
MRP	Management resource planning
ODD	Overview, Design Concepts, and Details
OFAT	One-Factor-At-a-Time
OMG	Object Management Group
PAIS	Process-Aware Information System
PEAS	Performance, Environment, Actuators, Sensors
PM	Process mining
PN	Petri net
PNML	Petri Net Markup Language
RL	Reinforcement learning
RPA	Robotic process automation
SD	System dynamics
SIR	Susceptible Infected Recovered
SLA	Service-level agreement
SNA	Social network analysis
TVM	Ticket vending machines
UML	Unified Modeling Language
XES	eXtensible Event Stream
WMS	Workflow management system

Part I
Introduction and Background

Chapter 1
Introducing Agent-Based Simulation for the Business Processes

Abstract This chapter provides an overview of agent-based modeling and simulation as applied to the analysis of organizations and their business processes. We introduce the topic that lies at the intersection of the three research areas of computational simulation, business process management, and agent-oriented analysis for simulation-based decision support. We particularly emphasize the interest in modeling and simulation with an agent-oriented perspective. Against this background knowledge, this chapter introduces the conceptual framework and contents of this book.

1.1 Motivation

There are many motivations for this work, but all of them can be traced to the profound recent changes impacting the world of work and organizations. Nowadays, business processes are increasingly interesting because of their impact on business performance. New technologies can refine business processes, having major repercussions on daily work, productivity, and quality improvement. On the one hand, recent relevant topics in organizational studies concern many different research areas. In recent years, the discipline focused on process-oriented approaches, which aims to extract knowledge about organization's business processes based on event data recorded in business information systems. On the other hand, modeling and simulation are typical methodologies adopted in organizational studies. Research is increasingly confronted with digitization and the need to investigate productivity improvements, automation, normative compliance, and optimization, including through the adoption of industry standards. These new challenges also require the exploration of innovative research practices.

The main motivation for this book is to systematize and explore an agent-oriented approach in the business and management research. Specifically, we propose the adoption of agent-based business process modeling and simulation to study the intersection between the disciplines of management, organizational modeling, and computational simulation. The main idea is to consider an agent-oriented perspective of computational simulation in addition to more standard approaches,

© Springer Nature Switzerland AG 2022
E. Sulis, K. Taveter, *Agent-Based Business Process Simulation*,
https://doi.org/10.1007/978-3-030-98816-6_1

Fig. 1.1 The main keywords and topics including simulation, business process management, and agent in agent-based business process simulation, with the intersection of three research areas

such as discrete-event simulation (DES) and system dynamics (SD). The broader context of application includes data science research, risk management, Internet-of-things, smart cities, and so on.

Research Trends To introduce the topics of the book, we propose an analysis which covers the terms included by the titles of research papers indexed on the Google Scholar database by searching for the following terms: agent-based, business process, and simulation. Figure 1.1 summarizes in a word cloud the main topics of interest that result as frequently used terms in recent research papers.

The adoption of an agent-oriented approach to business processes offers three major opportunities: providing simulation-based decision-support, performing holistic business process modeling, and utilizing the modeling abstraction of agent. We will next dwell on each of these opportunities because they also constitute some reasons for writing this book.

First, business process analysis and simulation are becoming more accessible and more easily understandable for a wider audience. More recently, a growing interest in business process analysis has focused on the adoption of innovative information systems that can track business activities. A lexical note: in this book, we will use interchangeably the terms *task* and *activity*, although the Object Management

Group (OMG)[1] uses mainly the term *task*. A common practice in some areas of business organization research considers to employ the term *task* for atomic operations and the term *activity* for a set of tasks. Alternatively, also the term *action* is used to denote atomic operations. As this is not a general rule, here, we prefer to adopt both terms that have a similar meaning without distinguishing between them. From the business process perspective, the focus has shifted to the ability to create algorithms that can discover sequences of business activities from logs of real events, as is further explained in Sect. 7.1. The Process Mining Manifesto [18] is a relevant starting point to address this kind of approaches. Against this background, simulation efforts have so far been primarily concerned with visualizing business processes based on business process models rather than with systematic ways of providing simulation-based decision support. In this context, employing an agent-oriented approach is highly relevant and provides a better understanding of concepts from management studies.

A second reason lies in the modeling perspective. For business process management, modeling is a necessary and preliminary step that can capture and visualize the flow of activities of a company, governmental institution, non-governmental organization, or an international organization. Typical business process management approaches have adopted discrete event simulation, with processes modeled using formal languages. This kind of formal approach requires the scrupulous modeling of each activity included by the business process from the start event until the end event of the process. Differently, agent-oriented approach focuses on the business process as a whole rather its individual constituent activities. Agent-oriented approach includes stochastic simulation that enables to mimic business activities in an artificial context very similar to the real situation. In addition, we study how to simulate the knowledge and resources of an organization and their utilization by different business activities. Our overall goal here is to improve the understanding of the workflow, as well as perform scenario analysis for future changes by simulating possible further improvements in the current business process.

Third, we strongly believe in the relevance of a method of analysis involving the idea of *agent*, which is a classical computer science term. This is a very powerful concept, but has recently been somewhat neglected after its decade-long heyday in the early 2000s, at the previous hype of artificial intelligence (AI) studies. Despite that, the agent concept remains one of the most popular notions in computer science, as can be seen from Google Trends detailed in Fig. 1.2. In particular, many techniques for agent-based simulation have been developed, such as search algorithms to generate a solution that explores the problem space, or a path from the initial state, as well as learning approaches like reinforcement learning. From the modeling perspective, agent is a powerful abstraction that helps capture and represent organizational and psychological issues, in addition to technical ones. From the organizational perspective, the notion of agent helps model and simulate how a complex business process delivers the product or service needed by the

---

[1] https://www.omg.org/.

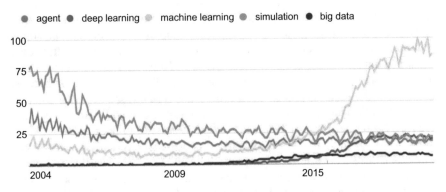

Fig. 1.2 Trends of topics in computer science based on the popularity of specific searches in Google Trends

customers. For example, the second author has participated in a research and development project, where a complex business process of business-to-business electronic commerce was modelled and simulated in an agent-oriented way. From the psychological perspective, the modeling abstraction of agent helps capture how humans behave within a complex sociotechnical system. For example, Boeing has funded research of designing and developing an agent-based simulation of how psychological profiles of airline dispatchers affect their behaviors within an Airline Operations Control Center. By this book, we aim to demonstrate how agent-oriented solutions can be very intuitive, easy to apply, and easy to understand for stakeholders such as practitioners or professionals, business analysts, and project managers.

Finally, another motivation for writing this book is our interest in bringing together for educational purposes the major findings of the three motivations outlined above. In our opinion, there is a need to disseminate current findings in management science to increase the popularity of terms, concepts, ideas, and algorithms of business process analysis, modeling, and simulation. Moreover, we believe that there is an opportunity to familiarize newcomers and professionals in areas other than computer science by adopting an agent-oriented approach to business process modeling and simulation. In this regard, this book proposes the adoption of an easy-to-use free and open-source software (FOSS) platform for developing multi-agent systems—the NetLogo tool. This is currently one of the most popular agent simulation platforms, which has been widely adopted in different disciplines due to its versatility and usability.

In the following section, we will introduce a general framework describing how the proposed agent-oriented modeling and simulation approach can be applied to business process analysis and simulation.

1.2   A General Framework

We introduce *agent-based business process simulation* (ABBPS) by outlining a general framework and practical applications to cope with real problems. Let us start from a realistic and dynamic representation of an actual system (AS) in an organization dealing with, for example, an order-to-cash process or a claims handling process. The building of this kind of model requires the construction of the simulated structure derived from the AS that would employ both (i) the analysis of the activities by all the operators of the AS and (ii) the event logs that reflect the operations of the AS. This step is close to how an initial analysis for developing a business process model is performed. The difference is that here we adopt an agent-based perspective by considering performers of the activities as active agents. New instances of orders or claims arriving into the process flow can be rendered as passive objects having attributes and behaviors that can be invoked by agents. In other terms, active agents perceive events originating in their environment, reason, and perform actions affecting their environment. At the same time, objects are passive entities without such capabilities that can be just manipulated by agents by, for example, invoking their methods.

The standard approach adopted in this book is to represent each AS using the Business Process Modeling Notation (BPMN) [11]. Using the business process models defined in BPMN, in Part II, we study the adoption of an agent-oriented approach considering both the perspective of software engineering (Chap. 5) and an agent-based simulation (Chap. 6).

In an agent-oriented approach, the focus is on individual units that of which the model consists. Broadly speaking, such individual units are divided into agents and objects. Agents are active entities, such as humans, organizations or organizational units, and robots. Objects are passive entities, such as raw materials, orders, claims, and software systems. Objects are manipulated by agents. Agent-oriented approaches emphasize the relationships between the individual parts—agents and objects—of the model. Consequently, the core of the simulation effort is capturing the interactions between agents at the micro-level that create consequences at the macro-level. Such consequences constitute emergent behavior of a multi-agent system. In a business-oriented analysis, a detailed model can typically simulate the real world at scale or use dimensions very close to the real world [9]. For such systems, requirements are elicited by applying several methods, such as interviews, document analysis, as well as mining activity logs. An agent-based business process model can be validated against the requirements by (i) interviews and (ii) checking the compliance of the simulation output with the logs of real business events, collected from the operation of the AS by applying mining techniques. After modeling the business process, an ABM of the business process is implemented (*ABM construction* in Fig. 1.3). Here there are two goals: (i) that of representing the effects of the changes to stakeholders and (ii) that of verifying the new records of the simulated system by comparing them with the previous ones. If the BPM analysis succeeds in improving the AS, we can try to apply them; if not, we have to repeat the whole process, looking for errors.

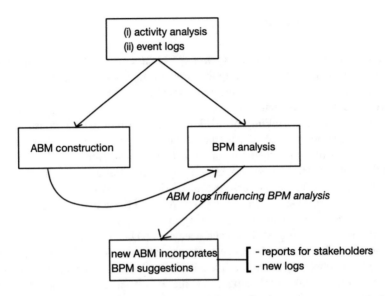

Fig. 1.3 The interactions between agent-based modeling and business process management

1.3 Simulation Tool Adopted in the Book

Simulation platforms are increasingly adopted in research, industry, services, and public administration. Nowadays, many simulation applications are proprietary software systems, which have often been integrated into other tools already used by organizations, such as enterprise resource planning (ERP) systems. In addition, many simulation applications take their input in international standard modeling languages, such as BPMN by OMG. To investigate more advanced research topics, such as optimization, planning, or reasoning, there are specific tools for each topic by both academia and industry available for such topics. Among them, many tools for computational simulation have been recently developed [1, 5, 14]. In most cases, they are proprietary software simulation platforms. Some of them include free versions for self-education purposes, as is the case with the leading proprietary simulation tool AnyLogic that has the corresponding free version called Personal Learning Edition [2]. In many cases, companies offer a free trial period, such as in the case of Arena [3] and iGrafx Process [6], or a personalized demo as in the case of Simul8 [16]. Some simulation tools are free, such as the web-based discrete-event Business Process Simulator BIMP [4, 7]. Other tools provide an open-source version, which enables to investigate multi-agent systems and agent-based simulations, as is described in Sect. 6.2.6. This book aims to provide practical suggestions for analyzing issues in business processes of an organization, to address management concerns. Considering this, we are mostly interested in exploiting open-source tools that have a certain degree of maturity and are easy to learn and adopt for immediate use. This is the case with NetLogo, the platform promoted and used in this book for agent-based business process simulation.

Why NetLogo?

A very typical tool for agent-based simulation is NetLogo,[2] which is currently used all over the world for several reasons. One reason for its success is the feature of animation that also includes optional graphical controls and displays [12]. Another success factor is the inclusion of its own programming language, which is easier to use than Java or C. NetLogo reflects its heritage as an educational tool, since its primary design goal has clearly been ease of use. Its programming language includes many high-level structures and primitives that greatly reduce programming effort and is complemented by extensive documentation. The language contains many but not all of the control and structuring capabilities of a standard programming language. One can also clearly see that NetLogo has been designed with a specific type of model in mind, consisting of mobile agents acting simultaneously on a grid space with behaviors dominated by local interactions on short timescales. The same feature is also the source of perhaps the biggest drawback of NetLogo: its lack of support for explicit exchange of messages between the agents. However, this missing feature can be compensated by other means in NetLogo. We can conclude that NetLogo is by far the most user-friendly tool for agent-based simulation in its look and documentation [12]. In comparison with other platforms, such as RePast [10], SWARM [8], or the new and promising GAMA platform [17], NetLogo is the most suitable one for educational projects in simulation mostly because of its programming language for coding agent-based simulation models. Therefore, it is easy and fast to build a model in NetLogo, as it is not necessary to have good skills in object-oriented programming languages like Java or C#, which is the case with the powerful simulation tool RePast. Compared to the SWARM platform, NetLogo can be easily configured and can be set up to run a model in just a few minutes [13]. NetLogo is therefore a very lightweight platform but also provides a set of extensions [15]. Moreover, NetLogo provides a free extension API for any programmer that may need to extend the functionalities of the platform. As is described in Sect. 9.3, we exploit this option to automatically import event logs. In addition, NetLogo includes tools for fast building a user-friendly graphical unit interface (GUI) using the available set of user interface components, such as buttons, sliders, text boxes, and so forth.

To summarize, some distinguishing features of NetLogo are:

- the capability of managing a collection of instances of a class of agents (traditionally named *turtles* as an inheritance from the Logo[3] language);[4]
- direct graphical representation of the agents' world;

---

[2] https://ccl.northwestern.edu/netlogo/.

[3] https://el.media.mit.edu/logo-foundation/.

[4] Due to the original purpose of Logo to program robots based on Grey Walters tortoises or turtles, as is explained at https://www.youtube.com/watch?v=lLULRlmXkKo (personal communication

- the ask construct, to execute the agents' procedures (each agent will take its turn in a random order);
- its openness, which enables to write general-purpose code with NetLogo, as well as connect programs written in NetLogo to those developed in R or Python, or add new extensions written in Java or Scala.

A NetLogo model can also take advantage of NetLogo's 3D graphical support. As we will see in the rest of the book, this allows, for example, to build in one step both the environment and the graph representing the agents' movements within it. This tool will be introduced in Chap. 4.

1.4   Examples and Applications

The book is self-contained, as it enables to learn how to use the tool and apply it in a practical way to the topic of business processes within or between organizations. For example, the book describes the agent-based models and simulations of business processes in different areas, e.g., ticket selling machine simulation; hospital emergency department; operations and queues; XES, BPMN, and Petri net import; reinforcement learning and genetic algorithms; process extraction and analysis; and network analysis.

Each program is presented with different granularity, mostly by describing the salient parts of the code, the main passages of the programming strategies, the output area of the program, and the diagrams or graphs of the results. To better distinguish the code in the book, we have adopted different character types and indentation, as in the following "hello world" example:

```
to greeting
    ask turtles [ print "Hello World" ]
end
```

All the applications discussed in the book and several other resources are freely available online at http://www.bpmagents.org.

1.5   Content Structure

The book starts with two introductory chapters in Part I. Chapter 2 provides a brief introduction to main BPM concepts. By introducing the business process lifecycle, this chapter describes the analysis of an organization by means of modeling and simulation, business process performance indicators, and recent efforts toward

---

with Joe Becker, co-founder of the Unicode project, who was a MIT student when Seymour Papert was developing Logo).

automatic extraction of information from event data. Chapter 3 offers a summary of the concept of agent and the studies concerning agent-based approaches that involve business process analysis and management studies.

Part II of the book introduces the NetLogo tool adopted in the book in Chap. 4. After that, Chap. 5 focuses on agent-oriented modeling as a problem domain analysis and design approach for creating decision-support systems based on agent-based simulations. This is followed by Chap. 6 that further describes the topic of agent-based modeling and simulation for business process analysis.

Part III proposes a wide spectrum of examples and practical applications of agent-based simulation of business processes. Chapter 7 reviews some BPM applications by introducing programs enabling to manage models represented in standard formats, such as BPMN and agent-based applications utilizing Petri nets. Section 8 describes a number of case studies from different areas, providing an idea of several practical applications. Finally, Chap. 9 introduces some exploratory examples of process mining topics and agent-based simulation with process discovery, conformance checking, and the eXtensible Event Stream standard language.

References

1. Allan, R.J., et al.: Survey of Agent Based Modelling and Simulation Tools. Science & Technology Facilities Council, New York (2010)
2. AnyLogic: Simulation modeling software tools & solutions. http://www.anylogic.com. Accessed 21 Jan 2022
3. Arena simulation software. https://www.rockwellautomation.com/it-it/products/software/arena-simulation.html. Accessed 21 Jan 2022
4. Bimp simulator. http://bimp.cs.ut.ee/simulator. Accessed 21 June 2020
5. Gajsek, B., Marolt, J., Rupnik, B., Lerher, T., Sternad, M.: Using maturity model and discrete-event simulation for industry 4.0 implementation. Int. J. Simul. Model. **18**(3), 488–499 (2019). https://doi.org/10.2507/IJSIMM18(3)489
6. iGrafx process. https://www.igrafx.com/products/process/. Accessed 21 Jan 2022
7. Kärgenberg, V.: Online Business Process Model Simulator. Ph.D. Thesis, University of Tartu (2012)
8. Minar, N., Burkhart, R., Langton, C., Askenazi, M., et al.: The swarm simulation system: a toolkit for building multi-agent simulations (1996)
9. North, M., Macal, C.: Managing Business Complexity: Discovering Strategic Solutions With Agent-Based Modeling and Simulation. Oxford University Press, Oxford (2007). https://doi.org/10.1093/acprof:oso/9780195172119.001.0001
10. North, M.J., Collier, N.T., Ozik, J., Tatara, E.R., Macal, C.M., Bragen, M., Sydelko, P.: Complex adaptive systems modeling with repast simphony. Complex Adapt. Syst. Model. **1**(1), 1–26 (2013). https://doi.org/10.1186/2194-3206-1-3
11. Object Management Group (OMG): Business Process Model and Notation (BPMN), Version 2.0.2. https://www.omg.org/spec/BPMN/2.0.2/PDF (2014). Accessed 30 April 2021
12. Railsback, S.F., Lytinen, S.L., Jackson, S.K.: Agent-based simulation platforms: review and development recommendations. Simulation **82**(9), 609–623 (2006). https://doi.org/10.1177/0037549706073695
13. Robertson, D.: Agent-based modeling toolkits NetLogo, repast, and swarm. Acad. Manag. Learn. Educ. **4**, 524–527 (2005). https://doi.org/10.5465/AMLE.2005.19086798

14. Rosenthal, K., Ternes, B., Strecker, S.: Business process simulation on procedural graphical process models. Bus. Inform. Syst. Eng. **63**, 569–602 (2021). https://doi.org/10.1007/s12599-021-00690-3
15. Salgado, M., Gilbert, N.: Agent Based Modelling, pp. 247–265. Brill Sense (2013). https://doi.org/10.1007/978-94-6209-404-8_12
16. Simul8. https://www.simul8.com. Accessed 21 Jan 2022
17. Taillandier, P., Gaudou, B., Grignard, A., Huynh, Q.N., Marilleau, N., Caillou, P., Philippon, D., Drogoul, A.: Building, composing and experimenting complex spatial models with the GAMA platform. GeoInformatica **23**(2), 299–322 (2019). https://doi.org/10.1007/s10707-018-00339-6
18. van der Aalst, W.M.P., Adriansyah, A., De Medeiros, A.K.A., Arcieri, F., Baier, T., Blickle, T., Bose, J.C., Van Den Brand, P., Brandtjen, R., Buijs, J., et al.: Process mining manifesto. In: International conference on business process management, pp. 169–194. Springer (2011)

Chapter 2
The Analysis of Business Processes

Abstract The discipline of Business Process Management is concerned with analyzing how an organization operates, beginning with activity modeling and ending with business process simulation. This chapter introduces the main concepts of the discipline, beginning with the business process lifecycle, examining how business processes are represented, managed, studied, and improved. We describe concepts related to the organizations involved in business processes, including measures to evaluate the performance characteristics of processes, i.e., time, quality, and cost. Recent advances in the discipline involve the exploitation of information system event logs, as well as the simulation of system operation from the *digital twin* perspective.

2.1 Business Process Analysis

2.1.1 The Boundaries of the Discipline

Studies of organizations are particularly relevant because of their great impact on the functioning of economic and social systems. While the earliest analyses emerged in the context of the industrial revolution of the nineteenth century [65], the spread of computers and the adoption of the Internet in the last years of the twentieth century led to a large-scale application of highly innovative tools and techniques. This kind of Fourth Industrial Revolution, also called Industry 4.0 [28], is rooted in the technological shift that pushes forward a renewed focus on the management perspective, largely concerned with understanding business processes, with the ultimate goal of improving quality, decreasing costs, and increasing revenues.

In this context, it is relevant to introduce the main topics of the BPM discipline, focusing more on concepts such as business analysis, performance metrics, and business process simulation. Any management project typically includes a modeling effort to represent the flow of the organization's major tasks that are performed by the workers of the organization. In conjunction with modeling, additional opportunities are offered by recent advances in computational simulation combined with the analysis of data consisting of process logs. With the new means, a

© Springer Nature Switzerland AG 2022
E. Sulis, K. Taveter, *Agent-Based Business Process Simulation*,
https://doi.org/10.1007/978-3-030-98816-6_2

company can easily investigate scenario analysis, planning, and decision-making, including decision support in a critical setting, as is described in [52]. Managers are increasingly exploring different topics related to Industry 4.0, digital twins, and smart manufacturing [41]. These days, the focus is mainly on activities such as monitoring, forecasting, and optimizing business processes [63]. Recently, a comprehensive definition describes BPM as: "The art and science of how work should be performed in an organization in order to ensure consistent outputs to take advantage of improvement opportunities, such as reducing costs, lead times, or error rates" [20].

2.1.2 What Does "Business Process" Mean?

The focus of organization studies has shifted more and more to the concept of *business process*. The Workflow Management Coalition provided a classic definition of the concept in the late 1990s: "A set of one or more linked procedures or activities which collectively realize a business objective or policy goal, normally within the context of an organizational structure defining functional roles and relationships" [64]. This definition is still very relevant today because, as we will show in Chap. 5, each business process has its main goal or purpose that can be elaborated into subgoals. Also, goals of business processes are achieved by performers of different organizational roles. More recently, one of the most widely adopted definitions of a business process states that a business process is "a collection of inter-related events, activities and decision points that involve a number of actors and objects, and that collectively lead to an outcome that is of value to at least one customer" [20].

The beginning of each instance of a business process corresponds to the occurrence of an event, which usually initiates many different activities within an organization. To provide three practical examples, the starting point may be the arrival of an order, the entry of a patient into a health service, or the intention to purchase new products with a purchase order. The flow of different activities may involve one or more departments of the same organization, until the business objective is fully achieved. The workflow specifies a certain pattern of activities, enabled by the utilization of resources, such as technology, equipment, materials, information systems, and machinery. The conclusion of a business process can manifest itself in one or more final events of the process. Referring to the three examples provided above, the ordering process may end with achieving the business goal of the process—sending out a purchase order. Alternatively, during the ordering process, a customer may interrupt the process by communicating an intention to withdraw the order. In a similar manner, a patient may complete a medical examination with admission to the hospital, discharge, or transfer to another service; a purchase order may be interrupted due to the unexpected lack of product or the lack of money.

2.1.3 Modeling Business Processes

The purpose of business process modeling is to obtain an overview of the flow of activities performed by workers of the organization with the help of the resources available for the organization. Different kinds of modeling methods can be used. Some particular approaches involve textual modeling languages, adopting a set of keywords to produce expressions that can also be understood by machines [31]. At the beginning of Chap. 5, we will provide an overview of three main types of business process modeling approaches: activity-oriented, agent-oriented, and product-oriented approaches. Notwithstanding the type, most of the business process modeling approaches used adopt a set of symbols and a graphical formalism to describe the flow of tasks connected by lines. Diagrams and flow charts have often been applied as useful graphical artifacts to support managers and stakeholders. In particular, the general-purpose Unified Modeling Language (UML) has been widely applied to provide documentation for various business activities or workflows (e.g., task diagram, a type of UML diagram) [44].

Business process modeling aims to complement the business process models with useful information regarding the process, such as estimated costs, key performance indicators, and resources to be utilized. In addition to the ability to provide an immediate understanding of the core business of a company, process modeling includes several elements and steps enabling to understand the corresponding mechanisms used for its operation [42]. For example, understanding of the company's business process can be significantly improved by considering the number of workers, the arrival distribution of instances, and the impact of technology on the process. An important point is concerned with the availability of a meaningful notation, i.e., a set of symbols and rules for represent processes which would be well-known and shared among managers and stakeholders and could also be "understood" by computers. In this direction, the international consortium of industry standards called the Object Management Group (OMG) has recently specified three standard modeling notations: Business Process Modeling and Notation (BPMN), Case Management Model and Notation (CMMN), and Decision Modeling Notation (DMN).[1] Among the various business process modeling techniques, BPMN is today probably the most widely adopted technique, largely due to its promotion by OMG.

BPM places a big emphasis on the capabilities offered by modern information technology to model workflow, as well as to study business processes according to the performance objectives of the organization in question. Recent efforts also address the construction of the process model directly from the business process data consisting of process logs. It has been recently pointed out: "As companies increasingly make use of business process models—formal graph-based business process description techniques such as Event-driven Process Chains (EPC) [46], Petri nets [36] or the Business Process Model and Notation [32] in order to

---

[1] OMG official website at https://www.omg.org/intro/TripleCrown.pdf.

design and document their business processes, Information Systems (IS) research reacts to this requirement with the development of (partly) automated model-based compliance-checking approaches and tools" [11]. In other words, with business process mining, the focus has shifted to exploiting the organization's information system, utilizing its ability to record data on the activities and workflows performed by staff members, and usage of resources and technological artefacts. The increased ability to manage this information vastly improves business process simulation results, as well as facilitates the understanding of the business processes. This way, modeling and simulation iteratively make business processes more consistent, repeatable, and valid. Creating a process model throughout the business process lifecycle involves several steps, which we will describe in more detail in the next section.

2.1.4   Introducing Business Process Modeling Notation

A business process model is specified by a process diagram. Several modeling languages have been proposed to represent the dynamics of business processes. For example, the ARIS [45] approach includes the following models: value-added chain diagrams (VAC), EPCs, and function allocation diagrams (FAD). The VAC model represents the value chain of the organization's macro-processes; the EPC model specifies the execution flow of activities, decisions, and events of each process; and the FAD model is used to detail each activity.

Among the different modeling languages mentioned in the last paragraph, the BPMN language is the "de facto" standard for modeling complex business processes. BPMN provides notations that are easily understandable for all stakeholders, ranging from business analysts to technical developers. BPMN is also accompanied by an open-source web-based editor https://bpmn.io. Another relevant tool is the Cawemo editor, which also allows for the creation of collaborative BPMN diagrams on the Camunda open-source platform.[2]

In addition, the BPMN language can be easily paired with a discrete-event simulator to build a powerful dynamic environment for process analysis and re-engineering, such as BIMP.[3] Figure 2.1 describes the most common graphical elements of the BPMN language.

BPMN consists of four basic categories of graphical elements: flow objects, connecting objects, swimlanes, and artifacts. *Flow objects* are events, activities, and gateways. An event is something that "happens" during the course of a business process. Ontologically, event is something that separates the state of the world before the event has occurred from the state of the world after its occurrence [49]. Events affect the flow of the process at different points in time: start, intermediate,

---

[2] Camunda website: http://camunda.com.

[3] The online BIMP simulator: https://bimp.cs.ut.ee/products/bimp-online-simulator/.

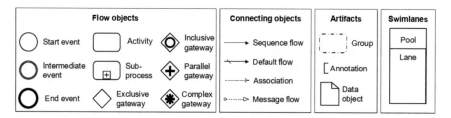

Fig. 2.1 BPMN main graphical elements

Fig. 2.2 Three main types of gateways and their description

and end. Events are simply represented by circles with open centers to allow internal markers to distinguish between different types of events. Business activities are represented as individual tasks or sub-processes. Task is represented by a rectangle with rounded corners. A sub-process is distinguished from a task by a small plus sign in the lower center of the shape. Finally, gateways are elements that control the execution flow of the process by means of the internal markers indicating the types of control behavior. A gateway is represented by a diamond shape. The most frequent gateways are parallel, exclusive, and inclusive (Fig. 2.2). Exclusive gateway represents a mutual choice between two (or more) branches in a process flow. An inclusive gateway specifies that one or more of the available paths will be taken. A parallel gateway specifies that all paths are always executed. For joining different branches, another gateway of the same type should be used.

Connecting Objects Connecting objects are used to specify how ow objects interact. A connector can be a sequence, a message, or an association. Sequence and message ows are represented by arcs which impose temporal constraints between ow objects. An association connects artifact objects to tasks and is represented by a dotted line. Artifacts are used to provide additional information about the process, such as data, text, and inputs and outputs of tasks.

Swimlanes Pools and lanes are used to group primary modeling elements related to functional capabilities or responsibilities. A pool represents a participant in a process and acts as a graphical container to partition a set of tasks from other pools. A lane is a sub-partition within a pool that is used to organize and categorize tasks.

2.1.5   An Overview of Petri Nets

A Petri net (PN) is a formalism introduced in 1962 by Carl Adam Petri in his doctoral dissertation [37]. Petri nets have found wide application in the design of a DES as a system consisting of states and state transitions [55]. Petri nets effectively define the evolution of event-driven systems.

A PN is a bipartite oriented graph with two types of nodes, places and transitions, which are connected by directed arcs. Places are graphically represented by circles and transitions by rectangles. An arc can join only nodes of different types, i.e., nodes with transitions and the other way around.

Each place can contain one or more tokens represented by dots. If the number of tokens that can be inside the place is limited, it is represented outside (above or below) the corresponding place. Each arc can be associated with a weight, which is a positive integer (if the writing is omitted, the weight will be considered unitary). The structure consisting of a place and a transition connected by two opposite arcs is called self-loop. Networks without self-loops are called pure PN. A PN model is typically recorded in a PNML file.[4]

The state (marking) of the PN is obtained by marking places with tokens. A transition is enabled if there is a distinct token for each arc from a place to the transition. If this is the case, a transition can be fired and produce a new marking. An enabled transition may fire any time. The firing of a transition is an atomic operation. When fired, the tokens in the input places are moved to the output places, according to the weights of the arcs and the capacities of the places. In Sect. 7.3.2, we provide an introductory demonstration to simulate a PN in NetLogo (*ABBPS_PN-Demo-example* model), as is depicted in Fig. 2.3.

2.1.6   Information Systems and Enterprises

According to a recent definition [47], an enterprise system can be viewed as a set of enterprise components, while the corresponding environment consists of humans and technical resources and actions. In this sense, an enterprise system utilizes an enterprise information system (EIS) by benefiting from the corresponding EIS services. These types of systems pursue the objective of offering enterprise products and/or services to entities belonging to the system's environment. In fact, the goal of the EIS is providing the corresponding enterprise system with the information support.

More broadly, an enterprise system can be viewed as a *work system* in which human participants and/or machines perform work (processes and activities) using

---

[4] PNML reference site: http://www.pnml.org/.

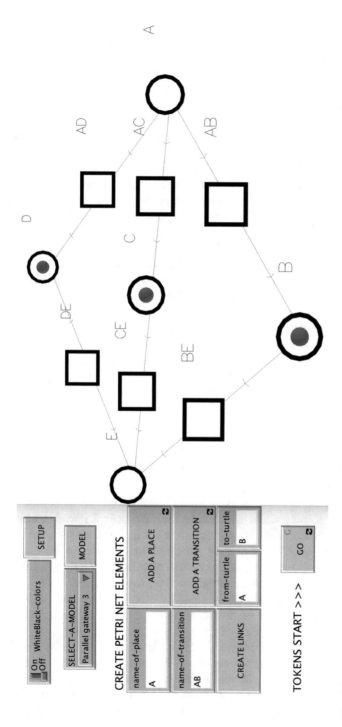

Fig. 2.3 Petri net simulation in a NetLogo model (3D view)

information, technology, and other resources to produce specific products/services for specific internal and/or external customers [2].

In recent years, information technology (IT) systems have integrated various hardware components and software applications (e.g., hardware and software applications). In the resulting enterprise resource planning (ERP) systems, developments in enterprise technologies have shifted the focus to business processes. A further step forward has been the adoption of workflow management systems (WMS), either as stand-alone applications or as integrated with enterprise systems. The set of enterprise IT applications can be also called business process management system (BPMS). A landmark case study—the Ford-Mazda case study—has largely contributed to the focus on the process-centric view of organizations based on BPMSs. We will provide an agent-based simulation of the Ford-Mazda case study in Sect. 8.1), paving the way for discussing business process re-engineering (BPR).

Business process data can be utilized by Process-Aware Information Systems (PAIS) [19], which are systems that are readily capable of producing event logs. Specific examples of such systems include enterprise resource planning systems, customer relationship management systems, and hospital information systems. Event log data is not simply limited to data generated by these systems, as many other systems can also generate useful data from process execution, such as personal devices that are able to store data about timestamps and tasks. Furthermore, for PAIS, it is relevant to specify how data about a complex business process can originate in more than a single source of information. The availability of real data has enabled to increase the application of simulation techniques to business process modeling, with the purpose of reproducing organizational structure and facilitating business process (re)engineering, which has attracted enormous interest among researchers [10, 60].

2.1.7   The Lifecycle of a Business Process

The discipline of business process management (BPM) is concerned with the analysis of a business process that includes several phases. The cycle usually begins with the identification step, after which all the other steps are repeated cyclically. Meanwhile, the BPM initiative must have a positive impact on the organization. The effort is evaluated by specific key performance indicators, such as performance improvement indicators (e.g., throughput time reduction and waste reduction), with measurement of the values provided by a business process. Setting of key performance indicators for evaluating business processes is further described in Chap. 5.

The steps of a business process lifecycle are represented in Fig. 7.1. We refer to Chap. 7 for an in-depth discussion of the topic. Agent-based modeling and simulation can be used at different stages of the business process lifecycle. The reason is that the analysis of activities and resources utilized by them, durations of delays, and interactions between organizational units can be elaborated at different stages of the business process lifecycle, depending on a particular decision-support task at hand.

Process Identification At the beginning of a business process lifecycle, managers must clarify the type of a problem to be solved. This can be done by delineating the scope of the business process and identifying its relationships with other processes. This initial step is usually called process identification.

The goal of business process identification is to identify the specific business process of interest. At this stage, it is important to distinguish between the steps of the business process being analyzed that are useful for the goals of the particular decision support tasks at hand and those that are less relevant. This is facilitated by applying the methodology that is described in Chap. 5 of this book. The main result of process identification is the so-called *process architecture* of an organization. This broad overview typically takes the form of a collection of processes and links between these processes that represent different types of relationships. In addition, another outcome is a *process portfolio* where processes are categorized according to relevant dimensions, such as importance and functions [20].

Process Discovery The outcome of a process analysis is process discovery— an activity geared toward capturing the current sequence of tasks by developing process models (*as-is*). Typically, this step provides the definition of diagrams describing the process. The process flow can be further explored using qualitative analysis techniques, such as stakeholder interviews and root cause analysis [43]. In a qualitative approach, the diagram usually reflects the particular understanding that people in the organization have of the process, including possible errors and misunderstandings. Quantitative techniques are more reliable for automatic exploration of the digital traces recorded in corporate databases.

The typical information transmitted by process diagrams include the types of activities performed, the points in which the flow diverges, the types of agents or actors involved in the process, and the types of resources utilized by the process. The most typical examples of diagrams reflecting business processes from different perspectives are UML activity diagrams, data-flow diagrams [16], and IDEF3 diagrams [30]. In the last decades, the most widely used process modeling notation has been BPMN 2.0.2, which was released as a standard notation by OMG in 2013 [35].

Process (Re)design The main output of the process redesign phase, starting from the *as-is* model, consists of a new and improved version of the business process model. Typically, we refer to such a new version as the *to-be* model. Scenario analysis and computer simulation provide different views of the current business process [17]. Some improvements can be tested, as in the case of new technologies [4, 5]. Here, the new process addresses problems identified in the previous phase to improve performance. Redesign efforts can impact one or more dimensions of the process, such as cost, time, quality, and flexibility.

Process Implementation The execution of the business process based on its description by diagrams involves at least two types of activities. First, the implementation may be tied to the corresponding software systems to perform and automate certain tasks. In addition, the implementation of the *to-be* process should consider organizational change management [15]. For example, it may be useful to redesign the work of people working on the process, train workers, or apply or develop a software system that would assist the manager in transitioning from the current process model to the new one. This step usually involves implementing process automation.

Monitoring and Controlling The last step of a BPM lifecycle involves the continuous observation of process performance. This is relevant for understanding to what extent the changes introduced to the process have achieved the desired impact, enabling to fine-tune the business process. The process monitoring and control phase can lead to new changes when performance has not achieved the intended impact. This phase includes a large set of key performance indicators, which facilitate business process fine-tuning. The goal is to achieve the objectives that have been defined for the process redesign phase.

2.2 The Management Perspective

2.2.1 Organization

A general definition of an organization is a group of people working together to achieve a common goal. The relevant dimensions of an organization are the coordination of work tasks, the distribution of skills and expertise, and the exercise of leadership, authority, and coordination of resources. Several types of organizations may be of interest for this work, from a public institution to a small private company. First, we can include governmental entities, such as municipalities, public agencies, as well as hospitals, schools, and airports. The interest of this type of organization typically relates to providing services to a large population, managing customers coming to a public office, and simulating administrative procedures, in a context of limited resources. Second, process analysis may be of interest to nonprofit organizations, such as voluntary associations or philanthropic entities. Their interest lies in improving steps to achieve an outreach goal through the involvement of people and third parties. Finally, a third type of organization of interest includes businesses and business-oriented companies that are interested in increasing their productivity, as well as optimizing costs, resources, and profit.

A traditional way of representing businesses is the functional perspective, where an organization is separated into its major parts or functions, depending on their specific expertise or roles, as individual building blocks (e.g., customer service, operations, marketing, warehousing, and so on). A business process perspective focuses on the series of activities that run through individual business functions, used to produce something, offer a service, or achieve a business goal (e.g., the order-to-pay process, the assembly line process).

2.2.2 Assets, Costs, and Time

Every business strategy consists of a plan for action that mixes the dimensions of resources, costs, and time concerns in order to achieve business goals. This can be examined for both established and start-up companies [34]. For example, the characteristics common to all companies include the involvement of agents or actors, the utilization of resources, the definition of costs, and the division of work time. Among the most relevant assets used by a company are automation equipment, as well as humans, including staff and different levels of personnel that may be directly involved.

A major concern in business management is the cost of operations required to produce goods or provide services. Cost variables can include several dimensions (e.g., fixed versus variable, humans versus equipment and machinery). A business process can be associated with fixed and variable costs. Fixed costs cannot be avoided because they do not vary with production volume, while variable costs are likely to change based on other dimensions, such as the number of goods produced or services provided by the company. Examples of variable costs include raw material costs, utility costs, and commissions. In contrast, fixed costs of a company remain the same regardless of other factors, even if no goods or services are produced. These include costs of production facilities, rent for machines and equipment, and insurance. Some considerations affect the entire management perspective, as in the case of the concept of economy of scale. This concept suggests that the fixed costs relatively decrease when production is increased because the price of a higher quantity of goods can be spread over the same amount of fixed costs. In a simulation, the costs of investments and depreciation of the assets can be inserted like parameters of the simulation.

Time is another relevant dimension that is needed for addressing various business issues. Business strategies must consider time in production processes and logistics, as well as in customer analysis and marketing. In a factory, working hours and shifts must be carefully planned with respect to other key activities, such as sourcing raw materials, shipping products to customers, receiving production orders, and so on. Simulations need to manage time accurately, as is described more thoroughly in Chap. 6.

2.2.3 Performance

The performance of a company is addressed by methods such as strategy maps and balanced scorecards (BSC). BSC is a well-known model of multidimensional performance measurement [27]. The four main dimensions of BSC applied to organizational performance are financial, customer, internal business process, and learning dimensions. To quantify both the performance and the outcome of a business process, one or more performance targets can be identified, leveraging different metrics of the business process.

Process Performance Metrics Before beginning to analyze any process in detail, it is important to clearly define process performance metrics [62]. Several indicators enabling to evaluate how the system is performing can be explored and combined to determine if a process conforms to expected behavior. Metrics can capture when some parts of the process are working better than others, as well as investigate business expenses and costs, which may be lower or higher than expected. While a typical qualitative metric is about analyzing error rates, most quantitative performance metrics are concerned with time and cost.

Time Main time-related metrics deal with the timing of the workflow. The main performance features are cycle time, waiting time, and not-value-adding time. They are further elaborated below:

- *Cycle time* refers to the average amount of time between the start and end of processes. It is among the most relevant measures of a business process, indicating its so-called throughput.
- *Waiting time* is the amount of time a process instance (e.g., a worker, a product being produced, or a document) is waiting for further processing.
- *Not-value-adding time* is the amount of production cycle time spent on activities that do not directly produce goods or services, i.e., do not add value to the organization.

Cost Cost-related metrics involve business process execution, resource utilization, and waste estimation.

- *Cost per execution* concerns the average cost of process throughput.
- *Resource utilization.* The number of work hours allocated to a resource or group of resources as a percentage of their availability in a given period.
- *Lean indicators* consist of (seven) waste metrics related to activity costs such as indicators of overproduction and defect identification.

Quality-related metrics are concerned with *quantitative* assessment of compliance with certain criteria of data quality, such as completeness, accuracy, and consistency. Some typical examples of quality indicators follow.

- *Quality measures* refer to the error rate, which is the percentage of times a process execution ends in a negative result.
- *Service-level agreement* relates to the rate of commitment violations between customers and service providers.
- *Customer feedback* refers to customer satisfaction metrics.

2.3 Mining Business Processes

2.3.1 Data Analysis of Event Logs

Analysis of the activities contained by the business process can be explored both online during their execution and offline by means of analyzing the reports. The spread of recent technological improvements has led to the adoption of both a large set of very different data-centric approaches and new algorithms for business process analysis. Features of interest are both structured and unstructured information [6, 54]. In this context, we introduce some concepts to specify the meaning of process mining within the broad set of research on knowledge extraction from data generated and stored in information systems' databases and the corresponding "event logs."

Digital traces registered in PAIS (see Sec. 2.1.6) are of increasing interest from a management perspective. Each **event** represents the execution of a particular activity by certain agents or actors, utilizing a certain set of resources within a specific time period, whereas the collection of events connected to each other is called a *case*. Each activity can be characterized by at least two events: start-of-activity event and end-of-activity event. From a project management perspective, activities are defined along the three main dimensions of time, cost, and scope [13]. An organization's historical instances of events can be recorded in the corporate information system. In turn, a collection of cases that capture a particular instance of the business process is called a *trace*. One set of traces is the *event log*, which can be stored in a log file, adopting, for example, the IEEE XES [66] standard format.

An event log consists of cases, where a case consists of a number of events. Finally, each event represents the execution of a particular activity in the process. Event attributes can be mandatory, such as case identifier, event class, timestamp, and transition. The case identifier specifies which case generated the corresponding event. The event class (or activity name) indicates the type of activity to which an event refers. Some attributes at the case level can be the type and expected duration of the case. The timestamp tracks the occurrence of a certain event. The timestamp of an event can refer to the completion time of the corresponding activity. Finally, the transition of an event refers to the execution state of the corresponding activity, where a *complete* transition means that the activity is finished and a *start* transition means that the activity has started. Additional attributes can be the payload, such as the name of the agent or actor performing the activity, or the data used as input/output. In Sect. 9.3, we introduce a model that can handle the XES file to extract information about an event log for analyzing activities, along with the performing agents (actors) and resources utilized, and summarizing case identifiers, activities, timestamps, and other relevant information.

Event Log Example

As was mentioned above, a log corresponding to a process consists of a set of traces—particular instances of process execution. Each trace, in turn, consists of a sequence of events. For example, a trace might be about a single instance served by a Help Desk process. Meanwhile, events can be described by several attributes, including the following: (i) The activity performed with which the event is associated; (ii) the organizational unit that performed the corresponding activity; (iii) the timestamp of the event; and iv. the transition of the event. The trace itself can be characterized by different attributes. For example, in a Help Desk system, case severity could be one of the attributes. An automated analysis of an event log may consider the earliest timestamp of its constituent events as the start timestamp of the trace and the latest timestamp of its events as the end timestamp of the trace. Most of the time, the corporate information system records only one (complete) transition, so that the trace could be described by the flow of its constituent activities. A recent XML-based initiative provides a standard format for event logs, which is a generally acknowledged format for the interchange of event log data between tools and application domains in both research community and industry. In fact, the purpose of the IEEE 1849-2016 XES Standard format for eXtensible Event Stream (XES) is to be suitable for business process analysis, process mining, statistical analysis, and text mining. In Sect. 9.3, a demo example of an agent-based model imports information in the XES format. Utilizing the information available in an event log file can be the first step in setting the simulation parameters, enabling to model and simulate a real business process more accurately.

2.3.2 Process Discovery

A process mining application is concerned with the possibility of reconstructing the real process starting exclusively or primarily from the data recorded in the corporate information system. In the context of PM in healthcare [21, 33], an example of practical application may be the discovery of the healthcare process related to patient admission to a hospital department [3]. One of the first algorithms that allow to reconstruct a business process is the Alpha algorithm, while subsequent efforts have extended and improved the quality of the results obtained. This is the case with the heuristic miner, inductive miner, and split miner algorithms [7].

Alpha Algorithm
The Alpha algorithm [59] for workflow discovery consists of the following three phases:

- *pre-processing*. Data analysis for exploring the activity names and the sequences of activities and inferring relations between the transitions.
- *processing*. The execution of the Alpha algorithm, leading to the identification of direct succession, causality, and parallel relationships between activities.
- *post-processing* Making some concluding arrangements, such as improving the visualization.

More formally, the event-log E of n tasks can be expressed in terms of the high-level activities $E = \{A, B, C, \ldots\}$.

The first step of the Alpha algorithm detects all of the *Direct successions* which includes $A > B$ if the log contains traces where A is followed by B.

The second step checks the *causality* relations, expressed with $A >> B$, when there are traces of $A >> B$ and no traces $B >> A$.

Finally, the last main step of the algorithm investigates the existence of *parallel* sequences of tasks, expressed with $A||B$, when there are both the occurrences of $A >> B$ and $B >> A$.

Quality Dimensions in Automated Process Discovery

Several measures assess the quality of discovered process models, by comparing the results of the discovery algorithm (model) to the real process (event log). Some of the measures we mention here are Precision, Recall (or Fitness/Sensitivity), F-Score, Generalization, Simplicity, and Complexity. Each metric investigates the quality of the algorithm from a different perspective. The adoption of the metrics depends on the specific interest of the project managers and the corresponding research questions.

Precision describes the extent to which the discovered model includes only the behavior found in the event log. A discovered model has a high precision if it contains only the event log paths, not allowing for completely unrelated behavior with respect to the event data stored in the log. The most accurate or best-fitting model is also called an "enumerating model." If any trace produced by the discovered model is contained by the event log, the accuracy score is 1, while it is 0 in the worst case situation, when no trace of the event log is present in the discovered model.

The *Recall* (or *Fitness*) metric evaluates how well the model reflects the behavior recorded in the event log. It does not matter if the model can replicate more traces than exist in reality: if all traces included by the event log can be replicated in the model, this metric anyway achieves the maximum score of 1. If no traces can be found in the model, the Recall/Fitness/Sensitivity score is 0. It is worth noting that a specific type of model, the so-called "flower model," can produce any sequence of traces. In this case, the precision is very low, while the recall is high. However, this type of model is not useful and can only be used as a baseline to compare process discovery metrics. Floral models introduce the concept of underfitting, which is overgeneralizing event log behavior by the process model.

2.3.3 Conformance Checking

Another interesting process mining application compares a process model with the real instances of a given process. The goal is to identify deviations between the expected model and the model derived from the process instances of the actual behavior. Conformance checking techniques have been proposed to evaluate specific process models for the compliance of an organization (e.g., for auditors). Combined with a process simulation, this kind of evaluation allows to compare the performance of the model in different scenario settings by means of a quantitative technique producing a set of statistical data in the form of, for example, a dashboard, about the *as-is* business process model.

2.3.4   Process Mining Tools

Tools for process modeling and analysis have always been many, including proprietary tools, free or open-source versions for both academic research and industry [58].

The following list is not exhaustive and includes some of the leading existing process mining companies and tools that address one or more aspects of process mining:

- Apromore https://www.apromore.org/
- ARIS https://aris-process-mining.com
- Celonis https://www.celonis.com/
- Fluxicon https://fluxicon.com
- IBM Process Mining https://www.ibm.com
- PM4Py https://pm4py.fit.fraunhofer.de
- PROM http://www.promtools.org/doku.php
- Nirdizati http://nirdizati.org
- Signavio https://www.signavio.com/
- Trisotech https://www.trisotech.com/

Within the tools that are based on extracting knowledge from event logs available in information systems, the areas of interest cover different aspects of data mining and simulation, starting from extracting process models from an event log, comparing the model and the log for monitoring deviations, extracting different types of information such as social/organizational networks, automated construction of simulation models, model enhancement, recommendations, and case prediction.

2.4   Simulation for BPM

One of the first computer applications was a simulation. Similarly, one of the first programming languages was Simula, which was developed precisely for programming simulations. A historical overview can be started from World War II, when the Manhattan Project dealt with the simulation of nuclear explosion processes. To investigate the topic, statisticians proposed "Monte Carlo Simulation" as a promising methodology that was then applied in several research areas. Today, simulation is also one of the standard analysis techniques in operations research and management. Here, the main advantages of simulation are versatility, few constraints, and easy-to-interpret results. Therefore, it is not a surprise that simulation is one of the most established business process analysis techniques, which is also supported by a wide range of tools [56].

Most business process simulation efforts adopt a workflow viewpoint, which aims to represent real-world work sequences [50]. We have already introduced some related modeling tools in Sect. 2.1.3, which are able to represent workflow using a discrete-event approach. The main advantages of this approach include clarity, ease of understanding, and process orientation [51]. However, researchers have also pointed out some flaws of the discrete-event approach.

Three criticisms of workflow-based discrete-event simulation are weakness in analyzing complexity, ignoring interactions, and difficulty to investigate changes [29]. The first issue is that enterprise is not considered as a whole. Workflow-based simulation occasionally delves too deeply into process details on how to?, lacking the addressing of other relevant questions, such as "why?" and "what?". Therefore, traditional business process modeling approaches (e.g., EPC, UML, BPMN, and flowcharts) are too "weak at providing the necessary means for identifying bottlenecks and for performance analysis and for generating alternative improved business processes that would meet specified objectives" [29].

The second criticism is concerned with the neglect of qualitative factors in the analysis of an enterprise. Most business process improvement projects do not consider a holistic view of the enterprise. As we will elaborate in Chap. 5 of this book, enterprises should be treated as highly complex sociotechnical systems. However, by simulating enterprises mostly at the implementation level, the workflow viewpoint can overlook the complexity of human interactions. To enhance a holistic view, *hybrid simulation* [12] has been recently proposed that combines two or more of the following methods: discrete-event simulation, system dynamics, and agent-based simulation. Hybrid simulation enables to better investigate the effectiveness and efficiency of a complete sociotechnical system [26].

Third, business process engineering has been proposed to investigate transformations. According to this approach, successful engineering follows design thinking, focusing on strategic goals to be operationalized [8, 14, 38]. An enterprise can be considered as the result of the cooperation of human beings with a certain societal purpose [18]. Therefore, the full picture of how the system works and the potential effects of changes emerge from the interactions between several actors. Such interactions are easy to explore by agent-based simulation, which is considered as a promising method for analyzing an enterprise as a social system [48].

2.4.1 Different Types of Simulation

At least three main categories of computational simulations have been conceived over the past four decades. First, system dynamics (SD) models are top-down approaches to modeling and simulation, where a set of mathematical (i.e., differential) equations defines the behavior of the input-output system. These types of models focus on how populations of agents behave as a whole by studying how different populations change over time [23]. SD was initially proposed in urban management studies [22], but was quickly applied to different types of systems. In a typical SD model, the current output of the system depends on both its past history and current state. The main modeling elements are accumulation of flows into stocks, time delays, and feedback. A recent attempt proposes the adoption of SD to predict the future behavior of business processes in an a scenario-based approach [39].

The second type of approach is discrete-event simulation (DES) [9], which focuses on an ordered chronological sequence of events occurring at precisely defined moments of time. The simulation is driven by events, and the system status is discrete in time and space [67]. This approach has been widely employed in practical applications of simulation for business process modeling [25], with increasingly powerful and effective tools. Business process simulation has been combined with BPMN, i.e., the state-of-the-art language for the graphical representation of business processes [40]. Several software simulators support the adoption of BPMN diagrams to compare different process alternatives in a scenario analysis perspective, such as the BIMP simulator [1]. Some authors have highlighted some recent critical issues, proposing integration with real data and process mining techniques [57, 61].

Finally, agent-based simulation (ABS) typically focuses on programming the behaviors of individual agents to observe phenomena emerging from their interactions. This type of approach has not been adopted as widely in management and organizational studies as in other domains. A recent review has suggested a demarcation for this field by proposing the term agent-based organizational simulation (ABOS). In fact, the authors argue that ABOS refers to the application of agent-based simulation in business and management [24]. We will further explore the agent-oriented approach in both Chaps. 5 and 6.

2.4.2   Technologies and Digital Twin

The increasing use of emerging technologies affects all industries. The digital transformation of processes under Industry 4.0 [28] has resulted in higher operational efficiency, interconnected machines, automation of manual tasks, and improvements of data analysis. In the so-called fourth industrial revolution, data and automation are the two most important components.

On the other hand, in computer science, simulations refer to digital models that mimic operations or processes within real-life systems. These simulations are used to analyze the performance of production systems and to test and implement new ideas. Engineers and technicians make use of simulations in a variety of industries to test products, systems, processes, and concepts [53].

The concept of digital twin was born in the intersection of Industry 4.0 and computational simulations. A digital twin can be defined as a representation of an organization to integrate all data produced by or associated with the main business process or system it mirrors. This way, the model is like a mirror of the events occurring in the real world. Data for a digital twin is typically collected from sensors (Internet of things devices), edge hardware, smartphones, and other embedded devices.

The real-time digital representation that a digital twin provides a virtual environment for planning, programming, and training to facilitate management, implement new strategies, and have new insights.

While a simulation can help understand what may happen when changes are introduced, a digital twin typically helps understand both what is currently happening and what may happen when the process evolves.

The main two application areas of digital twins are as follows:

- Real-time simulations. Typical simulations reproduce features of physical environments without using real-time data. Differently, a digital twin runs a simulation based on data collected in real time, in order to make predictions about processes or monitor the productivity of an enterprise.
- Optimizing real-world processes by applying predictive analytic based on data collected in real time with an emphasis on simulated scenarios involving physical entities.

The accuracy of a simulation or digital twin heavily relies on the accuracy of the data used in the design of its models. In today's industry, data acquisition by smart edge devices and human-machine interfaces has been made possible, and digital transformation can occur only with applying data acquired this way.[5]

References

1. Abel, M.: Lightning Fast Business Process Simulator. Master's Thesis. Institute of Computer Science, University of Tartu (2011)
2. Alter, S.: Work system theory: Overview of core concepts, extensions, and challenges for the future. J. Assoc. Inform. Syst. **14**, 72–121 (2013). https://doi.org/10.17705/1jais.00323
3. Amantea, I.A., Arnone, M., Di Leva, A., Sulis, E., Bianca, D., Brunetti, E., Marinello, R.: Modeling and simulation of the hospital-at-home service admission process. In: SIMULTECH, pp. 293–300 (2019). https://doi.org/10.5220/0007928602930300
4. Amantea, I.A., Sulis, E., Boella, G., Crespo, A., Bianca, D., Brunetti, E., Marinello, R., Grosso, M., Zoels, J., Visciola, M., Guidorzi, E., Miolano, L., Ratti, G., Mazzoni, T., Zani, E., Ambrosini, S.: Adopting technological devices in hospital at home: a modelling and simulation perspective. In: Rango, F.D., Ören, T.I., Obaidat, M.S. (eds.) Proceedings of the 10th International Conference on Simulation and Modeling Methodologies, Technologies and Applications, SIMULTECH 2020, Lieusaint, Paris, France, July 8–10, 2020, pp. 110–119. ScitePress (2020). https://doi.org/10.5220/0009970801100119

---

[5] https://www.exorint.com/en/blog/what-is-the-difference-between-a-simulation-and-a-digital-twin.

5. Amantea, I.A., Sulis, E., Boella, G., Marinello, R., Grosso, M., Crespo, A.: A modeling framework for an innovative e-health service: the hospital at home. In: International Conference
   on Simulation and Modeling Methodologies, Technologies and Applications, pp. 111–132.
   Springer, Berlin (2020). https://doi.org/10.1007/978-3-030-84811-8_6
6. Aringhieri, R., Boella, G., Brunetti, E., Caro, L.D., Francescomarino, C.D., Dragoni, M.,
   Ferrod, R., Ghidini, C., Marinello, R., Ronzani, M., Sulis, E.: Towards the application of
   process mining for supporting the home hospitalization service. In: Marrella, A., Dupré, D.T.
   (eds.) Proceedings of the 1st Italian Forum on Business Process Management co-located with
   the 19th International Conference of Business Process Management (BPM 2021), Rome, Italy,
   September 10th, 2021. CEUR Workshop Proceedings, vol. 2952, pp. 33–38. CEUR-WS.org
   (2021). http://ceur-ws.org/Vol-2952/paper_295a.pdf
7. Augusto, A., Conforti, R., Dumas, M., La Rosa, M., Maggi, F.M., Marrella, A., Mecella, M.,
   Soo, A.: Automated discovery of process models from event logs: review and benchmark. IEEE
   Trans. Knowl. Data Eng. **31**(4), 686–705 (2018). https://doi.org/10.1109/TKDE.2018.2841877
8. Baldoni, M., Baroglio, C., Boissier, O., Micalizio, R., Tedeschi, S., et al.: Engineering
   business process through accountability and agents. In: The 18th International Conference
   on Autonomous Agents and Multiagent Systems, AAMAS 2019, pp. 1796–1798. IFAAMAS,
   International Foundation for Autonomous Agents and Multiagent Systems (2019)
9. Banks, J.: Handbook of Simulation: Principles, Methodology, Advances, Applications, and
   Practice. Wiley, London (1998)
10. Barjis, J., Verbraeck, A.: The relevance of modeling and simulation in enterprise and
    organizational study. In: Workshop on Enterprise and Organizational Modeling and Simulation,
    pp. 15–26. Springer, Berlin (2010). https://doi.org/10.1007/978-3-642-15723-3_2
11. Becker, J., Delfmann, P., Eggert, M., Schwittay, S.: Generalizability and applicability of
    model-based business process compliance-checking approaches a state-of-the-art analysis and
    research roadmap. Bus. Res. **5** (2012). https://doi.org/10.1007/BF03342739
12. Brailsford, S.C., Eldabi, T., Kunc, M., Mustafee, N., Osorio, A.F.: Hybrid simulation modelling
    in operational research: a state-of-the-art review. Eur. J. Oper. Res. **278**(3), 721–737 (2019).
    https://doi.org/10.1016/j.ejor.2018.10.025
13. Daddey, F., Watt, A.: Working with individuals and teams. Project Management (2021)
14. Davenport, T.H., Short, J.E., et al.: The new industrial engineering: information technology
    and business process redesign (1990)
15. De Lellis, A., Di Leva, A., Sulis, E.: Simulation for change management: an industrial
    application. Proc. Comput. Sci. **138**, 533–540 (2018)
16. DeMarco, T.: Structure analysis and system specification. In: Pioneers and Their Contributions
    to Software Engineering, pp. 255–288. Springer, Berlin (1979)
17. Di Leva, A., Sulis, E.: A business process methodology to investigate organization manage-
    ment: a hospital case study. WSEAS Trans. Bus. Econ. (14), 100–109 (2017)
18. Dietz, J.L., Hoogervorst, J.A., Albani, A., Aveiro, D., Babkin, E., Barjis, J., Caetano, A.,
    Huysmans, P., Iijima, J., van Kervel, S., et al.: The discipline of enterprise engineering. Int.
    J. Organ. Design Eng. **3**(1), 86–114 (2013). https://doi.org/10.1504/IJODE.2013.053669
19. Dumas, M., van der Aalst, W.M., Ter Hofstede, A.H.: Process-Aware Information Systems:
    Bridging People and Software Through Process Technology. Wiley, London (2005). https://
    doi.org/10.1002/0471741442
20. Dumas, M., La Rosa, M., Mendling, J., Reijers, H.: Fundamentals of Business Process
    Management, vol. 1, 2nd edn. Springer, Berlin (2018). https://doi.org/10.1007/978-3-662-
    56509-4
21. Fernández-Llatas, C.: Interactive Process Mining in Healthcare. Springer, Germany (2021).
    https://doi.org/10.1007/978-3-030-53993-1
22. Forrester, J.W.: Urban dynamics. Ind. Manag. Re. (Pre-1986) **11**(3), 67 (1970)
23. Forrester, J.W.: System dynamics, systems thinking, and soft or. Syst. Dyn. Rev. **10**(2–3), 245–
    256 (1994)

24. Gómez-Cruz, N.A., Saa, I.L., Hurtado, F.F.O.: Agent-based simulation in management and organizational studies: a survey. Eur. J. Manag. Bus. Econ. (2017). https://doi.org/10.1108/EJMBE-10-2017-018

25. Hlupic, V., de Vreede, G.: Business process modelling using discrete-event simulation: current opportunities and future challenges. Int. J. Simul. Process. Model. **1**(1/2), 72–81 (2005). https://doi.org/10.1504/IJSPM.2005.007115

26. Jahangirian, M., Eldabi, T., Naseer, A., Stergioulas, L.K., Young, T.: Simulation in manufacturing and business: a review. Eur. J. Oper. Res. **203**(1), 1–13 (2010). https://doi.org/10.1016/j.ejor.2009.06.004

27. Kaplan, R.S., Davenport, T.H., Robert, N.P.D.K.S., Kaplan, R.S., Norton, D.P.: The Strategy-Focused Organization: How Balanced Scorecard Companies Thrive in the New Business Environment. Harvard Business Press (2001). https://doi.org/10.1108/sl.2001.26129cab.002

28. Lasi, H., Fettke, P., Kemper, H.G., Feld, T., Hoffmann, M.: Industry 4.0. Bus. Inform. Syst. Eng. **6**(4), 239–242 (2014). https://doi.org/10.1057/jos.2014.35

29. Liu, Y., Iijima, J.: Business process simulation in the context of enterprise engineering. J. Simul. **9**(3), 206–222 (2015). https://doi.org/10.1007/s12599-014-0334-4

30. Mayer, R.J., Painter, M.K., de Witte, P.S.: IDEF family of methods for concurrent engineering and business re-engineering applications. Knowledge Based Systems College Station (1994)

31. Mazanec, M., Macek, O.: On general-purpose textual modeling languages. In: Dateso, vol. 12, pp. 1–12. Citeseer (2012)

32. Model, B.P.: Notation (BPMN) version 2.0. OMG Specification, Object Management Group, pp. 22–31 (2011)

33. Munoz-Gama, J., Martin, N., Fernandez-Llatas, C., Johnson, O.A., Seplveda, M., Helm, E., Galvez-Yanjari, V., Rojas, E., Martinez-Millana, A., Aloini, D., Amantea, I.A., Andrews, R., Arias, M., Beerepoot, I., Benevento, E., Burattin, A., Capurro, D., Carmona, J., Comuzzi, M., Dalmas, B., de la Fuente, R., Francescomarino, C.D., Ciccio, C.D., Gatta, R., Ghidini, C., Gonzalez-Lopez, F., Ibanez-Sanchez, G., Klasky, H.B., Prima Kurniati, A., Lu, X., Mannhardt, F., Mans, R., Marcos, M., Medeiros de Carvalho, R., Pegoraro, M., Poon, S.K., Pufahl, L., Reijers, H.A., Remy, S., Rinderle-Ma, S., Sacchi, L., Seoane, F., Song, M., Stefanini, A., Sulis, E., ter Hofstede, A.H., Toussaint, P.J., Traver, V., Valero-Ramon, Z., van de Weerd, I., van der Aalst, W.M., Vanwersch, R., Weske, M., Wynn, M.T., Zerbato, F.: Process mining for healthcare: characteristics and challenges. J. Biomed. Inform. 103994 (2022). https://doi.org/10.1016/j.jbi.2022.103994

34. Muthuri, R., Capecchi, S., Sulis, E., Amantea, I.A., Boella, G.: Integrating value modeling and legal risk management: an it case study. Inform. Syst. e-Bus. Manag. 1–29 (2021). https://doi.org/10.1007/s10257-021-00543-2

35. OMG: Business Process Model and Notation (BPMN), Version 2.0.2 (2013). http://www.omg.org/spec/BPMN/2.0.2

36. Peterson, J.L.: Petri nets. ACM Comput. Surv. (CSUR) **9**(3), 223–252 (1977)

37. Petri, C.A.: Communication with Automata. Ph.D. Thesis, Universitt Hamburg (1966)

38. Polyvyanyy, A., Su, Z., Lipovetzky, N., Sardina, S.: Goal recognition using off-the-shelf process mining techniques. In: Proceedings of the 19th International Conference on Autonomous Agents and MultiAgent Systems, pp. 1072–1080 (2020)

39. Pourbafrani, M., van Zelst, S.J., van der Aalst, W.M.P.: Scenario-based prediction of business processes using system dynamics. In: Panetto, H., Debruyne, C., Hepp, M., Lewis, D., Ardagna, C.A., Meersman, R. (eds.) On the Move to Meaningful Internet Systems: OTM 2019 Conferences—Confederated International Conferences: CoopIS, ODBASE, C&TC 2019, Rhodes, Greece, October 21–25, 2019, Proceedings, Lecture Notes in Computer Science, vol. 11877, pp. 422–439. Springer, Berlin (2019). https://doi.org/10.1007/978-3-030-33246-4_27

40. Pufahl, L., Wong, T.Y., Weske, M.: Design of an extensible BPMN process simulator. In: Teniente, E., Weidlich, M. (eds.) Business Process Management Workshops—BPM 2017 International Workshops, Barcelona, Spain, September 10–11, 2017, Revised Papers. Lecture Notes in Business Information Processing, vol. 308, pp. 782–795. Springer, Berlin (2017). https://doi.org/10.1007/978-3-319-74030-0_62

41. Qi, Q., Tao, F.: Digital twin and big data towards smart manufacturing and industry 4.0: 360 degree comparison. IEEE Access **6**, 3585–3593 (2018)
42. Roeglinger, M., Poeppelbuss, J., Becker, J.: Maturity models in business process management. Bus. Process Manag. J. **18**, 328–346 (2012). https://doi.org/10.1108/14637151211225225
43. Rooney, J.J., Heuvel, L.N.V.: Root cause analysis for beginners. Quality Progress **37**(7), 45–56 (2004)
44. Rumbaugh, J.E., Jacobson, I., Booch, G.: The Unified Modeling Language Reference Manual—Covers UML 2.0, 2nd edn. (2005)
45. Scheer, A.W.: ARIS Business Process Modeling. Springer, Berlin (2000)
46. Scheer, A.W., Thomas, O., Adam, O.: Process modeling using event-driven process chains. Process-Aware Inform. Syst. **119** (2005). https://doi.org/10.1002/0471741442.ch6
47. Shishkov, B.: Designing Enterprise Information Systems. Springer, Berlin (2020). https://doi.org/10.1007/978-3-030-22441-7
48. Siebers, P.O., Macal, C.M., Garnett, J., Buxton, D., Pidd, M.: Discrete-event simulation is dead, long live agent-based simulation! J. Simul. **4**(3), 204–210 (2010). https://doi.org/10.1057/jos.2010.14
49. Sterling, L., Taveter, K.: The Art of Agent-Oriented Modeling. The MIT Press, Cambridge (2009). https://doi.org/10.7551/mitpress/7682.001.0001
50. Sulis, E., Amantea, I.A., Boella, G., Marinello, R., Bianca, D., Brunetti, E., Bo, M., Bianco, A., Cattel, F., Cena, C., Fruttero, R., Traina, S., Feletti, L.C., de Cosmo, P., Armando, L., Ambrosini, S.: Monitoring patients with fragilities in the context of de-hospitalization services: an ambient assisted living healthcare framework for e-health applications. In: 2019 IEEE 23rd International Symposium on Consumer Technologies (ISCT), pp. 216–219 (2019). https://doi.org/10.1109/ISCE.2019.8900989
51. Sulis, E., Amantea, I.A., Fornero, G.: Risk-aware business process modeling: a comparison of discrete event and agent-based approaches. In: 2019 Winter Simulation Conference (WSC), pp. 3152–3159. IEEE, Piscataway (2019). https://doi.org/10.1109/WSC40007.2019.9004822
52. Sulis, E., Di Leva, A.: Public health management facing disaster response: a business process simulation perspective. In: 2018 Winter Simulation Conference (WSC), pp. 2792–2802. IEEE, Piscataway (2018). https://doi.org/10.1109/WSC.2018.8632534
53. Tao, F., Cheng, J., Qi, Q., Zhang, M., Zhang, H., Sui, F.: Digital twin-driven product design, manufacturing and service with big data. Int. J. Adv. Manuf. Technol. **94**(9), 3563–3576. https://doi.org/10.1007/s00170-017-0233-1
54. Teinemaa, I., Dumas, M., Maggi, F.M., Di Francescomarino, C.: Predictive business process monitoring with structured and unstructured data. In: International Conference on Business Process Management, pp. 401–417. Springer, Berlin (2016). https://doi.org/10.1007/978-3-319-45348-4_23
55. van der Aalst, W.: The application of petri nets to workflow management. J. Circuits Syst. Comput. **8**(1), 21–66 (1998). https://doi.org/10.1142/S0218126698000043
56. van der Aalst, W.: Business process simulation revisited. In: Workshop on Enterprise and Organizational Modeling and Simulation, pp. 1–14. Springer, Berlin (2010). https://doi.org/10.1007/978-3-642-15723-3_1
57. van der Aalst, W.: Business process simulation revisited. In: J. Barjis (ed.) Enterprise and Organizational Modeling and Simulation—6th International Workshop, EOMAS 2010, held at CAiSE 2010, Hammamet, Tunisia, June 7–8, 2010. Selected Papers. Lecture Notes in Business Information Processing, vol. 63, pp. 1–14. Springer, Berlin (2010). https://doi.org/10.1007/978-3-642-15723-3_1
58. van der Aalst, W., Reijers, H., Weijters, A., Dongen, B., Medeiros, A., Song, M., Verbeek, H.: Business process mining: an industrial application. Inform. Syst. **32**(5), 713–732 (2007). https://doi.org/10.1016/j.is.2006.05.003

59. van der Aalst, W., Weijters, T., Maruster, L.: Workflow mining: discovering process models from event logs. IEEE Trans. Knowl. Data Eng. **16**(9), 1128–1142 (2004). https://doi.org/10.1109/TKDE.2004.47
60. Barjis, J. (ed.): Enterprise and Organizational Modeling and Simulation: 6th International Workshop, EOMAS 2010, held at CAiSE 2010, Hammamet, Tunisia, June 7–8, 2010. Selected Papers, 1 edn. Lecture Notes in Business Information Processing 63. Springer, Berlin, Heidelberg (2010). https://doi.org/10.1007/978-3-642-15723-3
61. van der Aalst, W.M.P.: Business process simulation survival guide. In: vom Brocke, J., Rosemann, M. (eds.) Handbook on Business Process Management 1, Introduction, Methods, and Information Systems, International Handbooks on Information Systems, 2nd edn. pp. 337–370, Springer (2015). https://doi.org/10.1007/978-3-642-45100-3_15
62. Van Looy, A., Shafagatova, A.: Business process performance measurement: a structured literature review of indicators, measures and metrics. SpringerPlus **5**(1), 1797 (2016). https://doi.org/10.1186/s40064-016-3498-1
63. Weske, M.: Business Process Management—Concepts, Languages, Architectures, 3rd edn. Springer, Berlin (2019). https://doi.org/10.1007/978-3-662-59432-2
64. WfMC: Workflow management coalition terminology and glossary. Workflow Management Coalition (1999)
65. Wren, D.A.: The History of Management Thought. Wiley, London (2005)
66. XES Working Group: IEEE standard for extensible event stream (XES) for achieving interoperability in event logs and event streams. IEEE Std. **1849**, 1–50 (2016). https://doi.org/10.1109/IEEESTD.2016.7740858
67. Zeigler, B.P., Muzy, A., Kofman, E.: Theory of Modeling and Simulation: Discrete Event & Iterative System Computational Foundations. Academic Press, New York (2018). https://doi.org/10.1016/C2016-0-03987-6

Chapter 3
Agents and Organization Studies

Abstract The notion of agent is one of the most relevant concepts in computer science, within its sub-disciplines of artificial intelligence and information systems. In this chapter, we introduce the main definitions of the concept in the computer science literature. We mention the idea of individual-based modeling. To better understand the topic, we propose an exploration of a database of academic research articles, with a survey of recent trending topics. Adopting "agent" and "business" as keywords, we consider abstracts of scientific articles from the last 20 years. We also report on a semantic graph analysis performed by us to explore the most frequent co-occurring concepts by using network metrics and clustering.

3.1 The Agent Idea

The concept of agent is one of the most relevant ones in the computer science literature. Since the origins of artificial intelligence (AI) research, the focus was on the construction of computational entities with a certain degree of autonomous behavior. The close relationship between agent and AI is well exemplified by Russell-Norvig's famous seminal work, first published in 1995 [39]. In fact, the textbook *Artificial Intelligence: a modern approach* by Russell and Norvig includes the term agent 1564 different times in 348 pages, out of the total of about 950 pages.

The concept of agent has begun to be relevant from the 1990s [38], particularly in the context of computer science. Nevertheless, the concept of agent has been quickly adopted with a wide-ranging set of meanings, including the following ones: a piece of software, an autonomous object, an intelligent system, a technological entity embedded (i.e., situated) in an environment, and a robot. In socioeconomics studies, agent mostly refers to active entities (individuals, groups, companies, etc.) possessing some private and shared knowledge, exhibiting certain behaviors and being involved in interactions with other agents.

Although the AI discipline has become increasingly popular in recent years, the concept of agent is no longer closely associated with AI. The feeling is that after the explosion in the early 2000s of "Big Data" studies, the focus quickly shifted to data analysis ("Data Science" is a trending topic in the 2020s) with automatic

© Springer Nature Switzerland AG 2022
E. Sulis, K. Taveter, *Agent-Based Business Process Simulation*,
https://doi.org/10.1007/978-3-030-98816-6_3

information extraction techniques, such as supervised or unsupervised methods, natural language processing (NLP), as well as the adoption of neural networks [35].

Nowadays, the "agent-oriented" research community is a wide niche area, with several practical applications. While considerable efforts have been made at the theoretical level, the implementation phase with respect to real-world problems remains an uncertain area [19]. Moreover, there are some lexical facets, as the term has been adopted with several meanings and synonyms. The agent research community actually includes at least two main subgroups: multi-agent systems (MAS) [51] and agent-based modeling and simulation (ABM or ABMS) [12]. The ABM and MAS research communities have historically proceeded on nearly independent tracks, while recently there are attempts to gather research contributions that serve the goals of both fields [20]. Anyway, in both cases, a substantial part of the available tools is not within the reach of non-experts, which causes the risk of isolating a large research area. In particular, MAS mostly refers to an engineering approach within the AI community, where the main research goal is designing robots or software agents acting under dynamic conditions.

It is worth mentioning here the concept of individual-based modeling (IBM), mostly adopted in ecological studies [25]. IBM has focused primarily on populations composed of individual discrete organisms, each of which has a specific set of attributes—state variables—and behaviors. The core idea of ABM is very similar to this type of modeling effort, where agents' state variables can include individual properties, behavioral or physiological traits, as well as features such as relationships to other agents and objects, and their spatial locations. In a more targeted way, the ABM community refers primarily to socioeconomic studies where "agent" is a synonym for "individual" or "actor."

To summarize, a clear shared definition of agent is not easy to come by. The existing literature usually starts by stating what an agent is not. For example, a very simple agent can be a thermostat, which senses the environment and changes its state, but has neither autonomy nor continuous operation [29]. In the next paragraphs, we describe some of the main facets of the agent term, starting with the accompanying concepts that are related to various application fields. We also present some of the main definitions of agent in different research areas of computer science.

3.1.1 Agents in Computer Science Studies

The classical AI book by Russell and Norvig defines the concept of agent right at the beginning, as the authors state in the preface: "We define Artificial Intelligence as the study of agents that receive percepts from the environment and perform actions" [39]. Nevertheless, the concept of agent assumes slightly different meanings in different areas of computer science, mostly depending on different research perspectives. In the following paragraphs, we provide a synthetic analysis of the

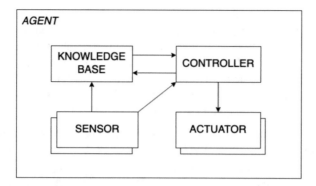

Fig. 3.1 Abstract agent architecture

concept of agent and some of the related concepts in different areas of computer science.

Autonomous Agents An agent's ability to change its own behavior is in the core of the concept of autonomy. By following the classical definition by Franklin and Graesser [23], an autonomous agent is "a system situated within and a part of an environment that senses that environment and acts on it, over time, in pursuit of its own agenda and so as to effect what it senses in the future." The autonomy of an agent depends on its ability to perceive its environment by using its sensors and act upon the environment by using its actuators. Both sensors and actuators can be real or simulated ones.

Abstract Agent Architecture The view of an autonomous agent described in Section *Autonomous agents* is illustrated by a simple abstract agent architecture shown in Fig. 3.1 from [45]. An agent receives information from its environment, including messages from other agents, through its *sensors* and stores information received from them in its *knowledge base*. The agent's behavior is determined by a *controller* that performs actions affecting the environment, including messages sent to other agents, through the agent's *actuators*. The controller receives its input knowledge from the knowledge base and from the sensors. Besides acting through actuators, the controller also performs local actions that change the knowledge stored in the agent's knowledge base [45].

Agent-Based System The idea of a system of agents mostly refers to many research areas in computer science, such as game theory, complex systems, multi-agent systems, evolutionary programming, and information systems [4, 7, 28]. The idea of a system mostly refers to architectural features, including features concerned with design and modeling [33]. According to this perspective, agent-based system is used as a synonym of multi-agent system, to emphasize the role of relationships between actors to achieve goals. This approach focuses on the interactions between autonomous agents in a network [5]. The idea of "system" has also been often adopted in modeling and simulation of manufacturing [36].

Software Agents Software agent is a kind of physical agent that is implemented in software [45]. The notion of software agent also refers to distributed computing [30]. The meaning of "software agent" in distributed computing is an abstraction that involves the idea of multiple threads or multiple processes in distributed systems. In this context, an agent is an autonomous software process or thread. Historically, interactions and coordination between different knowledge-based entities were at the core of multi-expert systems [26, 32].

Information Systems and Software Engineering Software engineering has proposed to extend the concept of "object" by introducing a whole set of new ideas, methodologies, and technologies to investigate interacting agents [41]. The notion of agent is also largely used as a useful modeling abstraction in the studies on information systems. In these areas, agent is ontologically defined as a kind of physical object that can act in the environment, perceive events, and reason [45]. The concept of agent was introduced to this area by the Zachman Framework [44, 54] and has been popularized by approaches, such as the enterprise model [14], the Tropos methodology [13], and others [48]. In this book, the usage of the term "agent" as a modeling notion is important because for agent-based business process simulation, agents participating in business processes first need to be identified and conceptually modelled.

Intelligence Many studies in AI investigate how a computational entity situated in an environment can make its own decisions. As was already explained in the section "Abstract Agent Architecture", an agent typically perceives the environment with its sensors. Based on the information perceived, an agent decides how to intervene in the environment through the actuators [21]. One of the simplest types of agents is "simple reflex agent," which is a computational entity that makes decisions only based on its current perceptions. On the other end of the "intelligence" spectrum is a learning agent that can automatically extract meaningful patterns and improve its actions through obtaining additional experience with the help of particular algorithms [24]. A weak position on intelligence by agents sees agents as tools that relieve humans of routine tasks suitable for computational solutions, but there is also a strong position according to which agents can be built to mimic or even surpass the cognitive capabilities of humans. Some application areas of intelligent agents are where the human user can benefit from continuous data analysis and monitoring data streams originating in large databases and where decision-support based on the data is required. Many applications of intelligent agents are tied to human-computer interaction, conversational agents, and the Internet.

Bot From the Internet-based view, an agent is often termed as a bot able to operate with a certain autonomy by, for example, traversing web pages or acting in a human-like fashion. A bot is performing tasks on behalf of its owner. A recent view of bots is robotic process automation (RPA) [2, 49]. From the perspective of robotics, agents learn and operate in a real-world environment. Robot can be defined as a kind of physical agent that is implemented in hardware. The behavior of a robot is optimized by tuning its sensors, actuators, and the controller [16]. Robot behavior must also be optimized with regard to energy consumption and physical performance parameters [31]. The terms "software robot" and "agent" are often used as synonyms [53].

3.1.2 Definition of Agent

The definition of agent can combine the concepts explained in different subsection of this section. However, it is difficult to include all the different perspectives. For example, while the concept of object seemed significant for capturing the interaction between entities, such as message exchange [27]), these objects are not necessarily autonomous. The autonomy of objects was taken further by other seminal work [1] that coined the term "actor" in the context of distributed systems.

In most systems, individual entities are clearly dependent on a central authority, but it is still relevant to assess how responsible they are for their own actions [8]. In the studies on artificial intelligence, there is currently a lot of debate about an agent's ability to reason, deliberate, and decide. A representative example is the ongoing debate about self-driving cars [6, 11]. Moreover, as agents are situated in a physical and social environment, perception and cognitive architectures become relevant areas of research [43, 47, 55].

In the context of this book, a general definition of *autonomous agent* refers to the idea of a software program that can act in the environment, perceive events, and reason. An agent responds to events occurring in the agent's environment. This response is independent of direct instructions provided by an external source, such as the owner or user of the agent. We refrain here from an attempt to provide a more elaborate definition of the term "agent," because its meaning can range from a simple program consisting of a small number of rules to a large and complex system.

We also mention here a classical contribution concerning the definition of tan agent. Michael Wooldridge and Nicholas Jennings started their book on intelligent agents with the following general definition of the concept:

> An agent is a computer system that is situated in some environment, and that is capable of autonomous action in this environment in order to meet its design objectives [52]

Based on the seminal definition stated above, the characteristics of an agent can be described, such as flexibility, autonomy, situatedness, adaptability, proactivity, and sociability [22]. An intelligent agent should be reactive, proactive, and social. An agent is reactive if it is able to perceive its environment and respond in a timely fashion to changes occurring in it. An agent is proactive if it does not simply act in response to its environment but is able to exhibit opportunistic, goal-directed behavior and take the initiative where appropriate. An agent is social if it is able to interact, when appropriate, with other man-made agents (software agents or robots) and humans in order to complete their own problem-solving, and to help others with their activities [45].

Types of Agents A typical classification of agents comes from the seminal work by Stuart Russell and Peter Norvig which introduced five types of agents based on their perceived degree of intelligence and ability. These are "table-driven agents" who use a table of stored actions to find the next action; "simple reflective agents" who act on the basis of condition-action rules, with no memory of past states of the world; "agents with memory" who use an internal state to keep track of past states of the world; "agents with goals" who have, in addition to state information, a description of desirable situations and consider future events; and "utility-based agents" who adopt utility theory to act more rationally [39].

Rationality The concept of rationality is crucial in social sciences, where it has been explained by the theory of bounded rationality by Herbert Simon [42]. However, later studies in this area have shown that an agent can also behave in an irrational or *seemingly* irrational way [34]. In particular, researchers have modelled irrational behaviors of traders in financial markets [18]. By adopting agent-based approaches, one can build simulation systems that are able to cope with influences arising from individual decisions and actions by humans. In other words, agents increase the psychological realism of complex simulation models, as well as improve the quality of the results of simulations [40].

Emergent Behavior Irrational behavior mentioned in the previous subsection can lead to emergent behavior. An example of collective irrational behavior is herding, where in a highly uncertain and stressful situation, an individual tends to follow others almost blindly [3]. Emergent behavior is a characteristic of a multi-agent system as a whole that cannot be determined by or predicted from the characteristics of individual agents, making up the multi-agent system. The purpose of ABM is mainly directed to understanding the functioning of a system as a whole based on both expected and emergent behaviors of the involved agents. In many cases, the output of the ABM results from the interactions between agents obeying simple rules. The result of running this kind of model is not easily predictable because of emergent behavior. For example, the spread of COVID-19 can be investigated by an ABM that represents randomly moving and interacting individuals, where each agent has been assigned a probability of getting infected upon interacting with another agent. This probability depends on the strength of one's immune system but currently also on vaccinations [17]. Further information on ABMs addressing the COVID-19 pandemic is presented in Sect. 8.5.1.

3.2 Agent in Business Management Research

Improvements in computing have widely influenced peoples' daily lives, as well as industry, business, and research. Terms such as algorithm and artificial intelligence have become increasingly common in both everyday life and scientific research. In this context, we investigated the recent trend of studies involving the concepts of "agent" and "business management." Our goal was to identify the most frequent research topics combined with agent-based approaches and business studies. To achieve that, we reviewed abstracts of scientific articles about agents and business process management. In particular, we collected all abstracts from the IEEE database, which is very relevant for these topics. We selected the abstracts that include both of the keywords "agent" and "business." Some pre-processing steps were initially applied by removing punctuation marks, numbers, and stop words. Finally, we applied stemming, which is the process of reducing inflected or derived words to their base or root form—stem. The analysis was performed by adopting the Python programming language with the NLTK [10] library. A further exploration done by us utilized the open-source software Gephi [9] for graph and network analysis.

3.2.1 Research Trends

At first, we counted the occurrences of terms in the titles and abstracts of publications in journals, conference proceedings, books, and magazines. Table 3.1 describes the trends in related research topics from 1999 to 2019. We can clearly notice the inverted parabola of the curve of the occurrence of terms, such as "agent-based," that peaked about 10 years ago. The terms "agent" and "multi-agent" observe a trend with the same peak followed by a decrease in the following 5 years and a new increase in the last 5 years. Finally, we observe the increasing trend of organization studies, including business management, simulation, and process mining. In particular, studies related to machine learning have had the biggest impact, with a very strong increase in recent years. Figure 3.2 describes the trends of some topics based on the occurrences of the related terms in the abstracts of scientific publications from 1996 to 2019.

Table 3.1 Number of research terms in the titles and abstracts of articles from the IEEE database, every 5 years from 1999 to 2019

Research term	1999	2004	2009	2014	2019
Agent	1,060	2,457	4,664	3,805	5,127
Multi-agent	238	814	1,749	1,676	2,518
Agent-based	135	362	670	490	439
Simulation	11,993	22,031	43,973	47,653	60,604
Business	1,313	2,466	7,061	5,560	6,953
Organization	1,086	1,736	3,994	4,818	5,367
Management	487	655	1,833	1,805	2,008
Mining	1,557	3,496	11,131	6,358	9,485
Process mining	0	1	29	58	135
Learning	3,179	6,187	12,390	14,742	47,184
Total	78,201	133,955	231,017	242,863	301,521

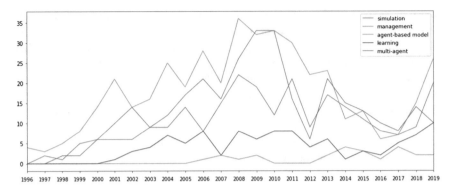

Fig. 3.2 Occurrence of stems in the IEEE abstracts from 1996 to 2019

3.2.2   A Semantic Network Analysis

To better describe the intersections of agent studies and organization and business process management topics, we focused on research works, the titles and abstracts of which contain both agent- and business-related terms. Some pre-processing steps were initially applied for removing punctuation marks, numbers, and stop words. We finally applied stemming to consider the root forms—stems—of terms.[1]

We analyzed the corpus by performing for each abstract a semantic network analysis of stems co-occurring in the same sentence. In particular, we created an edge between each pair of co-occurring stems, to represent that the two concepts are strongly interrelated [46].

The entire resulting indirect graph contains 3203 vertices (stems) and 134,379 edges, represented as one cohesive community of interconnected concepts. The diameter of the network is 4, indicating the longest of all computed path lengths. This is a *small-world network* [50], as our network has both a low-average shortest path length (also called average geodesic distance) and a high clustering coefficient (CC). In fact, the stems are very close to each other, because the average path length is 2.23. At the same time, the average CC (in the range from 0 to 1) is quite high −0.68.

Degree

A metric involving individual vertices representing stems refers to the number of connections. This measure is the *degree* of a vertex, which indicates the most connected stems. The two concepts that were used to collect data from the abstracts have the highest degree ("business" 1.456 and "agent" 1.415). Other strongly connected vertices include "system" (1361), "model" (1331), "service" (1046),

---

[1] The analysis was performed by adopting the Python programming language and NLTK library [10] as well as the open-source software Gephi for graph analysis [9].

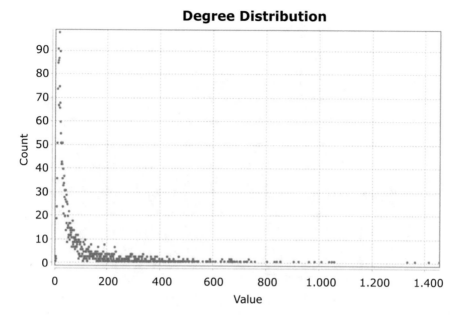

Fig. 3.3 Gephi diagram for the stem degree distribution in the IEEE abstracts

"data" (1036), "process" (1007), "technology" (981), "development" (960), and "management" (853).

The degree distribution clearly represents a typical feature of complex networks, with a few vertices having a high degree and most vertices having just a few connections. Figure 3.3 indicates our distribution with the long tail typical for these kinds of networks.

Centrality

Another relevant information of each vertex is concerned with its position in the network, i.e., with its role with respect to the topology of the network. In particular, the centrality metric affects the role of a vertex with respect to other groups of vertices connected to each other in the network.

By exploiting concepts like *betweenness* and *closeness centrality*, we identified some interesting features of the stems. In fact, by focusing on the sub-graph of the most connected vertices, where the degree of more than 300 stands for a high centrality, we notice how the following four stems act as structural holes [15]: "system," "model," "process," and "serv." We investigate the communities of these highly connected stems in the following subsection.

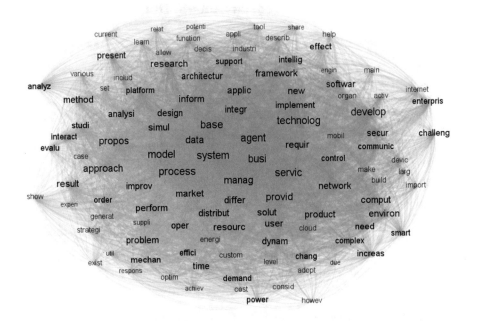

Fig. 3.4 The network of stems having a degree higher than 400

3.2.3 Communities of Concepts

The graph of terms (stems) and their connections are represented in Fig. 3.4. They can be further explored with clustering techniques to identify cohesive groups representing the core areas.

The community detection method allows for the identification of large groups focusing on the density-based modularity measure [37]. Within the 116 stems having a *degree* higher than 400, the clustering technique automatically identifies three large groups.

Two groups include our root terms and are, respectively, centered on "agent" and "business," while the third group is centered on "model" as a high-degree node.

Agent Group The first group of stems is described in Fig. 3.5. It refers to agent-related issues which mainly involve the following concepts:

- method (system, network, structure, architecture, development, platform, design)
- decision-making (decision, support, do, control)
- communication (communication, information, data, design, present
- practical applications (tool, software, industrial, device)

Business Group The second group of stems is represented in Fig. 3.6. It comprises the business and management perspectives. The main concepts here are concerned

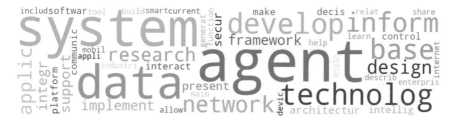

Fig. 3.5 Word cloud of the group of stems including *agent*

Fig. 3.6 Word cloud of the group of stems including *business* and *management* stems

Fig. 3.7 Word cloud of the group of stems including *model*

with process, services, organization, and the related elements time, requirements, environment, change, challenges, and dynamics.

Model Group A third group of stems is represented in Fig. 3.7 and describes a somewhat different set of concepts from the previous ones, not being related to the key terms of agent and business.

This word cloud focuses on the concept of model, as well as terms related to methodological issues. In fact, the group includes stems such as the following ones: approach, proposal, analysis, problem, results, performance, and simulation. In particular, some of these terms appear to be associated with management issues, involving the concepts of cost, market, operative, suppliers, and strategies. This group of terms referring to efficiency, evaluation, solution, and improvement typically concerns the modeling effort. Finally, our semantic analysis clearly highlights the applied, multi-faced, and practical nature, across a wide range of perspectives, of this type of researches involving agents and business management.

References

1. Agha, G.A.: ACTORS—A Model of Concurrent Computation in Distributed Systems. MIT Press Series in Artificial Intelligence. MIT Press, Cambridge (1990). https://doi.org/10.7551/mitpress/1086.001.0001
2. Agostinelli, S., Marrella, A., Mecella, M.: Research challenges for intelligent robotic process automation. In: Francescomarino, C.D., Dijkman, R.M., Zdun, U. (eds.) Business Process Management Workshops—BPM 2019 International Workshops, Vienna, Austria, September 1-6, 2019, Revised Selected Papers. Lecture Notes in Business Information Processing, vol. 362, pp. 12–18. Springer (2019). https://doi.org/10.1007/978-3-030-37453-2_2
3. Amores, D., Vasardani, M., Tanin, E.: Early detection of herding behaviour during emergency evacuations. In: Winter, S., Griffin, A., Sester, M. (eds.) 10th International Conference on Geographic Information Science, GIScience 2018, August 28–31, 2018, Melbourne, Australia. LIPIcs, vol. 114, pp. 1:1–1:15. Schloss Dagstuhl - Leibniz-Zentrum für Informatik (2018). https://doi.org/10.4230/LIPIcs.GISCIENCE.2018.1
4. Arazy, O., Woo, C.C.: Analysis and design of agent-oriented information systems. Knowl. Eng. Rev. **17**(3), 215–260 (2002). https://doi.org/10.1017/S0269888902000450
5. Arel, I., Liu, C., Urbanik, T., Kohls, A.G.: Reinforcement learning-based multi-agent system for network traffic signal control. IET Intell. Trans. Syst. **4**(2), 128–135 (2010). https://doi.org/10.1049/iet-its.2009.0070
6. Badue, C., Guidolini, R., Carneiro, R.V., Azevedo, P., Cardoso, V.B., Forechi, A., Jesus, L., Berriel, R., Paixão, T.M., Mutz, F., et al.: Self-driving cars: a survey. Expert Syst. Appl. 113816 (2020). https://doi.org/10.1016/j.eswa.2020.113816
7. Bai, Q., Ren, F., Fujita, K., Zhang, M., Ito, T.: Multi-agent and Complex Systems. Springer, Berlin (2017). https://doi.org/10.1007/978-981-10-2564-8
8. Baldoni, M., Baroglio, C., Boissier, O., May, K.M., Micalizio, R., Tedeschi, S.: Accountability and responsibility in agent organizations. In: International Conference on Principles and Practice of Multi-Agent Systems, pp. 261–278. Springer, Berlin (2018). https://doi.org/10.1007/978-3-030-03098-8
9. Bastian, M., Heymann, S., Jacomy, M.: Gephi: An open source software for exploring and manipulating networks. In: Proceedings of the International AAAI Conference on Web and Social Media, vol. 3 (2009). https://doi.org/10.13140/2.1.1341.1520
10. Bird, S., Klein, E., Loper, E.: Natural Language Processing with Python: Analyzing Text with the Natural Language Toolkit. O'Reilly, Beijing (2009). http://my.safaribooksonline.com/9780596516499
11. Bojarski, M., Del Testa, D., Dworakowski, D., Firner, B., Flepp, B., Goyal, P., Jackel, L.D., Monfort, M., Muller, U., Zhang, J., et al.: End to end learning for self-driving cars (2016). arXiv preprint arXiv:1604.07316. https://doi.org/10.1109/ICCE-Berlin.2018.8576190
12. Bonabeau, E.: Agent-based modeling: methods and techniques for simulating human systems. Proc. Nat. Acad. Sci. **99**(suppl 3), 7280–7287 (2002). https://doi.org/10.1073/pnas.082080899
13. Bresciani, P., Perini, A., Giorgini, P., Giunchiglia, F., Mylopoulos, J.: Tropos: an agent-oriented software development methodology. Auton. Agents Multi-Agent Syst. **8**(3), 203–236 (2004). https://doi.org/10.1023/B:AGNT.0000018806.20944.ef
14. Bubenko, J., Kirikova, M.: "worlds" in requirements acquisition and modelling. DSV (1994)
15. Burt, R.S.: Structural Holes: The Social Structure of Competition. Harvard University Press, Cambridge (1992)
16. Bösser, T.: Autonomous agents. In: Wright, J. (ed.) International Encyclopedia of the Social & Behavioral Sciences, pp. 1002–1006. Elsevier, Amsterdam (2015). https://doi.org/10.1016/B0-08-043076-7/00534-9
17. Cuevas, E.: An agent-based model to evaluate the covid-19 transmission risks in facilities. Comput. Biol. Med. **121**, 103827 (2020). https://doi.org/10.1016/j.compbiomed.2020.103827

18. Dhesi, G., Ausloos, M.: Modelling and measuring the irrational behaviour of agents in financial markets: Discovering the psychological soliton. Chaos Solitons Fractals **88**, 119–125 (2016). https://doi.org/10.1016/j.chaos.2015.12.015

19. Dignum, V., Dignum, F.: Agents are dead. long live agents! In: Seghrouchni, A.E.F., Sukthankar, G., An, B., Yorke-Smith, N. (eds.) Proceedings of the 19th International Conference on Autonomous Agents and Multiagent Systems, AAMAS '20, Auckland, New Zealand, May 9–13, 2020, pp. 1701–1705. International Foundation for Autonomous Agents and Multiagent Systems (2020). https://dl.acm.org/doi/abs/10.5555/3398761.3398957

20. Dignum, V., Gilbert, N., Wellman, M.P.: Introduction to the special issue on autonomous agents for agent-based modeling. Auton. Agents Multi-Agent Syst. **30**(6), 1021–1022 (2016). https://doi.org/10.1007/s10458-016-9345-5

21. Fortino, G., Guerrieri, A., Russo, W.: Agent-oriented smart objects development. In: Proceedings of the 2012 IEEE 16th International Conference on Computer Supported Cooperative Work in Design (CSCWD), pp. 907–912 (2012). https://doi.org/10.1109/CSCWD.2012.6221929

22. Franklin, S., Graesser, A.: Is it an agent, or just a program? A taxonomy for autonomous agents. In: International Workshop on Agent Theories, Architectures, and Languages, pp. 21–35. Springer, Berlin (1996)

23. Franklin, S., Graesser, A.: Intelligent Agents III. Lecture Notes on Artificial Intelligence, pp. 21–35. Springer, Berlin (1997)

24. Goodfellow, I.J., Bengio, Y., Courville, A.C.: Deep Learning. Adaptive Computation and Machine Learning. MIT Press, Cambridge (2016). http://www.deeplearningbook.org/

25. Grimm, V., Railsback, S.F.: Individual-based modeling and ecology. Princeton University Press, Princeton (2013). https://doi.org/10.1515/9781400850624

26. Hayes-Roth, F., Waterman, D.A., Lenat, D.B.: Building Expert Systems. Addison-Wesley Longman Publishing, Bostoorth (1983)

27. Hewitt, C.: Viewing control structures as patterns of passing messages. Artif. Intell. **8**(3), 323–364 (1977). https://doi.org/10.1016/0004-3702(77)90033-9

28. Janssen, M.: Complexity and Ecosystem Management: The Theory and Practice of Multi-Agent Systems. Edward Elgar Publishing, Cheltenham (2002)

29. Jennings, N., Sycara, K., Wooldridge, M.: A roadmap of agent research and development. Auton. Agents Multi-Agent Syst. **1**, 7–38 (1998). https://doi.org/10.1023/A:1010090405266

30. Jennings, N.R.: On agent-based software engineering. Artif. Intell. **117**(2), 277–296 (2000). https://doi.org/10.1016/S0004-3702(99)00107-1

31. Khalil, W., Dombre, E.: Modeling, Identification and Control of Robots. Butterworth-Heinemann (2004)

32. Liebowitz, J.: Introduction to Expert Systems. Mitchell Publishing, Los Angeles (1988)

33. Lin, H.: Architectural Design of Multi-Agent Systems: Technologies and Techniques: Technologies and Techniques. IGI Global, Pennsylvania (2007)

34. Masters, P., Sardina, S.: Expecting the unexpected: goal recognition for rational and irrational agents. Artif. Intell. **297**, 103490 (2021). https://doi.org/10.1016/j.artint.2021.103490

35. Mondal, B.: Artificial intelligence: state of the art. Recent Trends Adv. Artif. Intell. Internet Things 389–425 (2020). https://doi.org/10.1007/978-3-030-32644-9_32

36. Monostori, L., Váncza, J., Kumara, S.R.: Agent-based systems for manufacturing. CIRP Ann. **55**(2), 697–720 (2006)

37. Newman, M.E.J.: Modularity and community structure in networks. Proc. Nat. Acad. Sci. **103**(23), 8577–8582 (2006). https://doi.org/10.1073/pnas.0601602103

38. Poole, D.L., Mackworth, A.K.: Artificial Intelligence: Foundations of Computational Agents. Cambridge University Press, Cambridge (2010). https://doi.org/10.1017/9781108164085

39. Russell, S.J., Norvig, P.: Artificial Intelligence: A Modern Approach. Prentice Hall Series in Artificial Intelligence. Prentice Hall, Englewood Cliffs (1995). https://www.worldcat.org/oclc/31288015

40. Sibbel, R., Urban, C.: Agent-based modeling and simulation for hospital management. In: Cooperative Agents, pp. 183–202. Springer, Berlin (2001)

41. Silva, V., Garcia, A., Brandão, A., Chavez, C., Lucena, C., Alencar, P.: Taming agents and objects in software engineering. In: International Workshop on Software Engineering for Large-Scale Multi-Agent Systems, pp. 1–26. Springer, Berlin (2002). https://doi.org/10.1007/3-540-35828-5_1

42. Simon, H.A.: Bounded rationality. In: Utility and Probability, pp. 15–18. Springer, Berlin (1990)

43. Singh, D., Padgham, L., Logan, B.: Integrating BDI agents with agent-based simulation platforms: (JAAMAS extended abstract). In: Proceedings of the 16th Conference on Autonomous Agents and MultiAgent Systems, AAMAS '17, pp. 249–250. International Foundation for Autonomous Agents and Multiagent Systems, Richland (2017). http://dl.acm.org/citation.cfm?id=3091125.3091165

44. Sowa, J.F., Zachman, J.A.: Extending and formalizing the framework for information systems architecture. IBM Syst. J. **31**(3), 590–616 (1992). https://doi.org/10.1147/sj.313.0590

45. Sterling, L., Taveter, K.: The Art of Agent-Oriented Modeling. The MIT Press, Cambridge (2009). https://doi.org/10.7551/mitpress/7682.001.0001

46. Sulis, E., Humphreys, L., Vernero, F., Amantea, I.A., Audrito, D., Di Caro, L.: Exploiting co-occurrence networks for classification of implicit inter-relationships in legal texts. Inform. Syst. 101821 (2021). https://doi.org/10.1016/j.is.2021.101821

47. Sun, R., et al.: Cognition and multi-agent interaction: from cognitive modeling to social simulation. Cambridge University Press, Cambridge (2006). https://doi.org/10.1017/CBO9780511610721

48. Taveter, K., Wagner, G.: A multi-perspective methodology for modelling inter-enterprise business processes. In: Arisawa, H., Kambayashi, Y., Kumar, V., Mayr, H.C., Hunt, I. (eds.) ER 2001 Workshops, HUMACS, DASWIS, ECOMO, and DAMA, Yokohama Japan, November 27–30, 2001, Revised Papers. Lecture Notes in Computer Science, vol. 2465, pp. 403–416. Springer, Berlin (2001). https://doi.org/10.1007/3-540-46140-X_31

49. van der Aalst, W., Bichler, M., Heinzl, A.: Robotic process automation (2018). https://doi.org/10.1007/s12599-018-0542-4

50. Watts, D.J., Strogatz, S.H.: Collective dynamics of small-world networks. Nature **393**(6684), 440–442 (1998). https://doi.org/10.1038/30918

51. Weiss, G.: Multiagent Systems. The MIT Press, Cambridge (2013)

52. Wooldridge, M., Jennings, N.R.: Intelligent agents: theory and practice. Knowl. Eng. Rev. **10**(2), 115–152 (1995). https://doi.org/10.1017/S0269888900008122

53. Wright, J.: International Encyclopedia of the Social & Behavioral Sciences, vol. 11. Elsevier, Amsterdam (2015)

54. Zachman, J.A.: A framework for information systems architecture. IBM Syst. J. **26**(3), 276–292 (1987). https://doi.org/10.1147/sj.263.0276

55. Zimmer, N.: Socio-technical modeling and simulation of airline operations control. Doctoral Thesis, Technische Universität Braunschweig, Germany (2020)

Part II
The Agent-Based Perspective

Chapter 4
Agent-Based Simulation with NetLogo

Abstract This section introduces the NetLogo tool, which is currently one of the most widely adopted platforms for agent-based simulations. We first present an overview of the basic concepts used within NetLogo, such as commands and procedures for creating a modeling and simulation application. We then provide an introduction to the main components of a NetLogo program by introducing both the specific programming language and more advanced features. Understanding the tool is a necessary step to be taken to better appreciate the examples offered in the book.

4.1 Build and Learn with NetLogo

NetLogo's motto is "Low Threshold, No Ceiling." We believe this is also true in the context of business process modeling. The NetLogo platform was created at the turn of the last century by a team led by Uri Wilensky at Northwestern University. The main purpose was to provide a high-level platform that allows students to build and learn from simple ABMs. The platform includes a programming language based on Logo [5]. Having been continually improved, the current version of NetLogo contains many sophisticated capabilities, such as behaviors, agent lists, graphical interfaces, and extensions to run code written in Python or R. One of the success factors of NetLogo is a gentle learning curve. In addition, a large NetLogo community supports practitioners, and several manuals and tutorials are freely available both within the platform's help feature and as several external resources.

To support readers who have not yet tried out the tool, this section describes the main components of the platform while also providing a brief introduction to the NetLogo programming language in Sect. 4.2, as well as by introducing the extensions 4.3. We present three introductory NetLogo programs: a simple business process model, a tribute to the classical AI theme of the Wumpus world, and the simulation of an emergency department of a hospital as an ongoing case study often used in this book (Sect. 4.4). Finally, Sect. 4.4 introduces an online tutorial created specifically to introduce learning NetLogo.

© Springer Nature Switzerland AG 2022   53
E. Sulis, K. Taveter, *Agent-Based Business Process Simulation*,
https://doi.org/10.1007/978-3-030-98816-6_4

4.2   The Modeling Platform

NetLogo is a programmable modeling platform designed specifically for simulation modeling. In particular, the tool addresses ABM (or IBM, as is explained in Sect. 3.1) by managing the behavior of simple entities called agents or individuals acting in a certain environment, consisting of the grid or space of cells where agents can move around and interact with other entities. For the sake of clarity, we elaborate on the adoption of the term "entity." The world ontologically entails active entities—agents—like turtles and passive entities, objects, like patches of the turtles' environment.

The tool mostly deals with a "bottom-up" approach to model the interactions between entities in order to investigate the impact of micro-level behaviors at the macro-level. Nevertheless, the tool is very versatile and can be used also for other kinds of simulations in addition to ABM, such as discrete-event simulation and system dynamics.

The platform has been written primarily in Scala, while some parts have been written in Java and run on the Java Virtual Machine. In recent years, a version of the program (NetLogo Web) running on JavaScript has been developed, to execute models in a web browser. The web-based version supports a limited set of features of the desktop version. The Java platform, on which parts of NetLogo were initially written, enables using several libraries. The program offers also APIs for extending the code both in Java and Scala.

Desktop version can be downloaded and installed from the official website.[1] The platform includes hundreds of examples in the Models Library, as well as a very rich Help section including the User Manual, Dictionary, and Programming Guide.

4.2.1   Main Components

The NetLogo environment includes a programming language, a compiler, an interpreter, a syntax highlighting editor, and an interface builder. As has already been mentioned, NetLogo includes its own programming language that is simpler to use than other languages, such as Java or Objective-C, an animation display automatically linked to the program, and optional graphical controls and charts.

Each NetLogo program follows quite a conventional scheme. Figure 4.1 describes a hypothetical NetLogo screen that includes the following main parts: the top bar menu (1) including three tabs, which the top bar menu (1) including three tabs, which are Interface, Info, and Code; the setup area (2), with different buttons associated with the initial procedures to create a simulation; an input/output area (3) including monitors to present the results of the simulation, other buttons to

---

[1] http://ccl.northwestern.edu/netlogo/.

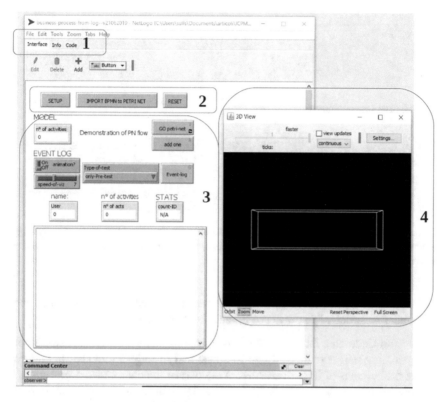

Fig. 4.1 The main parts of a NetLogo program

address the simulation, some sliders to define variable parameters of the simulation, and so on; the main area to visualize the simulation results called the "2D view," while the view area in the NetLogo 3D version is called the "3D view" (4). The visualization area is a black screen where agents move and interact with each other and other entities. When a new empty model is opened, this view is usually placed on the center-right of the screen.

The NetLogo Top Menu Bar

The NetLogo menu bar shown at the top of the screen has three main areas: Interface, Info, and Code, as is reflected by Fig. 4.2. The bar includes options for improving the visualization, such as a slider to set the simulation speed, as well as a checkbox to enable or disable the view area.

Interface The Interface usually contains the following elements: the output view of the simulation, some "buttons" for the user to interact with the simulation, several monitors, and graphs generated to illustrate the simulation results. Figure 4.3 describes a sample layout of buttons and monitors on the interface.

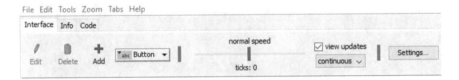

Fig. 4.2 The Interface menu

Fig. 4.3 A typical set of buttons on the Interface: switch ("with-infected?"), slider ("propagation-risk"), chooser ("preset-profiles"), procedure buttons ("setup" and "go"), and two monitors to show the results ("#people" and "#families")

Info The Info section includes a description of the purpose and the features, such as "what the model is," "how to use it," and "author references."

Code The Code area includes a NetLogo program written in the special-purpose programming language of NetLogo to create and manage the model. In addition to the declarations of initial variables, every part of the code called a procedure is enclosed between the keywords "to" and "end." Comments within the code begin with a semicolon ";". The next section focuses on the Code area.

4.2.2   A Glance to the Code

The NetLogo code serves primarily research and educational purposes, demonstrating a distinctive convenience of writing even by novice programmers. Because of the readability of the code even by someone completely inexperienced, the resulting simulation models can be easily understood. This aspect has facilitated the dissemination of ABM among many different research communities by communicating, comparing, and verifying simulation results.

Skeleton of a Program
The code can be written freely, and there are some conventions that make it easier to share among the research communities. A program can be typically separated into the following three main parts:

- *1. Variables declarations.* On the first line, a NetLogo program usually begins with the inclusion of libraries of interest, the so-called extensions. This is followed by the definitions of the classes or types of agents. In the NetLogo jargon, agents are termed as *turtles*, and classes or types of agents are called *turtle breeds*. Finally, the initial part defines both the global variables by the *globals* construct and the variables specific for each type of agent or other entity by the *turtles*-own, or *breed_name*-own constructs.

- *2. Initial settings*. A specific "setup" procedure, which by convention corresponds to the "setup" button of the NetLogo user interface, first cleans the simulation environment of previous values of the variables by executing the NetLogo command *clear-all*. This is followed by defining the initial values of the variables at the first step of running the simulation system, including resetting the time variable.
- *3. The main cycle*. Typically, the main procedure corresponds to the "go" button on the NetLogo user interface. The main loop includes procedures that are concerned with both the agents and the environment, to be repeated until the stop condition becomes fulfilled. The time variable is increased by one unit at a time with the *tick* command.

The NetLogo platform manages four types of entities, through specific variables of the corresponding types defined at the beginning of the program. These entity types are agents (*turtles*), the environment (*patches*) in which the agents move and interact, *links* between *turtles*, and the "observer" that refers to the kind of omniscient agent and controller having a "God's eye view" of the simulation. Also *patches* can contain variables and can be represented within a GIS to be imported as *shapefiles* (see Sect. 4.3.2). Similarly, the *links* between *turtles* can contain variables and are likewise modeled as entities to be added to or removed from to the simulation model.

A typical skeleton of the initial part of a NetLogo program is as follows:

```
extensions [ <name> ]   ; import specific libraries

globals [ <name> ]       ; global variables used in the program

turtles-own [ <name> ] ; turtles' local variables
patches-own [ <name> ] ; patches' local variables
links-own [ <name> ]    ; links' local variables
```

4.2.3 Setup and Go Procedures

The conventional names *setup* and *go* are commonly adopted to identify the main procedures for initializing and executing a NetLogo simulation.

The two procedures are associated with the two buttons—*setup* and *go*—on the Interface tab, as in Fig. 4.4. The setup typically procedure includes the following instructions: (i) initialize the simulation; (ii) set the patches of the environment; (iii) create the agents—turtles—of the environment by setting their positions, shapes,

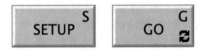

Fig. 4.4 Setup and Go buttons in the Interface. Note the loop symbol for Go button, as well as letters to assign an "action key" to the corresponding procedures

colors, orientations, and so on; and (iv) initialize the simulation time to 0 by means of *reset-ticks*. The following code provides an example of the setup:

```
to setup
  clear-all         ; clear the screen
  setup-patches     ; initialize the simulation environment
  setup-turtles     ; initialize the agents
  reset-ticks       ; reset the clock
end
```

4.2.4 Main Cycle

The *go* procedure executes the model and is performed in a loop. A standard configuration of the *go* procedure includes the following steps: (i) check the stop condition; (ii) simulate the environment, by affecting the patches; (iii) simulate agent behaviors by managing the turtles, as well as by performing the interactions between the turtles and their environment; (iv) update statistics by using monitors, charts, and plots; and (v) advance time by using internal counter tick.

The following code sample summarizes the content of the *go* procedure:

```
to go
    if <condition> [stop] ; the stop condition

    procedure-observer ; one or more general procedures
    procedure-turtles  ; procedures concerning the agents
    procedure-patches  ; procedures to update the environment

    tick                ; increment time
end
```

The program defines each different procedure as a portion of the code.

```
to procedure-observer
    <instructions>
    procedure-example    ; call the procedure
    set v procedure-return-a-value ; set a new variable v
end
```

A report function (keyword *to-report*) can return a value (keyword *report*) as follows:

```
to-report procedure-return-a-value
    <instructions>
    report value-resulting-from-some-calculation
end
```

4.2.5 Space and Time

Each simulation model typically occurs in space and evolves over time. This is also the case with the NetLogo simulation platform. In a discretized environment or "world" consisting of a grid or space (in 3D tool) of "patches," agents (or "turtles") perform different actions at discrete time steps, i.e., "ticks."

In some cases, the evolution of time or the spatial variations are of a particular interest. For example, the arrival of patients to the emergency department may depend on the hour of the day, the day of the week, and the month of the year. On the contrary, for instance, the arrival of orders to the chain of stores may vary from a city to another or may change over time. In addition, the agents manipulate variables related to time and space. For example, an employee's productivity may vary based on different internal and external factors. This is the case with individual job skills, but also with external events occurring at a certain time or involving space, such as economic incentives, office temperature, and satisfactory relationship with work colleagues.

Space The environment—"world"—created by NetLogo is composed of grid cells or "patches," where each "patch" has two coordinates or three coordinates in the 3D tool. The size of the display area can be changed by right-clicking on the display— the black area on the interface—and changing the maximum coordinates as well as the size of the patches to extend the grid. The NetLogo world wraps, meaning that when an agent crosses the edge of the world, it reappears from the opposite edge of the world. The model setup menu allows one to turn wrapping on and off horizontally or vertically, or in both ways at the same time.

Time The simulation environment is based on discrete time steps ("ticks"), where a tick counter is updated at each cycle of executing the simulation model. As was already mentioned before, the *setup* command initializes the tick using the instruction *reset-ticks*. To produce more realistic simulations, one can relate each tick to a unit of time, such as a second, minute, or day. Specific commands, such as *tick-advance*, allow to increase the tick counter to advance the simulation. This command allows to avoid wasting computation time in idle phases, as in the *ABBPS_Ford-Mazda* model discussed in Chap. 8. Another option is to exploit the Time library[2] that allows the simulation to manage real dates presented in various date-time formats. The Time extension has been recently developed, and it was not possible to include it in this work.

---

[2] https://ccl.northwestern.edu/netlogo/docs/time.html.

4.2.6 BehaviorSpace

The BehaviorSpace tool built into NetLogo is concerned with the design of ABM experiments. In particular, the BehaviorSpace tool addresses the verification, validation, and replication of an ABM. This tool simplifies the study of parameter variation in the model by automatically changing simulation parameters within predefined ranges.

Using the BehaviorSpace tool is often called *parameter sweeping*, intended as a quick way to conduct a series of simulations by varying parameters and displaying the output on a graph (see Sect. 6.2.3). As a matter of fact, the BehaviorSpace tool allows the users to easily visualize the output for the effect by varying simulation parameters. For instance, the research can specify a subset of values from the ranges of each variables included in the NetLogo model, in particular in the sliders of the model interface. The corresponding model can be run by the program modifying each possible combination of the selected values. In the execution of the model, the program records the results during each model run. This provides the researcher with a set of solutions from a subset of the model's parameter space, in order to be able to explore relationships between variables, as well as the general system behavior. We refer the interested reader to the detailed guide included in the program and available online, so as not to burden the reading of this Chapter (https://ccl.northwestern.edu/netlogo/docs/behaviorspace.html).

4.2.7 3D Visualization

The standard NetLogo desktop version provides by default a 2D visualization, which can be changed to 3D visualization by right-clicking on the display and then selecting the "Switch to 3D View" option. In addition, modelers can use the NetLogo 3D tool, which is a separate program included in the files downloaded from the NetLogo website. This tool allows one to create a model directly in a three-dimensional world. In that kind of world, each *patch* has three rather than two coordinates.

The ability to simulate in 3D a process or any other phenomenon has many advantages including a clear representation more appealing to the stakeholders, the ability to explore the 3D space by moving around within it, and visualization of variables that are otherwise difficult to visualize. The example *ABBPS_ED-map-building* in the website repository demonstrates how to create the walls of a building, as in the case of a real map of an emergency department.

The possibilities of improving the ease of understanding of business processes with a 3D visualization have already been explored [3]. The positive educational effects of 3D visualizations are also known [6]. Similar to the 3D Petri net business process visualization described in [1], we propose in Sect. 7.3.2 a 3D NetLogo business process visualization. In addition, the simulations that offer visualizations

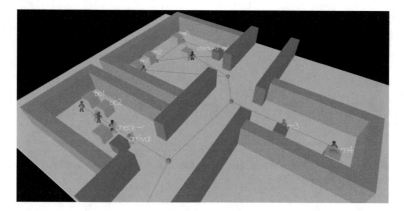

Fig. 4.5 Simulating agents moving in a building with the 3D NetLogo tool

of agents that move within a spatial structure, instead of an activity diagram, allow for immediate and better understanding. This is exemplified by the visualization represented in Fig. 4.5 concerning a 3D NetLogo model which uses "NW," i.e., the network extension. This is also similar to the ABM of a hospital emergency service included in the web repository of this book (*ABBPS_ED-3D* model).

4.2.8 NetLogo Web

NetLogo Web is a version of the NetLogo modeling platform that runs entirely in the browser. The advantages of being able to run a model on the web are the immediacy of spreading and sharing the model. NetLogo Web enables to represent the behavior of the simulation, as well as visualize the code. However, not all NetLogo models can yet be correctly executed in the Web version of NetLogo. In this book, we provide several examples of models that are directly executable on the web, such as the introductory business process example *ABBPS_Intro_Business_Process* model described in Sect. 4.4.1 and represented in Fig. 4.6.

4.2.9 BehaviorSearch

An experimental software bundled with NetLogo is BehaviorSearch [8], which is an open-source cross-platform tool to facilitate experiments with genetic algorithms. BehaviorSearch offers several search algorithms and representations of search spaces and can be used to explore the parameter space of any agent-based model created in the NetLogo language.

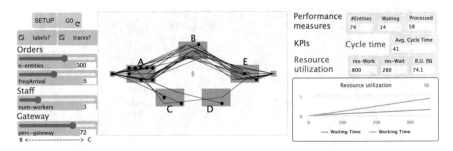

Fig. 4.6 The online version of the *ABBPS_Intro_Business_Process* model translated into HMTL and JavaScript by NetLogoWeb

The tool includes a GUI for providing a convenient way to facilitate design and execute advanced search and optimization techniques. BehaviorSearch exploits a combination of Boolean, numerical, and categorical parameters by adopting various search algorithms and search space representations. Finally, the tool provides a multi-thread support to improve the computational performance. An external, well-documented website makes it easy to approach the tool, also describing possible different practical experiments in this area.[3]

4.3 Extensions

In every programming languages, the integration of existing predefined procedures into the current program refers to the inclusion of "libraries." Regarding business process modeling, some libraries of interest enable the studies of networks with social network analysis (SNA), or the integration of geographic information systems (GIS). This is possible by using the respective NetLogo extensions "nv" and "gis." The users of NetLogo can also create their own extensions.[4] In the following subsections, we will provide an overview of the social network analysis and geographic information systems extensions.

---

[3] The BehaviorSearch website: https://www.behaviorsearch.org.

[4] See how to build a new extension at https://ccl.northwestern.edu/netlogo/docs/extensions.html, and how to exploit a built-in tool (extension manager) to share and install new libraries at https://ccl.northwestern.edu/netlogo/docs/extension-manager.html.

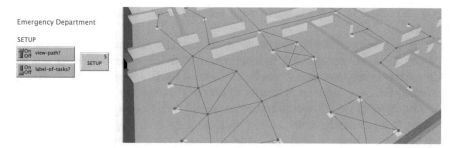

Fig. 4.7 An example that imports a *graphml* file to represent path trajectories in a building (*ABBPS_ED-Path-import-graph* model)

4.3.1 Social Network Analysis

In ABM, agents can be associated with other agents through links which can be used for representing relationships or contacts between the agents.

Links can be created by means of the `create-link-to` construct, which is thoroughly described in the user manual.[5] In addition, the network analysis benefits from a specific code extension provided by the `extensions [nw]` library.

The *NW* extension[6] is useful for calculating typical social network metrics, such as the degree or centrality. The library also allows to import or export the network in standard formats. For example, to import a network in the *graphml* format, the `nw:load-gexf "<name_of_the_file>.graphml"` construct should be used. The *ABBPS_ED-Path-import-graph* model represented in Fig. 4.7 imports vertex and edges from the *graphml* format, to create path between two distinct nodes in the emergency department. This approach is based on the campus model presented in [2]. Other work presented in this book adopt this library, as in the cases concerning the dissemination of information (*ABBPS_Dissemination-process*) or movements in a building (*ABBPS_ED-3D*) models.

4.3.2 Geographic Information Systems

As we have mentioned above, NetLogo agents can move on a grid or within a space of cells. In addition, they can also interact with a GIS (see also Sect. 8.3.2), using a special-purpose extension provided by NetLogo. The extension can be easily installed with the `extensions [gis]` command at the beginning of the program.

---

[5] https://ccl.northwestern.edu/netlogo/docs/dictionary.html.

[6] Visit: https://ccl.northwestern.edu/netlogo/docs/nw.html.

A guide enriched with examples helps the user understand how this extension works.[7]

The extension allows the import of pre-existing GIS data represented as vectors (points, lines, and polygons) or rasters (grids) into the current model. For example, the extension supports vector data in the form of ESRI shapefiles (.shp), which is probably the most common format for storing and exchanging vector data for GIS.

According to [9], "Simulations can be transformed from a basic representation to one that accurately replicates the characteristics of a map or population." In Sect. 8.3, we describe a NetLogo model of a basic reinforcement-learning project that uses a GIS.

4.3.3 Source Code and New Extensions

The source code of the NetLogo platform is hosted on GitHub.[8] This allows developers to explore and improve the platform, as well as to add new commands and reporters by writing code in Java and other languages that can be used in NetLogo. NetLogo provides some introductory examples that describe how to create extensions and use them in simulation models.[9]

A recent feature of NetLogo allows for easier management of new extensions.[10] In addition to the user's guide, some help is offered through the various channels of the NetLogo community, such as the official website, mailing lists, and Modeling Commons website.[11]

In this book, we propose an XES extension to NetLogo for handling the import and export of a business process event log in the standard XES format, as is described in Sect. 9.3.

4.4 Introductory Examples

This section introduces three basic examples for the beginners. The first example is a very simple business process modeling and simulation in NetLogo that handles patches as tasks and turtles as workers. The second example is the Wumpus world, which is concerned with classical AI. The third example is the simulation of

---

[7] https://ccl.northwestern.edu/netlogo/docs/gis.html.

[8] https://github.com/NetLogo/NetLogo.

[9] https://ccl.northwestern.edu/netlogo/docs/extensions.html.

[10] https://ccl.northwestern.edu/netlogo/docs/extension-manager.html.

[11] Modeling Commons website is for sharing and discussing agent-based models written in NetLogo and includes more than 1000 models http://modelingcommons.org.

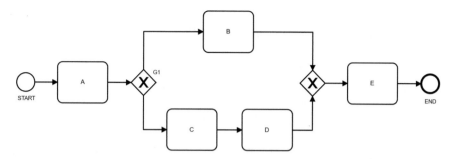

Fig. 4.8 A basic example of a business process model in BPMN

the business process of an emergency department, which can be considered as a practical running case study of this book.

4.4.1   A Basic Business Process

This section introduces a basic NetLogo program (*ABBPS_Intro_Business _Process.nlogo*) that can be used to begin exploring business process modeling and simulation. Specifically, we intend to simulate a simple business process consisting of five tasks ("A" through "E") with an exclusive gateway after the first task "A," as is represented by the BPMN model in Fig. 4.8.

Figure 4.8 shows how a business process in healthcare could look like, such as the registration phase of an emergency department business process. This kind of process starts with the arrival of a patient with the initial activity of reporting at the reception desk. After that, the flow of the business process follows two alternative paths. At the top, the flow consists of a single activity (e.g., involves patients already registered in the hospital IS), while the bottom flow consists of two activities (e.g., additionally includes registration of a new patient in the hospital IS). Finally, in both cases, the last activity concludes the process (e.g., adding the patient to the waiting list). Another type of business process that can be represented by the same model shown in Fig. 4.8 is that of production orders received by a company. In this scenario, the entities arriving in the process are orders (activity "A" may be the registration step), with two different possible treatments (e.g., two different shipping methods), before the final activity (e.g., invoice preparation) is performed.

Whichever case we want to represent, the process model can be translated to the constructs of the NetLogo platform. The activities of a business process can become *patches*, each of which is characterized by a name and a variable containing information about the average duration of the task. We join several cells together, so that they look like rectangles and have a uniform color. Workers can be *turtles* of a dedicated *turtle breed*. The entities arriving and going through the activities of

the process can be *turtles* of a different *turtle breed*. The corresponding NetLogo
program can start with the following initial code:

```
breed [ entities entity ]
breed [ workers worker ]

patches-own [          ; define the variables that all patches can use
  name                 ; their name
  service-duration     ; the (avg) duration time
]
```

The entity that enters the process is an agent, like a patient, or an object,
like an order, that goes through the activities of the flow. The entity may pos-
sess some local variables to characterize its state, such as the Boolean variable
`entity-service?` indicating if the entity is currently being served by the
simulation system, the `time-begin` to keep track of when serving an entity by
the simulation system will start, and the `CT-begin` to compute the cycle time (see
Sect. 2.2.3) at the end of the simulation. All entities remain in a waiting list (a global
variable `list-entities`), while they are not being served.

```
entities-own [         ; define the variables belonging to each breed
  entity-service?      ; is being served?
  time-begin           ; the moment serving an entity will start
  CT-begin             ; the starting time (for computing cycle time)
]
```

Workers are the agents that serve the entities in the simulation. When they are
free, they search for entities from the waiting list: if there are any, they will start
serving the first entity from the waiting list by performing their corresponding
activities. Therefore, each worker has a Boolean variable *is-working?* that identifies
the worker's status of *free* versus *busy*. Another variable of a worker agent keeps
track of the entity that the worker is currently serving. In our example, we also
introduced in a worker agent a few variables for managing the simulation, such
as the time to finish the current task *w-time-end-act*, as well as the variables (*w-
time-working* and *w-time-waiting*) for monitoring the working and waiting time.
Other variables could also be included in an entity to be served, such as the
complexity of the work required on the entity. This can be represented as a
dichotomous enumeration value—easy or difficult—or as a factor to be multiplied
by the processing time.

```
workers-own [ ; define the variables belonging to each worker
  is-working? ; a worker is working
  working-with ; the entity with which it is serving

  w-time-end-act ; the end of the working time on an activity
  w-time-working ; monitoring working time
  w-time-waiting ; monitoring waiting time
]
```

In a NetLogo program, the initial steps are typically included in a *setup*
procedure. In our *ABBPS_Intro_Business_Process* model, the *setup* includes different functions to initialize the main variables (`setup-variables`), patches

(setup-process), and agents (setup-workers), in addition to performing the default procedures ca and reset-ticks. The resulting code looks as follows:

```
to setup
  ca                    ; clear-all
  setup-variables       ; initialize main variables
  setup-process         ; create the environment and initialize the program
  setup-workers         ; initialize the agents
  reset-ticks           ; reset tick before to start
end
```

The *go* procedure, on the other hand, includes the main loop with the following procedures to introduce arrivals of new entities into the process (new-arrival), to check if workers are free to start serving an entity (workers-check-entities), and to check when the time of serving an entity is over and other activities of the business process can continue (check-time). The final set of procedures includes outputting some monitoring statistics (monitoring-stats). The main loop also includes the time increment (tick) and the stop condition.

```
to go      ; main cycle
  tick

  new-arrival               ; introduce new entities
  workers-check-entities    ; workers check for approved entities
  check-time                ; check the time taken to work on the entity
  monitoring-stats          ; update monitors

  if monit-entities = n-entities  [ stop ] ; the stop condition
end
```

In NetLogo, multiple variables can be initialized on the interface (see Fig. 4.9), such as the number of entities arriving in the simulation (*n-entities*) or the number of current workers. The monitors and diagrams generated allow for a quick review of the key results, including the average cycle time as a KPI. The *ABBPS_Intro_Business_Process* model is simple and understandable. In addition to this basic introductory example, Sect. 7.3.1 describes the ability of a particular NetLogo program to directly import a BPMN model into the program.

4.4.2 The Wumpus World

To better introduce the tool adopted in the book, and offer homage to classical work on agents in AI, we created in NetLogo the Wumpus World program (*ABBPS_Wumpus-World.nlogo*) represented in Fig. 4.10 for studying knowledge-based agents, proposed by Michael Genesereth [7].

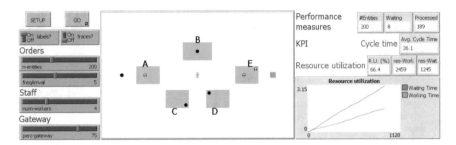

Fig. 4.9 An introductory business process modeling and simulation example in NetLogo

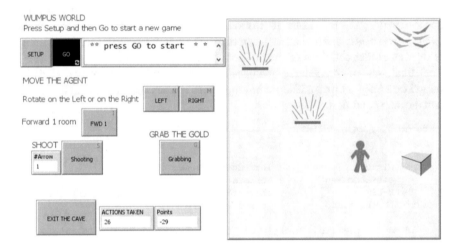

Fig. 4.10 Agent-based model of the Wumpus World—the main view

Description of the Game The Wumpus world takes place in a cave consisting of
rooms connected by passageways. Lurking somewhere in the cave is the terrible
Wumpus, a beast that eats anyone who enters its room. The Wumpus can be shot
by an agent, but the agent has only one arrow. Some rooms contain bottomless
pits that will trap anyone who wanders into these rooms (except for the Wumpus,
which is too big to fall in). The only mitigating feature of this bleak environment is
the possibility of finding a heap of gold. Although this program is rather tamed by
modern computer game standards, it illustrates some very important points about AI.
The typical Performance, Environment, Actuators, Sensors (PEAS) [4] description
about the environment is as follows:

- *Performance measure*: $+1000$ for climbing out of the cave with the gold, -1000
  for falling into a pit or being eaten by the Wumpus, -1 for each action taken, and
  -10 for using up the arrow. The game ends either when the agent dies or when
  the agent climbs out of the cave.

- *Environment* A 4 × 4 grid of rooms. The agent always starts in the square labeled [1,1], facing to the right. The locations of the gold and the Wumpus are chosen randomly, with a uniform distribution, from the squares other than the start square. In addition, each square other than the start square can be a pit, with the probability 0.2.
- *Actuators* The agent can move Forward, Turn-Left by 90°, or Turn-Right by 90°. The agent dies a miserable death if it enters a square containing a pit or the alive Wumpus. If an agent tries to move forward and bumps into a wall, then the agent does not move. The action Grab can be used to pick up the gold if it is in the same square as the agent. The action Shoot can be used to fire an arrow in a straight line in the direction the agent is facing. The arrow continues until it either hits (and hence kills) the Wumpus or hits a wall. The agent has only one arrow, so only the first Shoot action has any effect. Finally, the action Climb can be used to climb out of the cave, but only from the square [1,1].
- *Sensors* Each agent has five sensors, each of which gives a single bit of information: (i) In the square containing the Wumpus and in the directly (not diagonally) adjacent squares, the agent will perceive a Stench. (ii) In the squares directly adjacent to a pit, the agent will perceive a Breeze. (iii) In the square where the gold is, the agent will perceive a Glitter. (iv) When an agent walks into a wall, it will perceive a Bump. (v) When the Wumpus is killed, it emits a Scream that can be perceived anywhere in the cave.

The perceptions will be provided to the agent program in the form of a list of five symbols; for example, if there is a stench and a breeze, but no glitter, bump, or scream, the agent will get [Stench, Breeze, None, None, None].

4.4.3 Emergency Department

The last example that we introduce in this section is the modeling and simulation of an emergency department (*ABBPS_ED-simulation.nlogo*). The types of agents in the emergency department are workers or operators—nurses, physicians, and social workers—who are involved in a set of activities or tasks with patients.

An ABM focuses on agent behaviors, where active agents in ED are workers, who start the business process simulation when they are able to begin a service on a patient, or are engaged in back-office services. The flow of activities is defined by a business process model represented in the BPMN language. Figure 4.11 shows a basic diagram of the ED business process in BPMN that includes the main activities, starting from the arrival of a patient.

In Sect. 7.3.1, we demonstrate a NetLogo program enabling to automatically import a BPMN diagram to represent the workflow on a NetLogo screen. The ED business process model represents the 14 main tasks of the ED, containing two types of start events (i.e., arrival of patients by ambulance or on their own), as well as multiple gateways (all XOR decisions) of the flow.

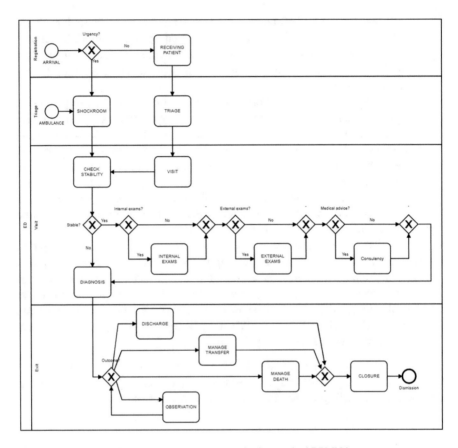

Fig. 4.11 Emergency department business process in the standard BPMN language

To improve the visualization of the activities, we also exploit the map of a real ED, as is shown in Fig. 4.12.

Here we have opted for the typical NetLogo Desktop (2D) version, which is the most traditional and stable version of NetLogo. The *ABBPS_ED-3D* model describes the importation of a map of an emergency department to create a realistic simulation environment. In the current 2D version, the "patches" or the pavement where the agents move can be colored according to the different ED sectors as follows:

- LightGreen—Waiting room
- Gray—Registration desk
- Green—Triage
- Blue—Observation area
- Red— Shock Room
- Pink—Consultation
- Purple—XRay exam

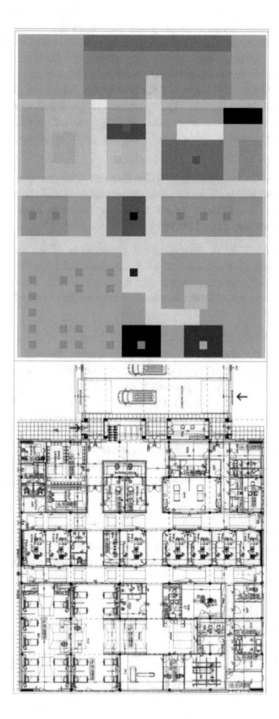

Fig. 4.12 Map of the real emergency department and NetLogo

Each patch has a variable for identifying the type of activity included by the business process. For example, the light green patches in the center correspond to the Triage activity. Each patch (corresponding to the activity) includes the number of workers, the types of workers, and the average and standard duration for completing the service. A Boolean variable *free?* determines whether the activity is available for a new patient. At the initial setup of the simulation, all the patches are vacant, which is represented by assigning the True value to the *free?* variable. A patch becomes busy after the workers have started serving a patient, which is represented by assigning the False value to the *free?* Boolean variable of the corresponding patch.

Agents in the ED ABM emphasizes the role of agents. The emergency department is staffed 24/7 by three physicians or clinical professionals and six nurses certified in emergency medicine. Patients arrive randomly but with certain regularities depending on the hour and day of the week.

Moving Agents within ED To determine the movements of the agents—patients and operators—we can import a graph with the paths between the nodes, where the weight of each edge corresponds to the time required to cover the distance between the two nodes by walking. For further information on graph importation, see Sect. 4.3.1.

Operators As in the real world, operators are the "engine" of the activities by the ED. The number of operators of different types—nurses, medical doctors, social workers—can be set by the corresponding sliders on the interface. There is a variable determining the "state" of each operator: it can perform a *service* with a patient ("S"); *take a break* ("P"); *look* for a new patient to serve ("L"); *move* from one location to another in the ED ("M"); or wait for a task to begin, as is represented in Table 4.1.

The simulation starts with the arrival of patients in the admission area, the first task being "Register Patient," and ends with the exit from the ED, the last task being "Closure." Similarly to workers, also each patient has a state variable corresponding to its current activity.

Regarding the process flow of activities, each agent has the "next task" variable that includes the name of the following task to be started at the next step. At the beginning of the simulation, the "next task" is set to "Registration." Whenever an agent finishes performing a task, it sets the "next task" variable according to the

Table 4.1 The worker states with the descriptions and names of the variables

Description	Var.	State
1-The worker looking for a patient to serve	W	Waiting for a patient to serve
2-Moving to/from ED areas	M	Moving to next ward
3-Pending/waiting to start working	P	Pending/Waiting to start
4-Busy, starting service on places with workers	S	Performing the service
5-Deciding to have a break—stop/pause	B	Having a break/pause

Table 4.2 The description and the variable names of the states of patients

Description	Var.	State description
1-The patient is waiting a call for the service	W	Waiting
2-Moving to/from ED areas	M	Moving
3-Pending/waiting to start working	P	Pending
4-Busy, starting service on places with workers	S	Service
5-Deciding to abandon	A	Abandon

flow of the business process. If there is a gateway, a function determines the next task according to the probabilities associated with different branches of the gateway.

Time Time scheduling is one of the most relevant aspects of ABM. NetLogo includes a tick variable for time discretization. We chose to simulate the emergency department at the time granularity of seconds. A procedure can easily map seconds to obtain hours (3600 ticks), days (86,400 ticks), and months (2,592,000). Alternatively, the time extension can be used to handle real data values,[12] for instance, the starting date (e.g.,"01.01.2020 00:00:00").

The Arrival of New Patients Patients arrive every day by following a specific distribution based on real life. In the model, every 24 h, the simulation computes an array with a stochastic set of arrival times. To manage different arrival times, we provide a specific model *ABBPS_Interarrival-times* on the website associated with the book.

Main Variables A patient has the following main variables: a status variable describing its current situation, such as waiting for a provider to arrive (Pending), being actively served by a worker (Service), or leaving the ED before being seen by a physician (Abandon); the Emergency Severity Index (ESI) corresponding to the patient's level of urgency, i.e., a number from 1 to 5 for the variable ESI; and a variable describing the next task in the flow (next-task). Table 4.2 describes the states of patients.

Some variables relate to key indicators of the healthcare process. In particular, we record the time of the arrival in the hospital time-of-arrival, in order to compute KPIs as the length of stay (Los) or the door-to-doctor time (DTDT). The LOS is the time spent by the patient from admission to the hospital to discharge. DTDT is the time elapsed by the patient from admission to the initial medical examination in the ED.

Rules The behavior of the ED simulation mostly depends on the behaviors of healthcare workers that are modelled as active agents. At each time unit, they check the environment: if a patient is waiting for a service, they will commit to the patient, whereby the variable "working-with" is set with the agent information. If needed, they also move to the next spatial area according to the flow of the business process.

---

[12] https://ccl.northwestern.edu/netlogo/docs/time.html.

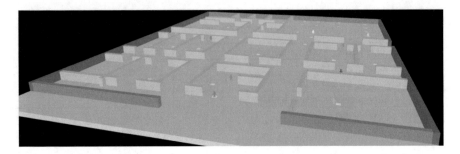

Fig. 4.13 A 3D visualization of a building in the *ABBPS_ED-3D* model

Finally, they may decide to have a break or work faster, depending on the number of patients in the waiting list.

Patients are primarily passive agents, as they must wait and follow the instructions by the healthcare workers. They remain in the queue corresponding to the activity of remaining in the common "Waiting-Area" until they are called to get the service. They become "active" when they decide to leave the ED before the normal end of the activities.

A 3D Model of an Emergency Department The web repository of the book includes also the *ABBPS_ED-3D* model describing how to get a nice 3D visualization. As mentioned before, a good visualization of the simulation improves the overall readability also to not BPM experts. For example, a 3D view can better describe the resulting paths or bottlenecks of a simulated scenario. The demo example provides the visualization of the same emergency department in a 3D perspective, as is shown in Fig. 4.13.

The code of the *ABBPS_ED-3D* model contains the creation of the walls based on a map concerning the healthcare hospital department, which allows to create a realistic simulation environment.

4.5   A Tutorial for Learning How to Program in NetLogo

To introduce learning NetLogo, we created a tutorial based on an introductory program called "Agents on the move" (Fig. 4.14). The tutorial provides six short lessons to perform a first ABM to simulate the connections between people moving in a world made of other people and objects (walls, puddles). In particular, people wander around by moving one step ahead in the world, which is full of walls, puddles, and other people.

The basic agent behavioral rules are: (i) When the agents hit a wall, they turn around and wander again. (ii) An agent on a puddle moves slower. (iii) If an agent meets other people, they both stop for a second and leave a trace by coloring the floor

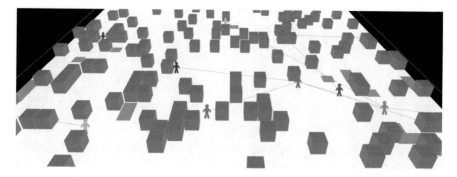

Fig. 4.14 "Agents on the move" model included in the tutorial for learning NetLogo

(patch). In addition, if they were not already connected, a link is created between them.

The tutorial with the corresponding model is publicly available at the following web address, https://abmsim.di.unito.it/tutorial-netlogo/, as well as on the book's website.

References

1. Betz, S., Eichhorn, D., Hickl, S., Klink, S., Koschmider, A., Li, Y., Oberweis, A., Trunko, R.: 3d representation of business process models. In: Loos, P., Nüttgens, M., Turowski, K., Werth, D. (eds.) Modellierung betrieblicher Informationssysteme (MobIS 2008), pp. 73–87. Gesellschaft für Informatik e.V., Bonn (2008)
2. Crooks, A., Malleson, N., Manley, E., Heppenstall, A.: Agent-Based Modelling and Geographical Information Systems: A Practical Primer. SAGE Publications Limited (2018). https://doi.org/10.4135/9781473916432.n4
3. Eichhorn, D., Koschmider, A., Li, Y., Sturzel, P., Oberweis, A., Trunko, R.: 3d support for business process simulation. In: 2009 33rd Annual IEEE International Computer Software and Applications Conference, vol. 1, pp. 73–80. IEEE, Piscataway (2009). https://doi.org/10.1109/COMPSAC.2009.20
4. Poole, D.L., Mackworth, A.K.: Artificial Intelligence: Foundations of Computational Agents. Cambridge University Press, Cambridge (2010). https://doi.org/10.1017/9781108164085
5. Railsback, S.F., Lytinen, S.L., Jackson, S.K.: Agent-based simulation platforms: review and development recommendations. Simulation **82**(9), 609–623 (2006). https://doi.org/10.1177/0037549706073695
6. Richards, D., Taylor, M.: A comparison of learning gains when using a 2d simulation tool versus a 3d virtual world: an experiment to find the right representation involving the marginal value theorem. Comput. Educ. **86**, 157–171 (2015). https://doi.org/10.1016/j.compedu.2015.03.009
7. Russell, S.J., Norvig, P.: Artificial Intelligence: A Modern Approach. Prentice Hall Series in Artificial Intelligence. Prentice Hall (1995). https://www.worldcat.org/oclc/31288015
8. Stonedahl, F., Wilensky, U.: Behaviorsearch [computer software]. Center for Connected Learning and Computer Based Modeling, Northwestern University, Evanston, IL (2010). http://www.behaviorsearch.org
9. Walker, B., Johnson, T.: NetLogo and GIS: a powerful combination. In: CATA, pp. 257–264 (2019)

Chapter 5
Agent-Oriented Modeling

Abstract The purpose of this book is to use agent-based simulations for studying business processes of any problem domain with the purpose to optimize them. When one is faced with a new problem domain and intends to model and simulate business processes of that domain, a natural question to be asked is "How should I start?" We answer this question in this chapter. The answer consists of three stages. First, the purpose and decisions to be supported by business process simulation and the stakeholders are identified. This entails identifying agents or active entities of the problem domain and representing their behaviors, knowledge, and interactions. Second, the models representing the problem domain analysis are mapped to the business process models. Third, the problem domain analysis models and business process models are mapped to the NetLogo program. To understand the problem domain and decisions to be supported, our approach uses a hierarchical abstraction to help deal with complexity in business processes. We take a typical top-down approach of focusing on high-level details early in problem domain analysis and exploring the lower-level details once the high-level understanding is sufficient. The purpose of this chapter is to describe how this can be done in a holistic and balanced manner. The methodology put forward in this chapter can also be used for agent-oriented problem domain analysis for different purposes separately from business process modeling and NetLogo.

5.1 Business Processes Modeling Approaches

Broadly speaking, business process modeling approaches can be divided into the following three categories [5]:

- Activity-oriented approaches define a business process as a set of ordered activities. The emphasis is on what activities take place.
- Agent-oriented approaches specify and analyze the role of the agents that participate in the process. The focus is on the entities that perform process elements.

© Springer Nature Switzerland AG 2022
E. Sulis, K. Taveter, *Agent-Based Business Process Simulation*,
https://doi.org/10.1007/978-3-030-98816-6_5

- Product-oriented approaches represent a process through the evolution of its products. The focus is on products and transformations made on them.

Historically, activity-oriented approaches such as Business Process Modeling Notation (BPMN) [1, 8] have become dominant over agent- and product-oriented approaches. However, to be successful in agent-based business process simulation and support decisions based on this kind of simulation, one needs to understand and model business processes with an agent-oriented mindset. In Sect. 5.1.1, we will describe how agent-oriented mindset can be achieved by the methodology of agent-oriented modeling (AOM) proposed in [13, 15].

5.1.1   The AOM Methodology

Far too often, agent-based simulations are developed in an ad hoc manner [6]. However, because of the complexity of agent-based simulations, application of systematic software engineering methodologies is necessary for developing useful agent-based simulations [2, 10]. A software engineering methodology defines a systematic process with steps that guide the developer from requirements elicitation to implementation, validation, and sometimes even maintenance of the software [11]. This chapter describes the AOM software engineering methodology that is tailored for designing and developing agent-based business process simulations. The AOM methodology addresses a problem domain at three different abstraction layers and from three complementary vertical perspectives. In general, many perspectives on the processes in an organization are possible. The Zachman Framework [12, 18] was one of the first conceptual frameworks to provide a comprehensive picture of the possible perspectives. The Zachman Framework classifies perspectives on a two-dimensional grid. The first dimension indicates the question being asked by a model's stakeholders: What? How? Where? Who? When? and Why? The second dimension indicates the stakeholder: Planner, Owner, Designer, Builder, and Subcontractor. Zachman proposes that every modeling approach may be categorized as a combination of one question and one stakeholder [17]. Proceeding from the philosophy of the Zachman Framework, Sterling and Taveter [13] defined the viewpoint framework. The viewpoint framework is also a grid with two dimensions but has only three vertical perspectives and three abstraction layers. The vertical perspectives are interaction, information, and behavior, and the abstraction layers are analysis, design, and implementation. The interaction perspective merges the Who and Where perspectives of the Zachman Framework, dealing with active entities or agents of the system[1] to be modelled and interactions between them. The information perspective directly corresponds to the What? perspective of the

---

[1] The term "system" is used in this section in the broad sense denoting both a social system—organization—and a technical system designed and built to support the organization. We elaborate the term "system" in Sect. 5.1.2.

Table 5.1 The viewpoint framework

Modeling concepts	Viewpoint aspect		
Abstraction layer	Interaction	Information	Behavior
Problem domain analysis	Roles and relationships between them	Domain entities	Goals
System design	Business process model		
System implementation	NetLogo program		

Zachman Framework and is concerned with the information to be represented within the system. The behavior perspective merges the Why? When? and How? perspectives of the Zachman Framework, focusing on the goals set for the system and the timed behaviors of the agents of the system for achieving these goals. The abstraction levels and perspectives are summarized by the viewpoint framework [13] represented in Table 5.1. The viewpoint framework consists of a matrix with three rows representing the abstraction layers of problem domain analysis, system design, and system implementation and three columns representing the interaction, information, and behavior perspectives. Each cell in this matrix represents a specific viewpoint, such as "interaction analysis," "information design," or "behavior implementation." Each viewpoint is captured by one or more models, which make use of the relevant concepts.

The central concepts used at the abstraction level of problem domain analysis are *roles*, *domain entities*, and *goals*, which correspond to the respective vertical perspectives of interaction, information, and behavior. *Goal* is a state of affairs to be achieved by the system. *Domain entity* is a modular unit of knowledge to be handled by the system or an environmental resource for the system. *Role* is a capacity or position that is required for achieving the goals set for the system. Role is played by an agent, which is defined as an active entity that can act in the environment, perceive events, and reason [13]. At the abstraction level of system design, business processes are modelled by mapping the concepts of problem domain analysis to the constructs of a business process modeling language. Finally, at the abstraction level of system implementation, business process simulations are built by mapping the concepts of problem domain analysis and the constructs of the BPMN business process modeling language to the programming constructs of the agent platform NetLogo that is used as a primer in this book. Please note that we do not distinguish between vertical perspectives for the system design and implementation layers because they are intermingled in BPMN and NetLogo representations. The AOM methodology is agile—several iterations are conducted at each abstraction layer and also between the layers. The AOM methodology addresses each abstraction layer by a number of questions to be asked when designing the agent-based simulation system, similarly to the questions asked by the system's stakeholders according to the Zachman Framework [12, 18]. These questions Q1–Q18 are presented and explained in Sects. 5.1.2–5.1.5. Moving within and between the three abstraction layers prescribed by the AOM methodology and the artefacts—models—created at each layer are illustrated in Fig. 5.1.

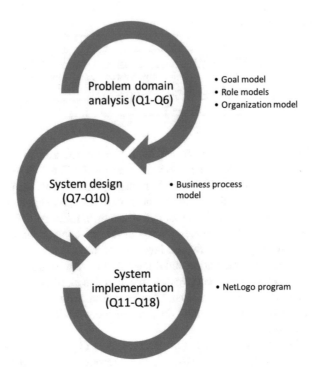

Fig. 5.1 The iterations of the AOM methodology for business process modeling and simulation

In Sect. 5.1.2, we explain how the problem to be addressed can be understood and modelled and how the stakeholders can be identified and represented with an agent-oriented mindset. This is followed by explaining in Sect. 5.1.3 how the problem domain can be rendered for agent-based business process simulation. In Sect. 5.1.4, we describe how the concepts of agent-oriented problem domain analysis are mapped to the constructs of a business process modeling language. In Sect. 5.1.5, we describe how a business process is mapped to the NetLogo simulation of the business process. Finally, in Sect. 5.2, we apply the methodology to another case study—the case study of purchasing business processes in a car factory.

5.1.2 Identifying the Problem and Stakeholders

Any agent-based simulation system is designed and developed with some purpose in mind. The purpose is usually concerned with making decisions of some kind. Such decisions can, for example, be made on where should electric vehicle charging stations be located, how should land be used in one or another location to minimize environmental impact, what types of services should be offered to tourists in a

Fig. 5.2 The iterations of the AOM methodology for business process modeling and simulation

particular destination, what would be the best way to evacuate the injured from the disaster zone, what are the most efficient isolation and vaccination strategies to slow down the spreading of COVID-19, and how to prevent the emergence of echo chambers of misinformation and fake news. Let us now consider a project where healthcare stakeholders should make a decision on how to organize in the most efficient way the work of a hospital's emergency department (ED). They need a sociotechnical system for supporting their decision. Sociotechnical system is defined as a software intensive system that supports human work processes within an organization and comprises both social and technical subsystems [11]. The decision-support system is called sociotechnical because it is supported by agent-based simulation decisions made by humans. A sociotechnical system of this kind can "try out" by means of its technical subsystem—agent-based simulation— the effects of decisions made by humans on how to organize the ED business process. The first step of designing and developing a decision-support system on ED business processes is to understand the problem domain and identify its stakeholders. We use goal models of AOM to represent the problem domain. Goal models consist of two types of goals—functional goals and quality goals—and roles. Functional goals indicate what the (sociotechnical) system should do or achieve. Quality goals present non-functional requirements of the system describing the quality aspects of the system—how the system should be. In addition, roles are identified which represent who are responsible for the attainment of which goals. All of this information is eventually presented as a simple graph where functional goals are rendered in a tree-like hierarchy. In the hierarchical goal model, each sub-goal represents a particular aspect of achieving its parent goal. Functional goals are represented with tilted rectangles, while roles and quality goals are attached to the appropriate functional goals. The notation for goal models is shown in Fig. 5.2. Quality goals and roles that are attached to the given functional goal apply to that goal and to all of the functional goals located below the given goal in the goal tree. Finally, a key performance indicator (KPI) is used for evaluating or measuring the attainment of a quality goal.

We use goal models for representing the motivations for the project as well as for designing the decision-support system and the agent-based simulation system included by it. Figure 5.3 presents the project motivation model for the simulation of the ED business processes. The goal of the project is to develop a system for decision support on ED business processes. Three quality goals were noted. First, the decision-support system must be developed using the agent-oriented paradigm. This is an important quality goal because the purpose of this book is to provide

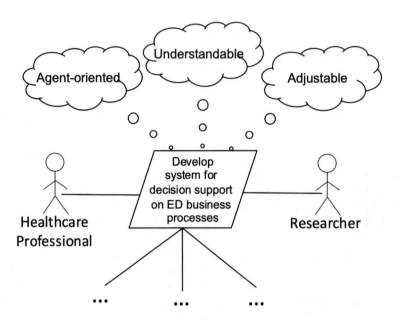

Fig. 5.3 Project motivation model

decision support by means of agent-based simulation of business processes. Please note that we use as the name of the quality goal the term "agent-oriented" rather than "agent-based" to represent that agent-based simulations should go hand in hand with agent-oriented mindset, which was explained in Sect. 5.1. The other two quality goals express that the ED business process simulator must be understandable and adjustable. The quality goal *understandable* is easy to achieve because it has been shown that the notion of agent is understandable also for people who are not experts in information technology [7, 13]. The quality goal *adjustable* can be achieved by *what-if* scenario analysis in business process simulation and by the variation of simulation parameters with the help of, for example, genetic algorithms [9, 14]. The goal model shown in Fig. 5.3 includes the stakeholder roles healthcare professional and researcher. Healthcare professionals define the decisions to be made with the help of the agent-based simulation system and establish the criteria for decision-making. Researcher designs and develops the system for decision support. We will return to the decision-making criteria shortly below. In addition to the project motivation, we also derive a high-level motivation model for the decision-support system. This outlines the goals of the entire sociotechnical agent-oriented system for decision support, rather than just of the agent-based simulation system to be built. For understanding the purpose of the simulation-based decision support system, we ask the following questions:

- What quality goals do we aim to optimize by means of agent-based simulation?
- What parameters do we intend to set up and vary to optimize the attainment of the quality goals?

- What key performance indicators do we plan to utilize to evaluate or measure the attainment of the quality goals by means of parameter optimization?
- How do we plan to optimize the values of the chosen parameters?

A goal model of decision support on ED business processes is shown in Fig. 5.4. This model identifies the key motivations of the healthcare professional and researcher—respectively, the main stakeholder and user of the system—and how the system fits into their workflow. We plan to optimize the attainment of the quality goal *efficient* that refers to the execution time of a business process. This quality goal can be elaborated into the measurable quality goals *minimal length of stay* and *maximal resource utilization*. Both of them positively contribute to the attainment of the quality goal *efficient*, which is denoted by the "+" signs in Fig. 5.4. The quality goal *minimal length of stay* represents efficiency from the patient's perspective and the quality goal *maximal resource utilization* from the management perspective. The parameters that are set up and varied to optimize the attainment of the quality goals are paths along which patients and healthcare workers move in the ED and the strategy of arranging the queue of patients. The key performance indicators that can be utilized for measuring the attainment of the *minimal length of stay* quality goal are *door-to-doctor time* (DTDT) and *length of stay* (LOS). DTDT is the number of minutes it takes for a patient to see a doctor from the arrival to the ED. LOS is the number of minutes from patient arrival to the exit from the ED. The key performance indicator that can be used for measuring the attainment of the *maximal resource utilization* quality goal is *time-worked-with-patients* (TWP), which represents the rate of minutes worked by doctors directly with patients. The key performance indicators DTDT, LOS, and TWP are depicted in Fig. 5.4. All of the key performance indicators explained above are important for designing the simulation system. The high-level motivation model of the decision-support system shown in Fig. 5.4 also reflects that we plan to optimize the parameters *minimal length of stay* and *maximal resource utilization* by means of varying paths how patients and healthcare staff move within the ED and varying the queue strategies for patients. In Sect. 5.1.3, we describe how a problem domain can be modelled in an agent-oriented way in the context of decision support obtained by agent-based simulations. We do this by describing how the goal *simulate ED business process* is elaborated into sub-goals along with the relevant quality goals and roles.

5.1.3 Agent-Oriented Problem Domain Modeling

In this subsection, we continue the top-down construction of the hierarchical goal model started in Fig. 5.4 by modeling the sub-goals of the goal *simulate ED business process*. In general, each business process should achieve a certain business goal, such as providing a service, finalizing a sales transaction, or producing a product. For example, the overall goal or purpose of a procurement business process is *procure*. As we introduced in Sect. 5.1.1, this kind of goal—functional goal or

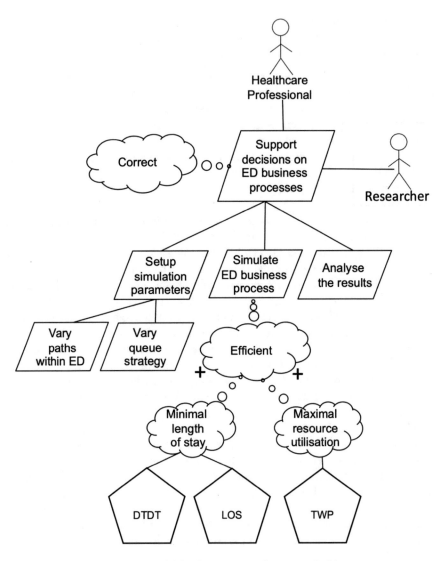

Fig. 5.4 High-level motivation model for the emergency department decision-support system

do-goal—answers the question "What should be done or achieved?" A functional goal can be elaborated into its sub-goals, each of which represents a particular aspect of achieving the higher-level goal. For example, in the procurement business process, the highest-level goal—*procure*—has been elaborated into the sub-goals *identify alternatives, find deal, order, receive product*, and *pay*, each representing a particular aspect of procurement. As we hinted in Sect. 5.1.1 and illustrated in Fig. 5.1, the AOM methodology addresses each abstraction layer of the viewpoint framework by a number of questions to be asked when designing the system. We now present questions Q1–Q6 that should be answered by the project stakeholders for agent-oriented problem domain analysis:

Q1. What is the purpose of the business process? This question aims to elicit the main functional goal of the business process to be modelled and simulated. Information elicited with this question is recorded as the root goal of the goal model. Example: the root goal of the ED business process is *treat a patient*.

Q2. For the goal identified in Q1:

Q2.1. Can achieving this goal be elaborated into different aspects? This question aims to identify sub-goals of the given functional goal. Information elicited with this question is recorded as the sub-goals in the goal model. Example: In the ED problem domain, the goal *treat a patient* has been elaborated into the sub-goals *register*, *triage*, *check-up*, and *exit*, each representing a particular aspect of treating a patient. If the answer to this question is "yes," add each identified sub-goal to the "stack" of sub-goals to be recursively analyzed and return to Q2.1 to identify sub-goals of lower levels of the goal tree.

Q3. For each goal identified in Q1 and Q2:

Q3.1. What are the quality aspects of achieving the goal, if any? This question aims to identify quality goals that characterize the attainment of the given functional goal. Quality aspects of achieving the goal are recorded in the goal model by quality goals attached to the given functional goal. Example: The quality goals *correct* and *fast* characterize the attainment of the functional goal *register*.

Q4. For each quality goal identified in Q3.1:

Q4.1. What are the key performance indicators required for measuring the attainment of this quality goal? The aim of this question is to elicit additional key performance indicators to the ones that were already identified in Sect. 5.1.1 and included in the high-level motivation model of the decision-support system. The key performance indicators are recorded in the goal model as associated with the respective quality goal. Example: The key performance indicator required for measuring the attainment of the quality goal *fast* is *time-to-registration* (TTR). The TTR indicator measures the time from the arrival of a patient to the ED to the start of the service at one of the registration desks.

Q5. For each goal identified in Q1 and Q2:

Q5.1. Which roles are needed to achieve this goal? This question aims to elicit the roles needed for achieving the goals defined for the problem domain. These roles are recorded in the goal model as attached to the corresponding functional goal. Example: The roles Medical Doctor, Triage Nurse, ED Nurse, and Healthcare Worker are required for achieving the goals set for the ED problem domain.

The answers to questions Q1–Q5 along with the respective sub-questions are recorded in the goal model. The goal model for the ED problem domain is shown in Fig. 5.5. The figure represents the highest-level motivational view of the problem domain, including the quality goals of the domain. The goal model depicted in Fig. 5.5 includes the roles required for achieving the goals of the problem domain. In goal models, we typically annotate roles to either goals that are leaf goals—that is, are not broken down further—or to non-leaf goals in which the role is responsible for the non-leaf goal and its sub-goals.

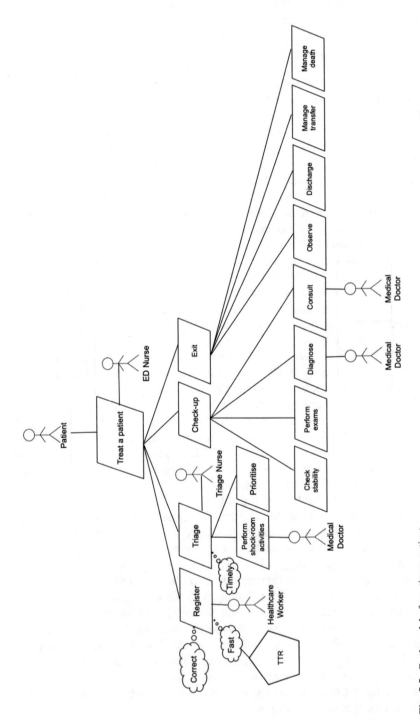

Fig. 5.5 Goal model of treating a patient

Role models describe the capacities or positions that facilitate the achievement of goals. Roles have responsibilities, which outline what an agent playing the role must do to achieve the related goals. Organization model represents how an agent performing a role depends on agents playing other roles for fulfilling its responsibilities. We now proceed with the question Q6 that helps model in more detail the roles, relationships between them, the knowledge needed by agents performing the roles, and the environment where the agents are situated.

Q6. For each role identified in Question Q5.1:

Q6.1. What responsibilities would an agent performing the given role have with respect to achieving the goals with which the role is associated? This question aims to elicit the responsibilities of the role. Information elicited with this question is recorded in the *responsibilities* attribute of the role model. Example: The responsibilities of the role Medical Doctor in the ED business process are *perform check-up*, *perform shock-room activities*, *diagnose*, and *consult*. Please note that responsibilities by roles are orthogonal to goals included by the goal model.

Q6.2. What other roles would an agent playing this role depend on for fulfilling its responsibilities? This question aims to elicit the dependencies between the roles of the problem domain. For determining a dependency, it is relevant if the exchange of information takes place between the agents performing the respective roles. Information elicited with this question is recorded in the organization model. Examples: For fulfilling its responsibility *diagnose*, Medical Doctor depends on the ED Nurse to inform it about the outcome of exercising its responsibilities *check stability* and *perform exams*. For fulfilling its responsibilities *observe*, *discharge*, *manage transfer*, and *manage death*, the ED nurse depends on Medical Doctor for the outcome of performing the responsibility *diagnose*. For fulfilling all of their responsibilities, Medical Doctor and ED Nurse depend on Healthcare Worker for exercising its responsibilities *register patient* and *move patient* if the patient is not capable of independent moving.

Q6.3. What knowledge would an agent require to successfully exercise the responsibilities defined by the corresponding role? Information about knowledge elicited with this question is recorded under the *knowledge* attribute of the role model. Example: To fulfil its responsibilities, a Medical Doctor is required to be aware of the Patient Information domain entity.

Q6.4. What resources would an agent require to successfully exercise the responsibilities of the corresponding role? This question aims to elicit the relevant aspects of the environment. Information elicited with this question is recorded in the *resources* attribute of the role model. Example: The roles Healthcare Worker, Triage Nurse, and Medical Doctor require the respective environmental resources Registration Area, Triage Area, and Check-up Area, and all of these roles require the environmental resource Health Information System. Table 5.2 models the roles included by the ED where the role name and its responsibilities, knowledge, and resources are represented in the respective columns of the table. Figure 5.6 depicts the organization model of the ED, which shows how agents performing particular roles depend on each other for fulfilling the responsibilities prescribed by the corresponding roles.

Table 5.2 The models of the roles included by the emergency department

Role	Responsibilities	Knowledge	Resources
Healthcare worker	Register patient Move patient (if not capable of moving)	Patient Information	Registration Area Health Information System
Medical Doctor	Perform shock-room activities Diagnose Consult		Triage Area Check-up Area Health Information System
Triage Nurse	Perform shock-room activities Prioritize		Triage Area Resuscitation equipment Health Information System
ED Nurse	Check stability Perform exams Observe Discharge Manage transfer Manage death		Check-up Area Observation Area Health Information System Radiology service Laboratory service
Patient	Move between the areas (if capable)		Registration Area Triage Area Check-up Area Observation Area

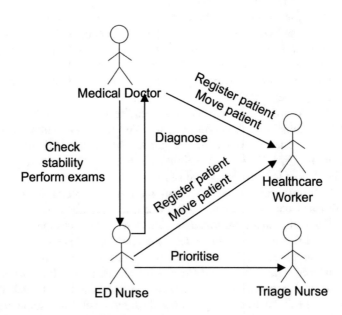

Fig. 5.6 Organization model of treating a patient

5.1.4 Mapping Agent-Oriented Problem Domain Models to BPMN

Goal model shown in Fig. 5.5 and role models contained by Table 5.2 represent the purpose and structure of a business process. They model the goals to be achieved by the business process and how agents performing the roles contribute to achieving the goals by fulfilling their responsibilities. A role model also represents the knowledge that is required for performing the role and the environment in which the role is to be performed. Organization model represents how roles depend on each other for fulfilling their responsibilities. Neither the goal model nor the role models specify the order in which the goals have to be achieved by exercising the corresponding responsibilities. We advocate delaying the definition of the order of achieving the goals because it leaves the door open for more solution alternatives until stakeholders have arrived at a shared understanding of the problem domain. The order is introduced by the business process model. A natural choice would be to follow an agent-oriented business process modeling approach, such as the one put forward in [16]. However, as we already stated at the beginning of Sect. 5.1, historically, agent-oriented business process modeling approaches have been supplanted by activity-oriented approaches such as Business Process Modeling Notation (BPMN) [1, 8], which has become an industry standard. Considering this, we transform agent-oriented problem domain models into a business process model represented in BPMN. This transformation is based on the mappings between the modeling constructs of high-level agent-oriented problem domain models and a business process model in BPMN. These modeling constructs are shown in the respective first and second column of Table 5.3. We now present Q7–Q10 that should be answered by the project stakeholders to map from agent-oriented problem domain models to the corresponding business process model in BPMN.

Q7. What is the overall title of the business process or the name of the organization whose business process is being modelled? Information elicited with

Table 5.3 Mapping between business process models and NetLogo programming constructs

Agent-oriented problem domain models	Business process model in BPMN	NetLogo program
Business process	Pool	NetLogo procedures
Role	Lane	Turtle breed or patch
Responsibility	Task	Procedure
Knowledge	Data object or Message	Local or global variable or turtle breed
Resource	Lane or Data store	Patch

this question is recorded as the name of the BPMN pool in which the business process is modelled. Example: the business process of the emergency department is modelled within the BPMN pool named "Emergency Department."

Q8. For each environmental resource identified in Question Q6.4 and included by Table 5.2:

Q8.1. If the resource is a geographical area or a logical area like a department, add the corresponding BPMN lane within the pool created in Question Q7. Example: In the business process model of the emergency department, separate lanes are added for the registration area, triage area, check-up area, and observation area. Q8.2. If the resource is an information system, add the corresponding BPMN data store to the pool. Example: In the business process model of purchasing in a car factory depicted in Fig. 5.12, the resource Purchasing Information System from Table 5.4 is mapped to the corresponding BPMN data store.

Q9. For each role identified in question Q5.1 and included by Table 5.2:

Q9.1. Create for the role a sub-lane within the lane representing the geographical or logical area where the role operates. If there is no lane for the area, create a lane for the role directly within the pool. Example: The sub-lanes Medical Doctor and ED Nurse are created within the lane created in question Q8.1 for the geographical area Check-up Area.

Q9.2. For each responsibility of the role, create a BPMN task with the same name. Example: The responsibilities *diagnose* and *consult* of the role Medical Doctor are represented as the corresponding BPMN tasks.

Q10. For each task identified in Q9.2:

Q10.1. What triggers the start of this task? This question aims to elicit the BPMN event that starts the task. Information elicited with this question is recorded as the trigger of the corresponding task in the business process model. Examples: The task *register patient* by a performer of the Healthcare Worker role is triggered by the arrival of the patient; the task *observe* by a performer of the ED Nurse role is triggered by the end of the task *diagnose* by a performer of the Medical Doctor role.

Q10.2. Under what conditions can this task be started? This question aims to elicit the precondition for the task, that is, the knowledge states of the environment that enable this task. Such conditions are recorded as BPMN gateway conditions, which ultimately define the flow of the business process. Examples: The task *register patient* can be performed if the patient is not in a critical condition; the task *perform exams* can be executed if the patient is stable.

Q10.3. What happens after this task has been completed? This question aims to elicit how the task changes the knowledge stored in the environment. Information elicited with this section is recorded as the post-condition of the corresponding task. Example: the post-condition of the task *diagnose* is "The patient has a diagnosis," which entails a change in the BPMN data object (not represented in Fig. 5.7) corresponding to the Patient Information domain entity of the agent-oriented problem domain models.

Q10.4. What information from performers of other roles would be required to successfully complete this task? This question aims to elicit possible information exchange with performers of other roles to complete this task. Information elicited with this question is recorded as a BPMN data input, message flow, or sequence flow **into** the task, where a data object or message, if any, refers to a domain entity of the agent-oriented problem domain models. Examples: The information from executing the task *perform exams* by a performer of the ED Nurse role is required to successfully complete the task *diagnose* by a performer of the Medical Doctor role; in the car factory case study described in Sect. 5.2, the message flow Invoice from a performer of the Vendor role is required to successfully complete the task *check documents* by a performer of the Accounts Payable role.

Q10.5. Performers of which roles should be informed that this task has been completed? This question aims to elicit the information to be exchanged with performers of other roles upon completion of this task. Information elicited with this question is recorded as a BPMN data output, message flow, or sequence flow **from** the task, where a data object or message, if any, refers to a domain entity of the agent-oriented problem domain models. Examples: A performer of the role ED Nurse has to be informed by a performer of the role Medical Doctor that the patient has been diagnosed; in the car factory case study described in Sect. 5.2, the message flow Purchase Order is required to be sent to a performer of the Vendor role upon completion of the task *send purchase order* by a performer of the Purchasing Office role.

The answers to questions Q7–Q10 are recorded in the business process model of the emergency department shown in Fig. 5.7. Please note the difference between the initial model of the emergency department business process represented in Fig. 4.11 and the business process model of the emergency department depicted in Fig. 5.7. The difference is due to using in the second case the systematic AOM methodology for problem domain analysis and business process modeling, resulting in Fig. 5.7.

5.1.5   Mapping Business Process Model to NetLogo

The final step that needs to be taken before we can start *what-if* simulation experiments with the business process model is mapping the business process model to NetLogo. This is accomplished by mapping the constructs of the agent-oriented problem domain models **and** the corresponding constructs of the business process model in BPMN to the constructs of NetLogo, as is shown in Table 5.3. This transformation results in the business process model represented as a NetLogo program. We make this transformation simpler by presenting questions Q11–Q15 that should be answered by the project stakeholders for mapping to NetLogo:

Q11. What types of agents are represented in the model? The answer to this question is recorded in NetLogo as turtle breeds, which are agent types in NetLogo. Turtle breeds correspond to roles of the agent-oriented problem domain models. Example: In the ED business process simulation, the role Patient is mapped to the

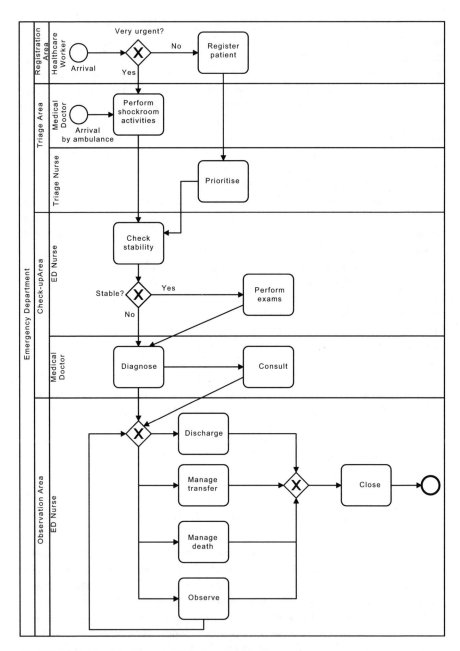

Fig. 5.7 The business process model of the emergency department

turtle breed *patients*, and the roles Medical Doctor, ED Nurse, Triage Nurse, and Healthcare Worker are mapped to the turtle breed *workers* whose local variable *name* defines if the agent models a Medical Doctor, an ED Nurse, a Triage Nurse, or a Healthcare Worker.

Q12. For each agent type identified in Q11:

Q12.1. By what attributes are agents of this type characterized? The answer to this question is recorded in NetLogo as local variables of the corresponding turtle breed. Local variables correspond to the knowledge that is represented for the corresponding role of the agent-oriented problem domain models. Example: In the ED business process simulation, the local variables defined for the turtle breed *patients* include *time-of-arrival* (time of entrance of a patient to the emergency department), *next-task* (next task of a patient), and *urgency-level*. These local variables are mapped from the domain entity Patient Information of the agent-oriented problem domain models.

Q12.2. What are the states that characterize agents of this type? The answer to this question is recorded as the local state variables of the corresponding turtle breed. A state variable is a variable that distinguishes an entity from other entities of the same type or category or traces how the entity changes over time [3, 4]. Example: In the ED business process simulation, the state of a patient, recorded in the corresponding local variable *state* defined for the turtle breed *patients*, can be "searching-for," "waiting," "moving," and "busy." State variables may or may not have their counterparts in the knowledge defined for the corresponding role of the agent-oriented problem domain models.

Q12.3. What are the actions by agents of this type? The answer to this question is recorded in NetLogo as procedures. Procedures correspond to responsibilities defined for the roles of the agent-oriented problem domain models. Example: In the ED business process simulation, the procedure *arrival-new-patients* corresponds to the responsibility *register patient* of the role Healthcare Worker, and the procedure *compute-urgency* corresponds to the responsibility *prioritize* of the role Triage Nurse.

Q13. What global knowledge should be represented in the simulation system? The answer to this question is recorded in NetLogo as global variables. Global variables correspond to the knowledge of which the agents performing different roles should be aware. Example: In the ED business process simulation, the global variables *monitor-duration-LoS* and *monit-dtdt* need to be represented. They correspond to the respective key performance indicators LOS and DTDT, which were introduced in Sect. 5.1.2 and of which all of the agents should be aware.

Q14. What environmental resources should be represented in the simulation system? The answer to this question is recorded in NetLogo as patches. Patches correspond to resources defined by the agent-oriented problem domain models. Example: In the ED business process simulation, the resources Registration Area, Triage Area, and Check-up Area are mapped to the respective patches bearing the names "Registration," "Triage," and "Visit."

Q15. What attributes of other agents and global knowledge are agents assumed to sense and consider in their decisions? The answer to this question is recorded in the

NetLogo program. Since NetLogo does not directly support interactions between turtles, this way information exchange by interactions can be indirectly represented. Examples: A turtle of the *workers* breed is assumed to sense and consider the value of the local variable *urgency-level* of a NetLogo turtle of the *patients* breed; a turtle of the *workers* breed is also assumed to sense and consider the value of the global variable *patients-in-waiting-area*, denoting the number of patients currently waiting to be checked and treated.

Having completed the mappings shown in Table 5.3, we also need to answer some additional questions that are concerned with agent-based business process simulation. These questions are based on the ODD protocol for designing agent-based simulations [3, 4], and they are represented as different aspects of the resulting NetLogo program. It is important to note here that we do not fully follow the ODD methodology because, as has been pointed out by [6], it is geared toward developing multi-agent simulations for ecology, in which organizational and social aspects are not so important. Differently, our emphasis is on agent-based simulations of business processes where organizational and social issues are crucial. We now present the additional questions Q16–Q18 that should be answered by the project stakeholders to complete transforming a business process model in BPMN to its representation in NetLogo:

Q16. How is time modeled in the simulation system? The answer to this question is recorded in the NetLogo program. Example: In the ED business process simulation, the emergency department is simulated at the time granularity of seconds, by making use of the NetLogo global variable *tick*.

Q17. How are instances of a business process generated, based on the arrivals of entities such as patients or orders? The answer to this question is recorded in the NetLogo program. Example: In the ED business process simulation, patients arrive randomly, depending on regularities caused by day of the week and hour of the day. The regularities are defined by a specific probability distribution, which is computed by the simulation system in advance for every simulated 24 hours, possibly based on the probability distribution of a real-life emergency department. The urgency levels of patients are also randomly set based on the corresponding probability distribution.

Q18. How is the simulation system initialized? How many agents of what type are there initially, and what are the values of their local variables? The answer to this question is recorded in the NetLogo program. Example: In the ED business process simulation, the ED is initially staffed with three medical doctors, five ED nurses, two triage nurses, and three healthcare workers, but these values can be changed through the simulation's NetLogo user interface. The simulation system can also be initialized with the actual number of medical doctors, ED nurses, triage nurses, and healthcare workers in the real-life emergency department. This data can be read from the corresponding data file.

5.2   The Case Study of Purchasing in a Car Factory

In this section, we describe another full-fledged case study of designing a simulation-based system of decision support for a car factory. In this case study, the management of a car factory needs to make a decision on how to organize in the most efficient way the business process of purchasing parts and materials from their vendors. They need a decision-support system that would enable them to run simulated *what-if* scenarios for different ways of organizing purchasing in the car factory. The goal model of decision support on purchasing is shown in Fig. 5.8. This model identifies the key motivations of the car factory management and researcher, who are, respectively, the main stakeholder and user of the system, and how the system fits into their workflow. Just like in case of supporting decisions on optimizing the work performed at ED (see Sect. 5.1.2), we plan to optimize for the car factory the attainment of the quality goal *efficient* that refers to the execution time of a purchasing process. For the car factory case study, this quality goal can be elaborated into the measurable quality goals *minimal turnaround time* and *maximal useful time*. Both of them positively contribute to the attainment of the *efficient* quality goal, which is denoted by the "+" signs in Fig. 5.8. The *minimal turnaround time* quality goal represents efficiency from the perspective of the car factory's external customer. The attainment of the *minimal turnaround time* quality goal can be measured by the *average-cycle-time* (ACT) key performance indicator, which represents the number of minutes from sending the order to the arrival of products—cars. The other quality goal—*maximal useful time*—represents efficiency from the factory management perspective. The attainment of the *maximal useful time* quality goal can be measured by the *average-time-worked* (ATW) key performance indicator. The ATW key performance indicator represents the average number of minutes worked by the workers directly on the orders. The key performance indicators ACT and ATW are depicted in Fig. 5.8.

The high-level project motivation model of the decision-support system shown in Fig. 5.8 also reflects that we plan to achieve the quality goals *minimal turnaround time* and *maximal useful time* by means of reorganizing the purchasing business processes and reorganizing the environment of these business processes. We started agent-oriented problem domain analysis by answering questions Q1–Q5 that were presented in Sect. 5.1.3. The answers were recorded in a goal model. In our case study, the highest-level goal—*purchase*—was elaborated into the sub-goals *prepare purchase order*, *send purchase order*, *send copy of purchase order*, *receive goods*, *confirm arrival of goods*, *check documents*, and *make payment*, each representing a particular aspect of purchasing. The goal model of purchasing is shown in Fig. 5.9.

We continued agent-oriented problem domain analysis by answering question Q6 that helped model in more detail the roles in terms of their responsibilities (Q6.1), the relationships between the roles (Q6.2), the knowledge needed by agents for performing the roles (Q6.3), and the resources provided by the environment where the agents are situated (Q6.4). Table 5.4 represents the role models of the car factory. The respective columns of the table describe for each role its name, and

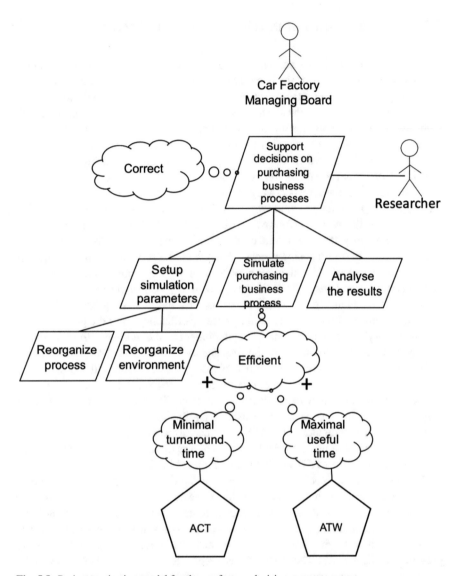

Fig. 5.8 Project motivation model for the car factory decision-support system

the responsibilities, knowledge, and resources of the role. Answering sub-question Q6.2 elicits relationships between the roles, which are recorded in the organization model. The organization model shown in Fig. 5.10 represents how the roles depend on each other for fulfilling their responsibilities in purchasing.

Next, we transformed the agent-oriented problem domain models to the business process model represented in BPMN by answering questions Q7–Q10, which were defined in Sect. 5.1.4. Answering these questions resulted in mapping the modeling

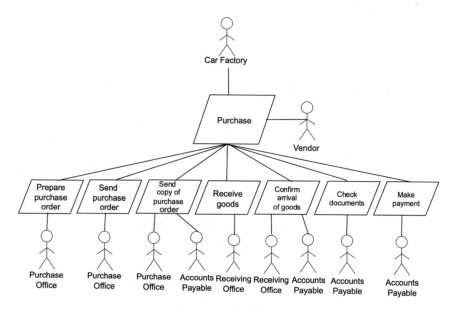

Fig. 5.9 Goal model of purchasing in a car factory

Table 5.4 The roles of the car factory

Role	Responsibilities	Knowledge	Resources
Vendor	Receive order		
	Send product		
	Send invoice		
	Receive payment		
Purchasing Office	Prepare purchase order	Purchase order	
	Send purchase order	Invoice	
	Send copy of purchase order	Product	
Receiving Office	Receive goods		
	Confirm arrival of goods		Purchasing Information System
Accounts Payable	Check documents		
	Make payment		

constructs of high-level agent-oriented problem domain models to the modeling constructs of BPMN. The modeling constructs of agent-oriented problem domain models and their counterparts in BPMN are shown in the respective first and second column of Table 5.3. The answers to questions Q7–Q10 were recorded in the business process models of the car factory. In the next paragraph, we will describe the mapping by providing in parentheses the number of the respective question of the methodology from Sect. 5.1.4.

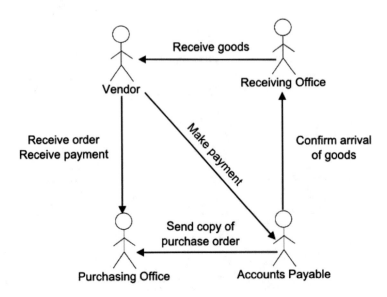

Fig. 5.10 Organization model of purchasing in a car factory

The agent-oriented problem domain models were mapped to two BPMN pools—"Car Factory" and "Vendor" (Q7). The resource Purchasing Information System identified in Table 5.4 was mapped to the BPMN data store of the same name (Q8.2). The roles modeled in Table 5.4 were mapped to the corresponding BPMN lanes Purchasing Office, Receiving Office, and Accounts Payable (Q9.1), whereby the responsibilities of each role were mapped to the corresponding tasks within the respective lane (Q9.2). After that, the triggers of the tasks (Q10.1) were defined, as well as their preconditions (Q10.2) and postconditions (Q10.3). Finally, incoming (Q10.4) and outgoing (Q10.5) message and sequence flows were specified for the tasks. In particular, the domain entities Purchase Order, Invoice, and Product representing the knowledge in the agent-oriented problem domain models were mapped to the respective message flows between the pools standing for the vendor and car factory (Q10.4 and Q10.5).

This case study included reorganizing the original business process, which is modelled in Fig. 5.11. The reorganized business process modelled in Fig. 5.12 has gotten rid of the *send copy of purchase order, confirm arrival of goods,* and *check documents* tasks due to introducing the data store Purchasing Information System that stores purchase orders and invoices and is accessed by performers of all three roles—Purchasing Office, Receiving Office, and Accounts Payable. Our intention was to perform agent-based simulation of both business processes to be able to compare their performance.

As the last step of the methodology, the business process model was transformed to NetLogo. This was done by answering questions Q11–Q18, which were defined in Sect. 5.1.5. In the next paragraph, we describe the mappings from the business

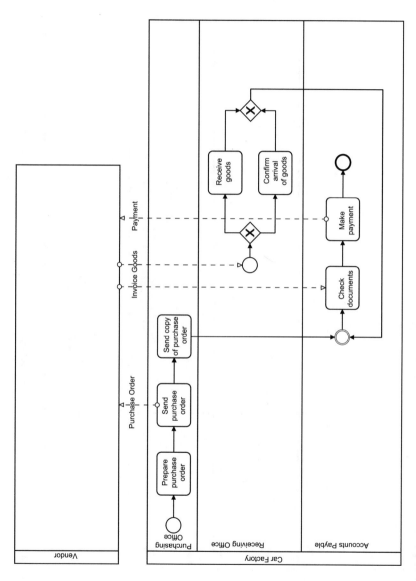

Fig. 5.11 Purchasing business process of the car factory before reorganizing

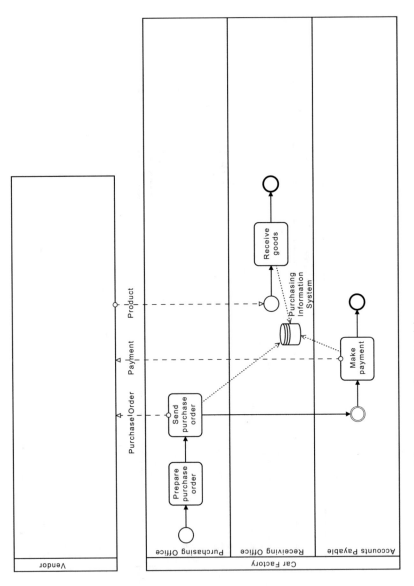

Fig. 5.12 Purchasing business process of the car factory after reorganizing

process modeling constructs to the constructs of NetLogo by providing in parentheses the number of the respective question of the methodology.

First, we mapped the roles Vendor, Purchasing Office, Receiving Office, and Accounts Payable to the turtle breed *workers* (Q11). Attributes of an agent belonging to the turtle breed *workers* include the local variable *working-with*, which refers to the purchase order on which the agent is working (Q12.1). The state of a worker, recorded in the corresponding local variable *state* defined for the turtle breed *workers*, can be one of the following: "waiting," "in-service," and "not-working-time" (Q12.2). The actions performed by agents of the turtle breed *workers* correspond to all of the responsibilities that are included by Table 5.4 (Q12.3). They are performed in the order defined by the business process models depicted in Figs. 5.11 and 5.12.

Considering the need to visualize on the NetLogo user interface the movements of purchase orders and invoices, we made an important design decision to represent the domain entities Purchase Order and Invoice shown in Table 5.4 as the respective turtle breeds *orders* and *invoices* (Q11), although purchase orders and invoices are conceptually passive objects rather than active agents [16]. For better visualization, we have also chosen to represent the roles Vendor, Purchasing Office, Receiving Office, and Accounts Payable as the respective NetLogo patches. This enables the user of the simulation system to observe the movements of purchase orders and invoices between the corresponding roles. Accordingly, the turtle breeds *orders* and *invoices* both include the local variable *destination-patch*, which refers to the order's or invoice's target patch corresponding to one of the following roles: Vendor, Purchasing Office, Receiving Office, or Accounts Payable (Q12.1). For the turtle breed *orders*, the additional local variable *working-with* was defined, which refers to the worker who is responsible for handling the order (Q12.1). The state of an order, recorded in the local variable *state* of the turtle breed *orders*, can be "waiting-for-worker," "in-service," "moving," or "delayed" (Q12.2). No action was defined for either the turtle breed *orders* or the turtle breed *invoices*, because, as was mentioned above, both of them define agents of a passive kind that are manipulated by other agents rather than being capable of performing autonomous actions (Q12.3).

In the car factory simulation system, the global variables *avgCycleTime* and *avgServiceTime* were represented (Q13). They correspond to the respective key performance indicators ACT and ATW, which were defined above. The resource Purchase Information System defined in Table 5.4, which was represented as a data store in the BPMN model shown in Fig. 5.12, was mapped to a separate NetLogo patch with the name "Information System" (Q14). Finally, an agent of the turtle breed *workers* is assumed to sense and consider the value of the global variable *working-time*, which keeps track of the simulated shifts by workers (Q15).

The simulation time is measured by ticks, whereas 60 ticks make up a simulated hour. By means of the global variable *working-time*, the time is divided into four slots: night time, morning working time, lunch break, and afternoon working time (Q16).

The generation of orders depends on the arrival frequency of a new bunch of orders and the number of orders in a bunch. By default, the value of the arrival

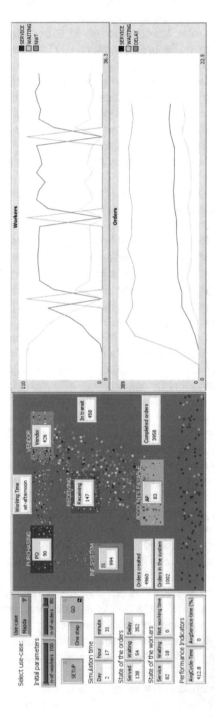

Fig. 5.13 The NetLogo visualization of the purchasing business process of the car factory

frequency of a bunch is set to 15, which means that every 15 simulated minutes, a new bunch of orders is generated. Similarly, the number of purchase orders in a bunch is set to 80. Both of these values can be changed by the respective sliders of the NetLogo user interface (Q17).

The simulation can be initialized with different numbers of workers (Q18).

A screenshot of the resulting NetLogo simulation of the car factory is depicted in Fig. 5.13. We will further discuss agent-based simulation of the business processes of the car factory in Sect. 8.1.

References

1. Dijkman, R.M., Dumas, M., Ouyang, C.: Semantics and analysis of business process models in BPMN. Inf. Softw. Technol. **50**(12), 1281–1294 (2008). https://doi.org/10.1016/j.infsof.2008.02.006
2. Fortino, G., North, M.J.: Simulation-based development and validation of multi-agent systems: AOSE and ABMS approaches. J. Simul. **7**(3), 137–143 (2013). https://doi.org/10.1057/jos.2013.12
3. Grimm, V., Berger, U., Bastiansen, F., Eliassen, S., Ginot, V., Giske, J., Goss-Custard, J., Grand, T., Heinz, S.K., Huse, G., Huth, A., Jepsen, J.U., Jørgensen, C., Mooij, W.M., Müller, B., Pe'er, G., Piou, C., Railsback, S.F., Robbins, A.M., Robbins, M.M., Rossmanith, E., Rüger, N., Strand, E., Souissi, S., Stillman, R.A., Vabø, R., Visser, U., DeAngelis, D.L.: A standard protocol for describing individual-based and agent-based models. Ecol. Model. **198**(1), 115–126 (2006). https://doi.org/10.1016/j.ecolmodel.2006.04.023
4. Grimm, V., Berger, U., DeAngelis, D.L., Polhill, J.G., Giske, J., Railsback, S.F.: The ODD protocol: A review and first update. Ecol. Model. **221**(23), 2760–2768 (2010). https://doi.org/10.1016/j.ecolmodel.2010.08.019
5. Kavakli, V., Loucopoulos, P.: Goal-driven business process analysis application in electricity deregulation. Inf. Syst. **24**(3), 187–207 (1999). https://doi.org/10.1016/S0306-4379(99)00015-0
6. Klügl, F.: "engineering" agent-based simulation models? In: Müller, J.P., Cossentino, M. (eds.) Agent-Oriented Software Engineering XIII—13th International Workshop, AOSE 2012, Valencia, Spain, June 4, 2012, Revised Selected Papers. Lecture Notes in Computer Science, vol. 7852, pp. 179–196. Springer, Berlin (2012). https://doi.org/10.1007/978-3-642-39866-7_11
7. Miller, T., Lu, B., Sterling, L., Beydoun, G., Taveter, K.: Requirements elicitation and specification using the agent paradigm: the case study of an aircraft turnaround simulator. IEEE Trans. Softw. Eng. **40**(10), 1007–1024 (2014). https://doi.org/10.1109/TSE.2014.2339827
8. Object Management Group (OMG): Business Process Model and Notation (BPMN), Version 2.0.2 (2014). https://www.omg.org/spec/BPMN/2.0.2/PDF. Accessed 30 Apr 2021
9. Podgorelec, V., Kokol, P.: Genetic algorithm based system for patient scheduling in highly constrained situations. J. Med. Syst. **21**(6), 417–427 (1997). https://doi.org/10.1023/A:1022828414460
10. Siebers, P.O., Klügl, F.: What software engineering has to offer to agent-based social simulation. In: Simulating Social Complexity, pp. 81–117. Springer, Berlin (2017). https://doi.org/10.1007/978-3-319-66948-9_6
11. Sommerville, I.: Software Engineering, 10th edn. Addison-Wesley, Reading (2015)
12. Sowa, J.F., Zachman, J.A.: Extending and formalizing the framework for information systems architecture. IBM Syst. J. **31**(3), 590–616 (1992). https://doi.org/10.1147/sj.313.0590

13. Sterling, L., Taveter, K.: The Art of Agent-Oriented Modeling. The MIT Press, Cambridge (2009). https://doi.org/10.7551/mitpress/7682.001.0001
14. Sulis, E., Terna, P., Di Leva, A., Boella, G., Boccuzzi, A.: Agent-oriented decision support system for business processes management with genetic algorithm optimization: an application in healthcare. J. Med. Syst. **44**(9), 1–7 (2020). https://doi.org/10.1007/s10916-020-01608-4
15. Taveter, K., Du, H., Huhns, M.N.: Engineering societal information systems by agent-oriented modeling. J. Ambient Intell. Smart Environ. **4**(3), 227–252 (2012)
16. Taveter, K., Wagner, G.: A multi-perspective methodology for modelling inter-enterprise business processes. In: Arisawa, H., Kambayashi, Y., Kumar, V., Mayr, H.C., Hunt, I. (eds.) ER 2001 Workshops, HUMACS, DASWIS, ECOMO, and DAMA, Yokohama Japan, November 27-30, 2001, Revised Papers, Lecture Notes in Computer Science, vol. 2465, pp. 403–416. Springer, Berlin (2001). https://doi.org/10.1007/3-540-46140-X_31
17. Wynn, D.C., Clarkson, P.J.: Process models in design and development. Res. Eng. Design **29**(2), 161–202 (2018). https://doi.org/10.1007/s00163-017-0262-7
18. Zachman, J.A.: A framework for information systems architecture. IBM Syst. J. **26**(3), 276–292 (1987). https://doi.org/10.1147/sj.263.0276

Chapter 6
The Agent-Based Business Process Simulation Approach

Abstract This chapter introduces the ABBPS modeling perspective in Sect. 6.1. Next, Sect. 6.2 explores the main concepts of practical applications and theoretical implications of agent-based simulations, while Sect. 6.3 provides a brief review of the related topics, such as complexity concepts. Finally, Sect. 6.4 describes some advanced features of ABM adopted in the remainder of the book.

6.1 Model Building

The previous chapter—Chap. 5—addressed the "Why" of business process modelling and simulation and described how business process models in BPMN can be systematically transformed to their agent-based simulations in NetLogo. This chapter complements it with various approaches, methods, and techniques for agent-based business process simulation.

6.1.1 Modeling the Real World

The need to model the reality around us has found valuable support in the recent development of computational and technological capabilities. Human activities and natural phenomena include behaviors and patterns that can be represented in an understandable way. This is known as *modeling*, which refers to the ability to retain the most salient features of the real world while discarding the non-essential parts. The need for simplicity is taken to an extreme in the famous dictum "All models are wrong, but some are useful," the phrase by the British statistician George E. P. Box [15]. In philosophy, one can argue by relying on the well-known problem-solving principle of Occam's razor which is interpreted as requiring that the simplest of competing theories should be preferred to the more complex ones. Following this principle, a model of a phenomenon is a simplified abstraction of reality, in which only the essential ingredients are preserved. In this context, the representation of a phenomenon should be simple but also maintain the accuracy, fidelity, and

© Springer Nature Switzerland AG 2022
E. Sulis, K. Taveter, *Agent-Based Business Process Simulation*,
https://doi.org/10.1007/978-3-030-98816-6_6

variability of the reality. For example, a simulation of business and economic activities, such as arrivals of purchasing orders in a trading company or sending out invoices, includes the mimicking of real arrivals of new orders in the system, and processing of each case in different tasks with the involvement of different workers in the process.

In recent years, there has been a growing interest in business process modeling and management. As we described in Sect. 2.1.3, a growing attention to these areas entails languages and tools able to represent a subset of human activities, work activities, and production processes [23]. Modeling languages are intended to explain the system being modeled to the stakeholders, such as customers, operators, analysts, and designers. Moreover, some of these modeling languages like UML or BPMN are executable by process engines, which are business process management tools that can provide service orchestration, human workflow management, and monitoring and reporting of process metrics and business performance indicators.

6.1.2 Modeling Phases

Each modeling technique aims to improve the overall comprehensibility of the real system. Typically, most modeling approaches break the construction of the model into several actions-steps to be taken [79]. We propose here a set of modeling steps to be performed in a practical business process analysis and simulation project:

1. the investigation and definition of the main questions that arise about the system;
2. the definition of what the system is, the elements of which it is composed, and their relationships;
3. establishing an experimental design according to the questions to be answered;
4. adopting one or more paradigms and the associated representation formats to construct a model of the system;
5. composing the parts of the model and the model as a whole;
6. simulating the model;
7. analyzing the simulation results.

Steps _i–vii_ should be performed in an iterative agile fashion [64].

Waterfall method. In addition to the above agile step-by-step approach, another approach called the "waterfall method" can be used [5]. According to the "waterfall method," each phase of the process should be executed based on the results of the previous phase. This kind of development methodology has recently been applied in an agent-oriented methodology for BPM [81].

A _de facto_ standard methodology widely used in the ABM community to document an agent-based model is the _ODD protocol_ [34]. The second version of the _ODD protocol_ was recently proposed for document projects of agent-based simulation [35]. The methodology consists of the three main components: overview, design concepts, and design details (ODD). These components include seven subtopics: Purpose, State Variables and Scales, Process Overview and Scheduling,

Design Concepts, Initialization, Inputs, and Sub-models. The purpose of ODD is to explain the model and make it reproducible by a third party. According to ODD, each component of a model must be documented in sufficient depth with respect to the purpose and design of the component. We already addressed in Sect. 5.1.5 the application of ODD for mapping a business process model to BPMN.

In the following sections, we provide an overview of some techniques of agent-based approaches, considering the main definitions of agents presented in Chap. 3.

6.2 Simulation-Based Analysis

A particular focus of simulation-based analysis is on simulation of real-world processes and phenomena. Traditional simulation techniques include mathematical modeling, mostly based on systems of differential equations as in SD approaches as introduced also in Sect. 2.4.1. Since the 1960s, the *discrete event simulation (DES)* approach has treated the system to be simulated as a sequence of discrete operations. More recently, the *agent-based modeling (ABM)* approach focuses on interactions, i.e., autonomous active entities—agents. This modeling approach emphasizes the interactions between agents through their environment. In a well-known ABM example, ants looking for food, as simple individual entities, interact by means of, for example, "pheromones," the trails of which the agents leave in their environment [67]. This modeling approach, also called individual-based modeling, emphasizes emergent behavior arising from the interactions between their elementary units, individuals, and agents.

6.2.1 Stochasticity

In deterministic simulations, such as differential equations and mathematical models with no random variables, the output of the model depends on the initial setup. On the contrary, a stochastic simulation possesses some inherent randomness, providing different results based on the probabilities randomly assigned to the values taken by the main variables. The output of this type of model can have different results under different conditions according to the adoption of random variables.

In particular, stochastic models produce different outputs when run repeatedly with the same inputs. Stochasticity can be based on agent behaviors or environmental responses triggered by random or probabilistic elements. This modeling perspective involves the assumption that agent behaviors or environmental responses are not known with complete certainty. Instead, the corresponding factors are characterized by ranges of possible values, means, variances, and other statistical measures.

Computer simulations typically rely on generating a sequence of pseudo-random numbers that have to be very similar to real random numbers. In fact, some algorithms generate a sequence of numbers that approximates the properties of random numbers. In this sequence, each number is computed based on its predecessor. The first number in the sequence is the *seed*, which specifies a particular stream from a set of possible streams of random numbers.

By using the same *seed* at each new run, the computer generates the same sequence of pseudo-random numbers. This means that the resulting numbers are no longer pseudo-random. To maintain pseudo-random numbers across different runs, a good practice is to change the *seed* with each new simulation. Another good practice is to generate a random *seed* from computer time by converting the clock value to an integer value. In NetLogo, the `random-seed` instruction sets the *seed* of the pseudo-random number generator to the integer part of the generated number.[1]

6.2.2   Verification and Validation

Verification and validation are two relevant activities that occur throughout the modeling effort. Verification is applied in the context of evaluating the computational implementation of a model in terms of the goals by the researchers, as was described in Chap. 5. Differently from verification, validation typically refers to an assessment of the credibility of the model as a representation of the subject.

Verification of the simulation model determines whether the output of each step meets the specification. In other words, the implementation of the model must conform to the conceptual description of the model, such as the conceptual description of the kind put forward in Chap. 5. Once the model can be considered as conforming to the conceptual description, the verification process focuses on the next step. About verification, a related question can be worded as "Has the right model been built?" For finding the answer, model verification involves checking the model with domain experts of the proposed model. The answer to the question suggests how well the model follows the behavior of actual real-world processes or phenomena that are to be simulated.

Simulation model validation focuses on the output of the model to investigate how accurately the model represents the real world. Validation compares the model and the associated data with real-world perspectives of employing the model. By analyzing a realistic set of input variables, this step is primarily concerned with the simulation output, which must be similar to real-world values. The validation question can be worded as follows: "Has the model been correctly built?" Since validation is a key issue in simulation modeling, many validation strategies have been put forward [44, 61]. For example, one of the simplest validation strategies is ensuring *face validity* which is based on a subjective assessment to investigate whether the model appears to be an accurate representation of the real-world process or phenomenon. More accurate validation strategies include data analysis to focus

---

[1] http://ccl.northwestern.edu/netlogo/docs/dict/random-seed.html.

on comparing the results of the data generated by the model to the actual data [44], as well as cognitive analysis [30].

Validity entails asking domain experts whether the model performs reasonably, as well as making subjective judgments about whether the model is sufficiently accurate. Finally, we mention here that the concept of model validity has been extensively adopted in studies of management science [29, 47, 53].

6.2.3   Parameter Sweeping

Every simulation run produces results that are not reliable considered alone because of the possibility that they are due to the chance. Similarly, if a model with random elements is executed only a few times, the performance distribution is not completely reliable. A deeper analysis should include multiple runs, to be jointly analyzed by means of statistical measures. Recent improvements in the infrastructure available for computing have enabled massive increase in the repetition of such simulations to systematically test the behavior of a model across a range of different parameters setting. If a model is run multiple times, the relative distribution of results becomes more precise. Typically, with additional runs of the model, the mean and standard deviation become more stable, and the standard error of the mean becomes smaller. Parameter sweeping is the technique of varying a set of initial values to conduct a series of simulations for analyzing the results. Parameter sweeping is facilitated by the BehaviorSpace tool built into NetLogo, which is further described in Sect. 4.2.6. The BehaviorSpace tool allows the users of NetLogo to run a predefined number of agent-based simulations, making it easy to set and vary parameters.

6.2.4   Scenario Analysis

Scenario analysis is a technique for investigating possible future outcomes based on the impact of different configuration settings by simulating different scenarios. This type of analysis is typically employed for estimating changes in an existing organization to assess the expected behavior due to favorable or unfavorable events.

In change management [10], scenario analysis explores practical changes in business process performance by, for example, comparing a best-case scenario with a worst-case scenario. Some examples of typical applications of scenario analysis are minimization of risks by financial investment strategies, maximization of the profit by company management strategies, and the optimization of the shifts by the staff. From the perspective of ABM, this type of analysis is foremost based on modeling interactions between organizational roles. In ABM, some changes in the characteristics of the agents and environmental parameters may occur, having an impact on the simulated future state of a particular business organization, an industrial sector, or even the whole economy.

Managers typically adopt scenario analysis in decision-making to compare the impacts of different strategies on the actual output of a model [1]. Typical cases involve setting model parameters to achieve outputs that are from the current situation. In a *base-case scenario*, the management considers the underlying assumptions that are most likely to hold in the case envisioned by the model. Variations in the initial parameters can be tested to obtain a *best-case scenario*, i.e., the projected ideal scenario which can be implemented by the management with respect to particular goals. The goals could have been modelled in the context of decision-making as has been described in Chap. 5. In contrast to the *best-case scenario*, the *worst-case scenario* focuses on the most severe outcome that can occur in a given situation. For example, the reader can explore the *ABBPS_TVM-queues* model provided in the web repository of the book. This model is concerned with the arrivals of customers to ticket vending machines (TVM), as is shown in Fig. 6.1. The adoption of BehaviorSpace would facilitate the analysis of different scenarios (as described in Sect. 4.2.6).

Performing scenario analysis provides managers with insights about the evolution of the business processes of the organization being studied in the near future. Typically it is relevant to explore different plausibly possible events that can occur and have an impact on the business processes of the organization [27]. Benefits of scenario analysis include the ability to predict the future based on the expected outcomes when planning changes to the business processes [71]. Based on the results of scenario analysis by ABM, managers can also strengthen certain procedures to avoid worst-case scenarios by taking a proactive approach to prevent a problem. Risk management considers both best- and worst-case outcomes with the purpose to make informed decisions [2, 3]. The main drawbacks of scenario analysis are concerned with the difficulty of considering unforeseen events that may occur in the future, such as the outbreak of the COVID-19 pandemic. The technique mostly

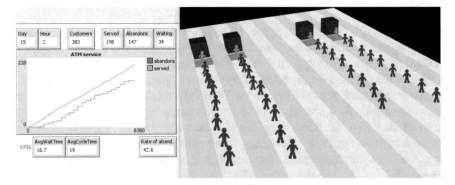

Fig. 6.1 Interface on the left and the view area with queues of customers to TVMs on the right in the *ABBPS_TVM-queues* model

depends on the management and stakeholders ideas and requires the availability of high-level expertise. However, a simulation model by ABM can be easily redesigned to enrich the model with new parameters and unforeseen behaviors.

6.2.5 Sensitivity Analysis

Sensitivity analysis, also called *factor screening*, is a technique for evaluating the performance of simulation output with respect to changes in initial simulation parameters. Following the experimental design terminology proposed by Averill Law [43], this type of analysis defines the *factors* as input parameters and structural assumptions of a model. The measures of output performance are *responses*. The purpose of sensitivity analysis is to study the impact of changing the *factors* on the *response*, i.e., investigating the change in the simulation output with respect to the change in the input parameters.

The simplest form of sensitivity analysis is where all factors are set to fixed values, except for one factor which can be varied. This approach is called One-Factor-At-a-Time (OFAT). In our model of the emergency department of a hospital, the arrival of ED patients is an important factor that should be carefully considered. For example, let us focus on the response to the initial registration phase of the business process. A possible question of interest to be asked is: "How is the performance of the registration task affected by changes in the values of the input parameters?" Focusing on the throughput time of the registration phase, the following three factors appear to be of interest in a *sensitivity analysis*: (i) the average number of patients arriving to the ED (in the example mentioned in Sect. 4.4.3, the mean value is 7.5, but this value depends on several circumstances); (ii) the implicit severity of patients (some patients can be more difficult to be registered than others); and (iii) the qualification of the nurses in terms of their experience and skills (an intern, for instance, may be slower in her or his job than an experienced caregiver). We have addressed this example more thoroughly in the *Arrivals-to-ED* model that is available in the web repository.

In this case, a *sensitivity analysis* is performed by the 2^k factorial design approach where two levels are chosen for each factor. This allows for better management of the simulation runs, which can execute $2x^k$ possible factor-level combinations. To explain this approach more clearly, the following paragraph provides a concrete example.

Example of Sensitivity Analysis

The *ABBPS_ED-Patients-Arrival* model in the companion website describes the arrival of patients at the Registration Office (REG). This is a typical problem addressed through the use of modeling and process simulation [28, 41]. In particular, the example proposed here considers three variables of interest: the frequency of patient arrivals (Factor 1); the inherent complexity (Factor 2) concerned with the type of the patient; and the skills of the operator working at the counter based on their experience (Factor 3). First, the frequency of the arrivals can be computed based on real data. Our model considers the average number of arrivals per hour, which is about seven to eight new patients. This value may change throughout the day. Moreover, this value can increase in case of some emergency situation. An improved version of the model takes into account different arrival frequencies in the course of a day. As a matter of fact, the distribution of arrival frequencies typically follows a specific pattern. Second, the duration of the registration process depends on the type of a patient (e.g., an elderly patient typically takes more time than a young patient). Third, the level of skills of the operator working at the counter affects the duration of providing the service (an intern or a new operator is less confident in the procedures). The model considers the last two factors to increase or decrease the total duration of registration for each patient. In this example of *sensitivity analysis*, the 2^k factorial design approach reduces each factor into pairs of values.

Figure 6.2 describes the interface of the model for addressing the OFAT analysis. On the left, the interface has a slider for each factor. The first factor is the arrival frequency of patients. We represent it in a discrete manner as "high-freq" (in our simulation, about 12 patients in an hour) or "low-freq" (in our case, five patients in an hour). Furthermore, patients may be "easy" or "difficult" to handle. "Easy" and "difficult" patients are created with the respective probabilities of 25% and 75%. In a similar manner, "skilled" workers are created with the probability of 75% and "new" workers—with the probability of 25%.

Table 6.1 represents the 2^k factorial design performed by us. In the table, the response R_i varies in the range of i from 1 to 8. Each row implies the execution of the simulation with the i_{th} combination of factor levels. The combination C1, for example, considers Factor 1 (frequency of arrivals) at the "low" level, Factor 2 at the "easy" level, and Factor 3 at the "skilled" level. The corresponding Response is R1, resulting from running the simulation with the combination C1. The analysis continues with examining the change in the response upon changing the value of one factor while keeping the values of the other factors fixed. For instance, we can investigate the impact of a change in the experience factor (i.e., the *effect* of Factor 3) by moving the level of the factor from "skilled" to "new." We compute this *effect* by investigating all responses for which pairs of other factors—Factor 1 and Factor 2—remain the same. This is the case with the pairs (C1, C2), (C3, C4), (C5, C6), and (C7, C8). Ultimately, we compute the average value of the differences between these responses to estimate the variation of Factor 3.

More generally, we estimate the effect of the factor Fj denoted by e_{Fj}, as the average change in the response while holding other factors fixed. Formula 6.1 describes the 2^k factorial design to estimate the effect of Factor 3 in our *ABBPS_ED-Patients-Arrival* model.

$$e_{F3} = \frac{(R2 - R1) + (R4 - R3) + (R6 - R5) + (R8 - R7)}{4} \qquad (6.1)$$

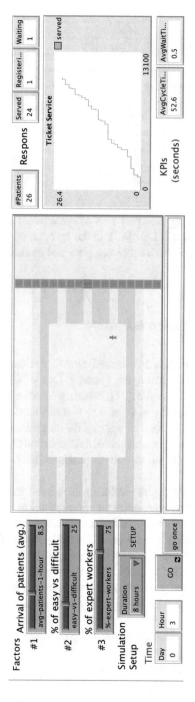

Fig. 6.2 Interface of the *ABBPS_ED-Patients-Arrival* model

Table 6.1 Sensitivity analysis with a factorial design approach. Design matrix of the ED-arrivals model

	Factor 1	Factor 2	Factor 3	
Combination	*Frequency*	*Complexity*	*Experience*	Response
C1	Low	Easy	Skilled	R1
C2	Low	Easy	New	R2
C3	Low	Difficult	Skilled	R3
C4	Low	Difficult	New	R4
C5	High	Easy	Skilled	R5
C6	High	Easy	New	R6
C7	High	Difficult	Skilled	R7
C8	High	Difficult	New	R8

A further discussion on the interpretation of *sensitivity analysis* main effects is presented in the work by Averill Law [43]. In the companion website, we also offer a more complicated example, with more counters and queues, as is represented by Fig. 6.1.

6.2.6   Agent-Based Simulation Tools

Several tools have been proposed to model human societies, as well as natural and artificial phenomena as multi-agent systems. One of the first object-oriented programming language was Simula [24], which was developed in the 1960s by Kristen Nygaard at the University of Oslo. The features that were added to previous languages, such as ALGOL, aimed to address the simulation of real-world events and systems of discrete actors. Simula included the creation of an entity, which could represent either an object or an agent, with the encapsulation of their properties and actions.

Since the late 1990s, many agent platforms have been developed to model phenomena in fields as diverse as economics and finance, urban planning, engineering, healthcare, and social sciences [56]. In the same period, the concept of intelligent agent was developed, but what it really entails is still debated today. Nowadays, the agent-oriented research community benefits from many heterogeneous platforms of agent-based modeling and simulation. A recent review that includes 25 existing tools states: "Hence, a common problem is how people interested in using multi-agent systems should choose which platform to use in order to benefit from agent technology" [42].

Table 6.2 provides an overview of the most popular agent platforms, starting from the commercial tool AnyLogic, and continuing with the open-source tools Brahms, Jason, Mason, Repast Symphony, NetLogo, and Swarm. The tools are described according to the following categories: implementation language, development

Table 6.2 Overview of the most popular agent platforms

Agent platform and conditions for its usage	Implementation language	Development interface	Complexity of model creation	Scalability	Scope or problem domains
AnyLogic (closed source code; commercial product; free version for personal studying)	Java	Visual	Average	From high to very high	Interactive 2D and 3D models for different problem domains, including complex adaptive systems
Brahms (open-source code; free for studying and research work)	Java	Special purpose development language	High	From high to very high	Agent-based models rooted in activity theory [39, 65] for different problem domains
Jason (open-source code; free)	Java	Special purpose development language	Average	Average	Agent-based organizational models and models of cognitive agents
Mason (open-source code; free for studying and research work)	Java.net	Java	High	From average to high and very high	2D and 3D models for different problem domains
NetLogo (open-source code; free)	Scala and Java	Special purpose development language	Low	From average to high	2D and 3D models for different problem domains
Repast symphony (open-source code; free)	Java	Visual	High	From high to very high	2D and 3D models for different problem domains, including complex adaptive systems
Swarm (open-source code; free)	Java and Objective-C	Objective-C and Java	High	Extremely high	*Complex adaptive systems for problem domains in social sciences and biology*

interface, complexity of model creation, scalability, and the scope or problem domains.

This section further provides a brief overview of a selection of the existing agent-oriented platforms according to the evaluation criteria of usability, extensibility, and ease of learning.

- *NetLogo* can be considered as the reference tool for ABM. The platform has been developed since the late 1990s and has continuously been improved and enriched with new features. The software was born as "a multi-agent programming language and modeling environment for simulating natural and social phenomena (...) particularly well suited for modeling complex systems evolving over time" [72]. Designed for both education and research, NetLogo has become a powerful research tool that is also suitable for students at both the undergraduate and graduate levels. The author, Uri Wilensky, has stated as follows: "Modelers provide instructions to hundreds or thousands of independent 'agents' all operating concurrently. This makes it possible to explore connections between micro-level behaviors of individuals and macro-level patterns that emerge from their interactions. NetLogo enables users to open simulations and play with them, exploring their behavior under various conditions. NetLogo is also an authoring environment that is simple enough to enable students and researchers to create their own models, even if they are not professional programmers" [72].

  One of the reasons for the broad success of this modeling platform stems from the fact that it is an Integrated Development Environment (IDE) allowing one to move very easily from writing code for the model—modeling perspective—to running the simulation, simulation perspective. The ABM researcher Patrick Taillandier has pointed out on this feature: "This possibility has a deep impact on the modeling process and on the modeler habits: rather than waiting to have a complete model before running simulations, NetLogo allows modelers to experiment very quickly the impact of the modification of the model code, and consequently favors a test and try modeling approach" [70]. One of the main drawbacks of the tool is concerned with the computational capabilities. In fact, it is not the most powerful of the existing ABM tools, but it is certainly the most popular and reliable one of the tools for developing agent-based simulations. Another drawback of NetLogo is that it does not explicitly support exchanging messages between agents. Therefore, the effects of the message exchange have to be arranged by the modeler by exchanging the information between agents through global variables.

- *Repast* stands for Recursive Porous Agent Simulation Toolkit. Repast Simphony [55] is a set of libraries for creating and running agent-based simulations and for visualizing and collecting data from them.[2] Repast has been created by the Social Science Research Computing Division of the University of Chicago

---

[2] Repast web site: http://repast.sourceforge.net.

and has been further developed by the Argonne National Laboratory. It is a very powerful tool that can incorporate external code written in Java and work in a parallel distributed environment [20]. In the opinion of the authors, the weaknesses are disadvantages of Repast which are the incomplete documentation for newcomers and the relatively big effort required for obtaining a working simulation model. In fact, the adoption of the toolkit requires quite high-level programming skills, which makes this tool not the first choice for the purpose of disseminating ABM to different research communities. Nevertheless, the tool is among the most advanced ones and definitely constitutes a possible next step after in projects that require advanced ABM.

- The *GAMA* platform is a recent modeling and simulation development environment for building agent-based simulations with the features enabling to represent the simulation results in a three-dimensional space.[3] The tool comes with an easy-to-learn modeling language (GAML) that can be readily used by researchers from other fields than computer science. GAMA is well suited to handle large numbers of agents—up to millions of agents—initialized from many types of dataset in large-scale projects. An interesting feature is the ability to include GIS analysis, such as data from shapefiles or open street map data, and incorporate in the models the files of Building Information Modeling (BIM) [51].

- *Jason, Jade* and *JaCaMo* are three very relevant agent platforms [8, 11, 14]. They are one step beyond the other tools described above in their ability to model also cognitive agents including the support for exchanging messages between agents according to the standards by the Foundation for Intelligent Physical Agents.[4] They are also ahead of other agent platforms in their support for the BDI [33] and AgentSpeak agent architectures [59]. However, the documentations of these platforms are not easy to grasp for a broader audience, and the simulation results are not immediate to obtain and share. Agent platforms like *Jason, Jade*, and *JaCaMo* are typical references used in the MAS research community for Agent-Oriented Software Engineering (AOSE) [74].

- *AnyLogic* is a "multimethod simulation modeling" proprietary platform, developed by the AnyLogic Company, which presents the tool as "the leading simulation software for business, utilized worldwide in many industries, including logistics, manufacturing, mining, healthcare, etc."[5] The tool supports agent-based, discrete event, and system dynamics simulations. The company provides some facilities for beginners and students, as well as support for academics and professionals.

---

[3] GAMA website: https://gama-platform.github.io.

[4] FIPA website: http://www.fipa.org/.

[5] AnyLogic website: https://www.anylogic.com/.

6.3 The Agent-Based Modeling Perspective

Agent-based computational models mostly involve populations of individual agents that have been implemented as computational entities. A natural way to design and implement agent-based models is starting from individual active entities—agents—and passive entities, objects, representing the environment. This kind of modeling and simulation effort looks for systematic regularities that emerge at the macro-level from interactions between the agents. In this kind of computational modeling, the overall social structure does not depend on equations that govern the whole system, but instead depends on the macro-level regularities that emerge from agent behaviors. Typically, ABM programmers focus on creating relatively simple individual agents with limited computational capabilities. However, in some cases, agents may include a bit more complex equations to model their behaviors and decision-making.

This kind of approach typically relies on low-entry high-ceiling programming languages, such as NetLogo, which facilitate the modeling of entities that are governed by simple behavioral rules. Such entities may operate in the context of heterogeneity, non-equilibrium dynamics, and spatial processes [37]. As was already stated, the overarching principle of ABM is that the whole is greater than the simple sum of its constituent parts [13]. Many real systems or organizations can be easily understood as collections of interacting components, where each of these components has its responsibilities and behavioral rules. Some of these components may be more influential than others, but none of them completely controls the behavior of the entire system. All of these components to a greater or lower degree contribute to the overall behavior of the system. This is also the meaning of a complex adaptive system (CAS), the overall behavior of which emerges from the behaviors of its constituent components [17].

6.3.1 Emergent Behavior and Micro-Macro Analysis

A key aspect of individual entities behavior is concerned with their interactions throughout the system, paying attention to the emergence of bottom-up patterns. Agents can represent individuals, but also groups or organizational units or organizations as a whole. The approach of agent-based business process modeling focuses on the role of different entities—agents and objects—in modeling business processes of an organization as a whole. The difference between objects and agents is that objects, such as orders, machines, and products, are passive entities, while agents, such as workers and customers, are active discrete entities that have their own specific goals and behavior rules. Objects are invoked and manipulated by agents. An example of manipulation is calling the method of a computational object in object-oriented programming. From the business process perspective, agents can represent workers involved in different tasks of a business process, such as operators in a company, workers in an industry, or employees in an office. Other entities can be modeled as passive computational objects, such as orders, raw materials, and invoices. More recently, agents can also represent robots that operate in a problem domain to be modelled and simulated. Once the elementary actions of which the process model is composed have been identified, the simulation allows new entities to be incrementally introduced into the modeling and simulation process. Incremental introduction is necessary because otherwise the complexity of the whole model would fast grow beyond a manageable level. The following paragraphs introduce some relevant concepts from complexity studies.

Emergent Behavior As was mentioned in Sect. 6.3, in a typical ABM, individual entities are modeled by adopting for them simple behavioral rules. In the resulting ABM, the output of the interactions between the entities may give rise to collective properties based on the individual properties of the parts. Moreover, a system consisting of many interacting parts typically has a *micro-level*, where agents operate, and a *macro-level*, where emergent rules arise that make the system more than just the sum of its parts. In business and management studies, the emergent behavior is typically defined as a *side effect*, where an order emerges out of chaos. In economics, the unintended consequences of individual actions are said to give rise to the so-called *externalities*, which can be positive or negative. In the real world, a case of negative *externalities* is the unattended effects of manufacturing activities, which cause air pollution, threaten health, and increase healthcare and social costs in a society. Conversely, there can be cases of positive *externalities*. For instance, individuals who choose to protect their homes from fire usually implicitly provide also their neighbors with the benefits by protecting their homes from the spread of fire. Simple rules-based interactions of the described kind are at the heart of ABM [4].

Self-Organization Another relevant concept in complexity studies is the ability of the system to generate a stable order from interactions between entities, which can be viewed as constituting the chaos [25]. Self-organization is a well-known feature in different areas, such as studies in cognitive psychology and neurosciences, as well as in biology. In a typical example, billions of neurons are connected in the human brain without any central control [50]. In natural systems, this is the case with simple individuals like insects who cooperate to organize themselves, without any central coordination for building tunnels or bridges within their nest [66]. A simple example concerns the analysis of the behavior of insects, as the ant model included in the Models Library of NetLogo [19].

Micro-macro analysis focuses on "the effects of referring to properties, behaviors, structures, or patterns that are located at a higher macro-level and that result from (inter)actions at the lower micro-level of the system. We call such properties 'emergent'. In other words, the overall behavior of the system (i.e., the emergent behaviour) is the result of interactions among the individual entities in the system" [48]. The idea of focusing attention on the synergies between the micro- and macro-levels is also important in social sciences and economics [31, 62].

6.3.2   Complexity

In computer science, the notion of complexity comes in many disguises. Abstract complexity is based on the ease or difficulty of perceiving visual structures. Computational complexity is concerned with the amount of computational resources required for the execution of algorithms. Programming complexity is a measure of the interactions between various components of software. In network theory, complexity is a measure of different possible connections between components of a system. This is close to the notion of complexity most relevant for this book that is concerned with phenomena emerging from interactions between different parts of a system. In the words of Mark Newman, a complex "system of interacting parts exhibits emergent behavior" [54]. As was already mentioned in Sect. 6.3.1, it is often said that the behavior of the system is not the sum of individual behaviors. In particular, there is a general agreement among physicists in defining complexity as a system composed of a large number of elements interacting without central coordination and spontaneously leading to the emergence of "complex structures," i.e., stable structures with patterns that may occur on several spatial or temporal scales [6]. This is an accepted concept in social sciences, where a society can be defined as a structure that cannot be deduced from its parts in a simple way [63]. Complexity concerns these kinds of systems where small changes in input can often lead to different results. ABM is perfectly suited for modeling these types of systems. In his recent introduction to ABM for modeling complex natural, social, and engineered systems [78], Uri Wilensky clearly states:

> ABM, in particular, are distinctive from other modeling approaches in that they were designed in order to understand and explain complex phenomena that otherwise could not be explained through traditional approaches

A typical example of ABM is the *Termites* model, where hundreds of individual entities representing termites perform simple movements that result in creating a complex structure—nest— in their environment [60].

6.4   Advanced Features

6.4.1   Agents and Georeferenced Systems

The integration of an ABM with a georeferenced system can be a relevant improvement for the ABM. In particular, we refer to a geographic information system (GIS) as a computer system for managing data on a map. Typical spatial representations are *raster models*, based on grid data structures, or *vector models*, based on points, lines, and polygons [18]. A common format for storage of vector data was defined by the Environmental Systems Research Institute (ESRI)—the ESRI shape format to store the location, shape, and attributes of geographic features [52]. In particular, a shape feature class consists of at least three main files with the same name having different suffixes: first, the main file (shp) containing the geometries; second, an attribute table in the dBase-format (dbf); and finally, an index file for linking geometries and attributes (shx). In addition, some information can be stored in other files, such as projected coordinate system or spatial reference system (prj) or spatial index (sbn/sbx), or other kind of metadata (shp/xml). The information represented this way in the ESRI shape format is usually about the physical environment, such as roads, buildings, and vegetation. GIS has emerged as an essential tool for resource planning and management by capturing, storing, and displaying data about the locations of the resources [12]. In ABM, agents and objects can directly interact with the GIS environment [16].

Addressing georeferenced environments by ABM has rapidly increased in the last decades [7]. Several works have integrated GIS and ABM [37] in a practical way by exploiting NetLogo [21]. The applications cover different areas, such as agent behaviors, georeferenced networks, and spatial statistics [22]. GIS can show many different kinds of data on a map, such as streets, vegetation, and buildings. Figure 6.3 describes the integration of data sources of GIS with ABM. This enables users to more easily analyze patterns and relationships within the GIS data. In Sect. 8.3, we introduce an example of a self-driving vehicle moving within a georeferenced environment.

Georeferenced systems also play an important role in the business processes of an organization [45], where the business and organizational environment may include GIS applications [58]. Some studies have already investigated modeling business processes that incorporate context information, including ecological and geographical information [80]. Furthermore, spatial decision-making can be connected to enterprise information systems [32], as well as to customer relationship management (CRM) systems [73]. An interesting piece of recent work is concerned

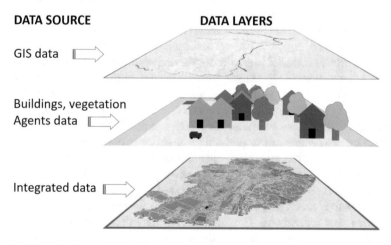

Fig. 6.3 GIS and ABM: Integration of data from different sources with the corresponding data layers

with the interoperability of geoprocessing workflows by converting the workflows to a standard notation [40]. Finally, we mention here the proposal of integrating GIS into ERP as suggested in [57]:

> including GIS into business process offers features that fall into the following categories: (i) Provision of geographic context to business decisions by integrating business data with geo-databases and feature tables. (ii) Linking business functions in an ERP system with geo-processes combined functionality that is distributable across the software architecture. (iii) Fusion of business and geographic information and functionality in the common operational picture on both high and low levels.

6.4.2   ABM and Heuristic Search

Problem domain analysis in ABM to a considerable degree can benefit from heuristic search. It reduces complexity by performing the *what-if* analysis of the problem domain by gradually and systematically modifying the conditions and parameters of the ABM.

The essence of search problems is investigating a large search space to generate high-quality solutions. Some algorithms involve search strategies that are based on the graph theory. A typical example is the *breadth-first* search, where the target node in a search tree is found by storing and utilizing a queue of visited nodes. Similarly, the *depth-first* search algorithm recursively explores a branch in the tree, starting from the initial node until the end node is found. After that, the algorithm continues with backtracking to explore in the same way other branches of the tree. In the *best-first* search, the algorithm starts from a node to find a given goal node following the path with the smallest cost based on a criterion, such as the shortest distance travelled. A good solution for this kind of search problem is the A* algorithm [36] for finding the best moving paths for agents. We have adopted the A* algorithm in the ED simulation to model the movements of operators and patients in the facilities of the ED (see *ABBPS_ED-3D* model in the web repository).

Another relevant class of heuristics for solving optimization and search problems consists of evolutionary algorithms, which evolve over time. In particular, genetic algorithms (GA) [38] are search algorithms inspired by biology that involve concepts related to natural selection like mutation, crossover, and selection. In ABM, a typical goal is to achieve an optimal or a near-optimal solution. GA starts with the construction of a *genetic code* representing the structure of different individuals. The population in each iteration is called a *generation*. Starting from an initial population of randomly generated *individuals*, an iterative process evaluates at each step the *fitness* of each individual. A specific value (*fitness score*) is computed obtaining a ranking of individuals. Then, some individuals are selected by the current population to generate new individuals. This mating pool may depend on the *fitness* values of the selected individuals—in fact, the new generation is a combination of two individuals. A typical solution includes a randomly modified genome to guarantee the differentiation of a new specie. At the next steps of the algorithm, a new generation of candidate solutions is adopted. The algorithm terminates either when a satisfactory fitness level has been reached or a maximum predefined number of generations has been produced for the population [77]. The technique has already been successfully applied to business processes [26, 49].

Applications of Genetic Algorithms   An application of genetic algorithms in ABM may involve a system with a population consisting of agents [46, 68, 69]. A solution to a problem is found by focusing on a strategy consisting of a set of rules, each of which specifies an action for each possible situation. ABM encodes a strategy for all possible situations, resulting in an action for each situation, which is represented by a number. For example, a vector of binary numbers—zeroes and ones—of a fixed size provides an appropriate representation of each candidate solution. A fitness function evaluates the domain of the solution, measuring the quality of the represented solution. Thereafter, a portion of the existing population is selected to breed a new generation, i.e., the most suitable agents are selected to continue the algorithm. A specific tool is BehaviorSearch, a software to help with automating the exploration of ABM by using genetic algorithms and other heuristic techniques (e.g., random search, hill climbing algorithms) to search the parameter space.

6.4.3   Learning Agents

A possible application of ABM is concerned with learning by agents. In particular, reinforcement learning (RL) is a widely used technique, according to which an agent learns the most beneficial actions, considering its goals, based on the feedback the agent has received from its environment [9]. Typical RL practical applications are inventory production and management, conversational agents, finance, and stock portfolio management. The RL technique concerns to behavioral psychology, where a reinforcement occurs to strengthen future behaviors depending on a particular positive or negative antecedent stimulus, constituting a reward or punishment.

   In machine learning, a reward may follow a certain action performed by the agent. In particular, an action gets a positive score if it is successful and a negative score if the agent is "punished" for an impermissible action. A well-known RL algorithm is Q-learning [76], where agents pay attention not only to the immediate rewards but also to the long-term rewards. The algorithm is based on an iterative process that considers each state-action pair using a table mapping the states of the world to the actions and rewards by the agents [75]. Finally, a specific table—Q-table—contains all the rewards called Q-values including the long-term payoffs. In a training phase, at each iteration, the long-term reward is computed by adopting the following variants of the Bellman equation. Formally, given a state s of the agent and an action a by the agent, the expected reward computed by the algorithm is $Q(s, a)$.

$$Q(s, a) = R(s, a) + \alpha \times (\gamma \max_{a} Q(s', a) - R(s, a)), \qquad (6.2)$$

In Eq. 6.2, α is the learning rate, i.e., a weight given to the new information compared with the already known information. The new long-term reward is the current reward $R(s, a)$ plus all future rewards in the next state s' and in the following states, assuming that the agent always performs its most beneficial actions. The discount factor γ is a number in the range 0,1 to weigh the immediate rewards and future rewards.

An introductory example in Chap. 8 describes an agent—a self-driving vehicle SmartCab—that is supposed to learn the path between the starting and ending points, by using a grid search algorithm. The basic concepts are the *State space*, which is the set of states for an agent; the *Action space* which is the set of all the actions that an agent can perform in its given state; a *Reward table* which includes for each actions the corresponding reward; and, finally, the *Q table* which contains for each pair of states and actions the corresponding Q-values (initialized to 0 and updated after training).

References

1. Abubakar, A.M., Elrehail, H., Alatailat, M.A., Elçi, A.: Knowledge management, decision-making style and organizational performance. J. Innovation Knowl. **4**(2), 104–114 (2019). https://doi.org/10.1016/j.jik.2017.07.003
2. Amantea, I.A., Di Leva, A., Sulis, E.: A simulation-driven approach to decision support in process reorganization: a case study in healthcare. In: Exploring Digital Ecosystems, pp. 223–235. Springer, Berlin (2020). https://doi.org/10.1007/978-3-030-23665-6_16
3. Amantea, I.A., Leva, A.D., Sulis, E.: A simulation-driven approach in risk-aware business process management: A case study in healthcare. In: Rango, F.D., Ören, T.I., Obaidat, M.S. (eds.) Proceedings of 8th International Conference on Simulation and Modeling Methodologies, Technologies and Applications, SIMULTECH 2018, Porto, Portugal, July 29–31, 2018, pp. 98–105. SciTePress (2018). https://doi.org/10.5220/0006842100980105
4. Axelrod, R.: Advancing the art of simulation in the social sciences. In: Simulating social phenomena, pp. 21–40. Springer, Berlin (1997). https://doi.org/10.1002/(sici)1099-0526(199711/12)3:2
5. Balaji, S., Murugaiyan, M.S.: Waterfall vs. v-model vs. agile: a comparative study on sdlc. Int. J. Inform. Technol. Bus. Manag. **2**(1), 26–30 (2012). https://doi.org/10.17950/ijer/v4s4/405
6. Barrat, A., Barthelemy, M., Vespignani, A.: Dynamical Processes on Complex Networks. Cambridge University Press, Cambridge (2008). https://doi.org/10.1017/CBO9780511791383
7. Batty, M.: Agent-based models for geographical systems: a review (2019). https://doi.org/10.1007/978-90-481-8927-4. Accessed 15 Jan 2021
8. Bellifemine, F.L., Caire, G., Greenwood, D.: Developing Multi-Agent Systems with JADE, vol. 7. Wiley, London (2007). https://doi.org/10.1002/9780470058411
9. Bengio, Y.: Learning deep architectures for AI. Found. Trends Mach. Learn. **2**(1), 1–127 (2009). https://doi.org/10.1561/2200000006
10. Binci, D., Belisari, S., Appolloni, A.: Bpm and change management: an ambidextrous perspective. Bus. Process Manag. J. (2019). https://doi.org/10.1108/BPMJ-06-2018-0158
11. Boissier, O., Bordini, R.H., Hübner, J.F., Ricci, A., Santi, A.: Multi-agent oriented programming with JaCaMo. Sci. Comput. Program. **78**(6), 747–761 (2013). https://doi.org/10.1016/j.scico.2011.10.004
12. Bolstad, P.: GIS fundamentals: a first text on geographic information systems. Eider (Press-Minnesota) (2016)

13. Bonabeau, E.: Agent-based modeling: Methods and techniques for simulating human systems. Proc. Nat. Acad. Sci. **99**(suppl 3), 7280–7287 (2002). https://doi.org/10.1073/pnas.082080899

14. Bordini, R.H., Hübner, J.F., Wooldridge, M.: Programming multi-agent systems in AgentSpeak using Jason, vol. 8. Wiley, London (2007). https://doi.org/10.1002/9780470061848

15. Box, G.E.: Science and statistics. J. Am. Stat. Assoc. **71**(356), 791–799 (1976). https://doi.org/10.1080/01621459.1976.10480949

16. Brown, D.G., Riolo, R., Robinson, D.T., North, M., Rand, W.: Spatial process and data models: toward integration of agent-based models and GIS. J. Geograph. Syst. **7**(1), 25–47 (2005). https://doi.org/10.1007/s10109-005-0148-5

17. Buckley, W.: Society as a complex adaptive system. In: Systems Research for Behavioral Science Systems Research, pp. 490–513. Routledge, London (2017). https://doi.org/doi.org/10.4324/9781315130569

18. Burrough, P.A., McDonnell, R., McDonnell, R.A., Lloyd, C.D.: Principles of Geographical Information Systems. Oxford University Press, Oxford (2015). https://doi.org/10.1111/j.1745-7939.2000.tb01582.x

19. Caillou, P., Rey Coyrehourq, S., Marilleau, N., Banos, A.: 6—exploring complex models in netlogo. In: Banos, A., Lang, C., Marilleau, N. (eds.) Agent-Based Spatial Simulation with NetLogo, vol. 2, pp. 173–208. Elsevier, Amsterdam (2017). https://doi.org/10.1016/B978-1-78548-157-4.50006-6

20. Collier, N., North, M.: Repast HPC: a platform for large-scale agent-based modeling. Large-Scale Comput. 81–109 (2012). https://doi.org/10.1002/9781118130506.ch5

21. Crooks, A., Malleson, N., Manley, E., Heppenstall, A.: Agent-Based Modelling and Geographical Information Systems: A Practical Primer. SAGE Publications Limited (2018). https://doi.org/10.4135/9781473916432.n4

22. Crooks, A.T., Castle, C.J.: The integration of agent-based modelling and geographical information for geospatial simulation. In: Agent-Based Models of Geographical Systems, pp. 219–251. Springer, Berlin (2012). https://doi.org/10.1007/978-90-481-8927-4_12

23. Curtis, B., Kellner, M.I., Over, J.: Process modeling. Commun. ACM **35**(9), 75–90 (1992)

24. Dahl, O.J., Nygaard, K.: Simula: an algol-based simulation language. Commun. ACM **9**(9), 671–678 (1966)

25. De Wolf, T., Holvoet, T.: Emergence versus self-organisation: different concepts but promising when combined. In: Brueckner, S.A., Di Marzo Serugendo, G., Karageorgos, A., Nagpal, R. (eds.) Engineering Self-Organising Systems, pp. 1–15. Springer, Berlin (2005). https://doi.org/10.1007/11494676_1

26. Di Francescomarino, C., Dumas, M., Federici, M., Ghidini, C., Maggi, F.M., Rizzi, W., Simonetto, L.: Genetic algorithms for hyperparameter optimization in predictive business process monitoring. Inform. Syst. **74**, 67–83 (2018). https://doi.org/10.1016/j.is.2018.01.003

27. Di Francescomarino, C., Ghidini, C., Maggi, F.M., Petrucci, G., Yeshchenko, A.: An eye into the future: leveraging a-priori knowledge in predictive business process monitoring. In: International Conference on Business Process Management, pp. 252–268. Springer, Berlin (2017)

28. Di Leva, A., Sulis, E., De Lellis, A., Amantea, I.A.: Business process analysis and change management: the role of material resource planning and discrete-event simulation. In: Exploring Digital Ecosystems, pp. 211–221. Springer, Berlin (2020). https://doi.org/10.1007/978-3-030-23665-6_15

29. Dumas, M., La Rosa, M., Mendling, J., Reijers, H.: Fundamentals of Business Process Management, vol. 1, 2nd edn. Springer, Berlin (2018). https://doi.org/10.1007/978-3-662-56509-4

30. Effken, J.A., Brewer, B.B., Logue, M.D., Gephart, S.M., Verran, J.A.: Using cognitive work analysis to fit decision support tools to nurse managers' work flow. Int. J. Med. Inform. **80**(10), 698–707 (2011). https://doi.org/10.1016/j.ijmedinf.2011.07.003

31. Eliasson, G.: Modeling the experimentally organized economy: complex dynamics in an empirical micro-macro model of endogenous economic growth. J. Econ. Behav. Organ. **16**(1–2), 153–182 (1991). https://doi.org/10.1016/0167-2681(91)90047-2

32. Farkas, D., Hilton, B., Pick, J., Ramakrishna, H., Sarkar, A., Shin, N.: A tutorial on geographic information systems: a ten-year update. Commun. Assoc. Inform. Syst. **38**(1), 9 (2016). https://doi.org/10.17705/1CAIS.03809
33. Georgeff, M., Pell, B., Pollack, M., Tambe, M., Wooldridge, M.: The belief-desire-intention model of agency. In: International Workshop on Agent Theories, Architectures, and Languages, pp. 1–10. Springer, Berlin (1998). https://doi.org/10.1007/3-540-49057-4_1
34. Grimm, V., Berger, U., Bastiansen, F., Eliassen, S., Ginot, V., Giske, J., Goss-Custard, J., Grand, T., Heinz, S.K., Huse, G., Huth, A., Jepsen, J.U., Jørgensen, C., Mooij, W.M., Müller, B., Pe'er, G., Piou, C., Railsback, S.F., Robbins, A.M., Robbins, M.M., Rossmanith, E., Rüger, N., Strand, E., Souissi, S., Stillman, R.A., Vabø, R., Visser, U., DeAngelis, D.L.: A standard protocol for describing individual-based and agent-based models. Ecol. Model. **198**(1), 115–126 (2006). https://doi.org/doi.org/10.1016/j.ecolmodel.2006.04.023
35. Grimm, V., Berger, U., DeAngelis, D.L., Polhill, J.G., Giske, J., Railsback, S.F.: The ODD protocol: a review and first update.Ecol. Model. **221**(23), 2760–2768 (2010). https://doi.org/10.1016/j.ecolmodel.2010.08.019
36. Hart, P.E., Nilsson, N.J., Raphael, B.: A formal basis for the heuristic determination of minimum cost paths. IEEE Trans. Syst. Sci. Cybern. **4**(2), 100–107 (1968). https://doi.org/10.1109/TSSC.1968.300136
37. Heppenstall, A.J., Crooks, A.T., See, L.M., Batty, M.: Agent-Based Models of Geographical Systems. Springer, Berlin (2011). https://doi.org/10.1007/978-90-481-8927-4
38. Holland, J.: Adaptation in natural and artificial systems: an introductory analysis with application to biology. Control and artificial intelligence (1975)
39. Kaptelinin, V., Nardi, B.A.: Acting with Technology: Activity Theory and Interaction Design. MIT Press, Cambridge (2006). https://doi.org/10.5210/fm.v12i4.1772
40. Kechagioglou, X., Lemmens, R., Retsios, V.: Sharing geoprocessing workflows with business process model and notation (BPMN). In: Proceedings of the 2019 2nd International Conference on Geoinformatics and Data Analysis, pp. 56–60 (2019). https://doi.org/10.1145/3318236.3318239
41. Kleijnen, J.P.: Sensitivity analysis and optimization in simulation: design of experiments and case studies. In: Winter Simulation Conference Proceedings, 1995., pp. 133–140. IEEE, IEEE (1995). https://doi.org/10.1109/WSC.1995.478715
42. Kravari, K., Bassiliades, N.: A survey of agent platforms. J. Artif. Soc. Soc. Simul. **18**(1), 11 (2015). https://doi.org/10.18564/jasss.2661
43. Law, A.M.: Simulation Modeling & Analysis, 5th edn. McGraw-Hill, New York (2015)
44. Law, A.M.: How to build valid and credible simulation models. In: 2019 Winter Simulation Conference (WSC), pp. 1402–1414. IEEE, Piscataway (2019). https://doi.org/10.1109/WSC40007.2019.9004789
45. Longley, P.A., Clarke, G.: GIS for Business and Service Planning. Wiley, London (1996). https://doi.org/10.1016/S0969-6989(97)81473-7
46. Macy, M.W., Willer, R.: From factors to actors: Computational sociology and agent-based modeling. Ann. Rev. Sociol. **28**(1), 143–166 (2002). https://doi.org/10.1146/annurev.soc.28.110601.141117
47. Mansar, S.L., Reijers, H.A.: Best practices in business process redesign: validation of a redesign framework. Comput. Ind. **56**(5), 457–471 (2005). https://doi.org/10.1016/j.compind.2005.01.001
48. Marchiori, M., Possamai, L.: Micro-macro analysis of complex networks. PLoS ONE **10**(1), 1–27 (2015). https://doi.org/10.1371/journal.pone.0116670
49. de Medeiros, A.K.A., Weijters, A.J., van der Aalst, W.: Genetic process mining: an experimental evaluation. Data Mining Knowl. Discovery **14**(2), 245–304 (2007). https://doi.org/10.1007/s10618-006-0061-7
50. Meisel, C., Gross, T.: Adaptive self-organization in a realistic neural network model. Phys. Rev. E **80**(6), 061917 (2009). https://doi.org/10.1103/PhysRevE.80.061917

51. Micolier, A., Taillandier, F., Taillandier, P., Bos, F.: Li-bim, an agent-based approach to simulate occupant-building interaction from the building-information modelling. Eng. Appl. Artif. Intell. **82**, 44–59 (2019). https://doi.org/10.1016/j.engappai.2019.03.008
52. Mitchel, A., et al.: The ESRI Guide to GIS Analysis, vol. 2: Spartial Measurements and Statistics. ESRI Press (2005)
53. Naylor, T.H., Finger, J.M.: Verification of computer simulation models. Manag. Sci. **14**(2), B–92 (1967). https://doi.org/10.1287/mnsc.14.2.B92
54. Newman, M.E.J.: The structure and function of complex networks. SIAM Rev. **45**(2), 167–256 (2003). https://doi.org/10.1137/S003614450342480
55. North, M.J., Collier, N.T., Ozik, J., Tatara, E.R., Macal, C.M., Bragen, M., Sydelko, P.: Complex adaptive systems modeling with repast simphony. Complex Adapt. Syst. Model. **1**(1), 1–26 (2013). https://doi.org/10.1186/2194-3206-1-3
56. Pal, C., Leon, F., Paprzycki, M., Ganzha, M.: A review of platforms for the development of agent systems. CoRR abs/2007.08961 (2020). https://arxiv.org/abs/2007.08961
57. Pászto, V., Jürgens, C., Tominc, P., Burian, J.: Spationomy: Spatial Exploration of Economic Data and Methods of Interdisciplinary Analytics. Springer, Berlin (2020). https://doi.org/10.1007/978-3-030-26626-4
58. Pick, J.B.: Geo-Business: GIS in the Digital Organization. Wiley, London (2008). https://doi.org/10.1002/9780470259955
59. Rao, A.S.: Agentspeak (l): Bdi agents speak out in a logical computable language. In: European Workshop on Modelling Autonomous Agents in a Multi-Agent World, pp. 42–55. Springer, Berlin (1996)
60. Sakellariou, I.: Agent based modelling and simulation using state machines. In: SIMULTECH, pp. 270–279. https://doi.org/10.5220/0004164802700279
61. Sargent, R.G.: Verification and validation of simulation models. J. Simul. **7**(1), 12–24 (2013). https://doi.org/10.1109/WSC.2010.5679166
62. Sawyer, R.K.: Artificial societies: multiagent systems and the micro-macro link in sociological theory. Sociol. Methods Res. **31**(3), 325–363 (2003). https://doi.org/10.1177/0049124102239079
63. Sawyer, R.K., Sawyer, R.K.S.: Social Emergence: Societies as Complex Systems. Cambridge University Press, Cambridge (2005). https://doi.org/10.1017/CBO9780511734892
64. Sharifi, H., Zhang, Z.: Agile manufacturing in practice-application of a methodology. Int. J. Oper. Prod. Manag. (2001). https://doi.org/10.1108/01443570110390462
65. Sierhuis, M., Clancey, W.J., Van Hoof, R.J.: Brahms: a multi-agent modelling environment for simulating work processes and practices. Int. J. Simul. Process Model. **3**(3), 134–152 (2007). https://doi.org/10.1504/IJSPM.2007.015238
66. Solé, R.V., Bascompte, J.: Self-Organization in Complex Ecosystems.(MPB-42). Princeton University Press, Princeton (2006). https://doi.org/10.1515/9781400842933
67. Soon, K.L., Lim, J.M.Y., Parthiban, R., Ho, M.C.: Proactive eco-friendly pheromone-based green vehicle routing for multi-agent systems. Expert Syst. Appl. **121**, 324–337 (2019). https://doi.org/10.1016/j.eswa.2018.12.026
68. Stonedahl, F.J.: Genetic algorithms for the exploration of parameter spaces in agent-based models. Ph.D. Thesis, Northwestern University (2011)
69. Sulis, E., Terna, P., Di Leva, A., Boella, G., Boccuzzi, A.: Agent-oriented decision support system for business processes management with genetic algorithm optimization: an application in healthcare. J. Med. Syst. **44**(9), 1–7 (2020). https://doi.org/10.1007/s10916-020-01608-4
70. Taillandier, P., Gaudou, B., Grignard, A., Huynh, Q.N., Marilleau, N., Caillou, P., Philippon, D., Drogoul, A.: Building, composing and experimenting complex spatial models with the gama platform. GeoInformatica **23**(2), 299–322 (2019). https://doi.org/10.1007/s10707-018-00339-6
71. Teinemaa, I., Dumas, M., Maggi, F.M., Di Francescomarino, C.: Predictive business process monitoring with structured and unstructured data. In: International Conference on Business Process Management, pp. 401–417. Springer, Berlin (2016). https://doi.org/10.1007/978-3-319-45348-4_23

72. Tisue, S., Wilensky, U.: NetLogo: A simple environment for modeling complexity. In: International Conference on Complex Systems, vol. 21, pp. 16–21. Boston (2004)
73. Treiblmayr, M., Tso-Sutter, K.H.L., Krüger, A.: Interfacing business processes and spatial processes. In: Proceedings 2011 IEEE International Conference on Spatial Data Mining and Geographical Knowledge Services, pp. 174–180. IEEE, Piscataway (2011). https://doi.org/10.1109/ICSDM.2011.5969027
74. Uhrmacher, A.M., Weyns, D.: Multi-Agent Systems: Simulation and Applications. CRC Press (2009). https://doi.org/10.1201/9781420070248
75. Watkins, C.J., Dayan, P.: Q-learning. Mach. Learn. **8**(3-4), 279–292 (1992). https://doi.org/10.1007/BF00992698
76. Watkins, C.J.C.H.: Learning from Delayed Rewards. King's College, Cambridge (1989). https://doi.org/10.1201/9781420070248
77. Whitley, D.: A genetic algorithm tutorial. Stat. Comput. **4**(2), 65–85 (1994). https://doi.org/10.1007/BF00175354
78. Wilensky, U., Rand, W.: An Introduction to Agent-Based Modeling: Modeling Natural, Social, and Engineered Complex Systems with NetLogo. MIT Press, Cambridge (2015). https://doi.org/10.1063/PT.3.2884
79. Wynn, D.C., Clarkson, P.J.: Process models in design and development. Res. Eng. Design **29**(2), 161–202 (2018). https://doi.org/10.1007/s00163-017-0262-7
80. Zhu, X., Zhu, G., vanden Broucke, S., Recker, J.: On merging business process management and geographic information systems: modeling and execution of ecological concerns in processes. In: International Conference on Geo-Informatics in Resource Management and Sustainable Ecosystem, pp. 486–496. Springer, Berlin (2014). https://doi.org/10.1007/978-3-662-45737-5_48
81. Zouad, S., Boufaida, M.: An agent-oriented methodology for business process management. In: International Symposium on Business Modeling and Software Design, pp. 287–296. Springer, Berlin (2020). https://doi.org/10.1007/978-3-030-52306-0_19

Part III
Agent-Based Modeling for Business Process Management

Chapter 7
Multi-Agent Systems and Business Process Management

Abstract This chapter provides an insight into applying autonomous agents and multi-agent systems (MAS) to BPM. The first section presents an overview of recent applications of agents in BPM. After that, some tools are introduced that enable to import to NetLogo models represented in typical BPM formats, such as BPMN, Petri nets, and the eXtensible Event Stream standard language.

7.1 Agents in BPM

Recent research directions of organizational studies include methods for discovering, modeling, analyzing, measuring, improving, optimizing, and automating business processes [4]. As was already mentioned in Chap. 2, recent efforts in BPM have focused the attention on business process analysis and data mining, resulting in proliferation of studies in process mining (PM) [34]. In particular, the main research interests in BPM have shifted to automatic discovery of business processes (*process discovery*) from workflow data stored in information systems in the form of event logs [1, 12]. A related research topic addresses algorithms and techniques for comparing the observed real behaviors with the process model by *conformance checking* with the aim of improving the operation of the real organization [17]. In addition, data can be used for on-the-fly deviation detection, predictions, and recommendations in the *operational support* phase. Once the model has been obtained by mining and analyzing the real data, machine learning algorithms can be applied to it, such as the methods of *predictive process monitoring* [3] for predicting the behaviors of new process instances. This section investigates the intersection between BPM and agent-oriented research.

Applications of MAS in BPM
Several applications in BPM can benefit from the research techniques and tools that have been coined and successfully applied in the community of autonomous

© Springer Nature Switzerland AG 2022
E. Sulis, K. Taveter, *Agent-Based Business Process Simulation*,
https://doi.org/10.1007/978-3-030-98816-6_7

agents and MAS. Accordingly, we list below the main areas where agent-oriented approaches have demonstrated promising results:

- *Multi-agent (deep) reinforcement learning.* Applying the techniques of reinforcement learning [30] and deep learning to MAS [18] is one of the recent research areas that is relevant for BPM. For example, [37] describes a multi-agent Q-learning algorithm for service composition. Moreover, neural networks have been applied to improve the learning processes [5].
- *Conversational applications.* A proactive chatbot [7] can interact with its users in a natural language, performing actions on their behalf, and initiating interactions to inform users about the relevant behaviors of the information system. Moreover, conversational agents or chatbots in human-computer interaction [7] can employ natural language processing for business process automation. One way to do this is to create a multi-agent system consisting of conversational assistants [23].
- *Cognitive agents.* The adoption of cognitive agents in BPM relies on "proactivity and self-adaptation of the running processes against the evolving conditions of the application domains in which they are enacted" [14]. Cognitive agents may adopt the Belief, Desire, and Intention (BDI) architecture in an agent-based business process management framework [10, 38]. A promising area to apply cognitive agents is modeling and simulating humans within business processes as software agents emulating different personality traits and varying emotions and moods [9, 24, 25]. A good recent example is the simulation study based on cognitive agents of how the job performance of airline employees is affected by personality traits, such as conscientiousness, extroversion, and neuroticism [42].
- *Micro-macro interactions in complex systems.* Complexity studies are co-interactions between agents and also between agents and objects of their environment. Practical applications of business process complexity are investigated in ABMS [19], whereas typical examples are markets, organizations, and emergency services [27]. More recently, the research on Internet of things has also focused on complex systems involving interactions between autonomous agents [8].
- *Agent-oriented decision-support systems.* As we have emphasized in Chap. 5, a typical scenario of conducting an agent-based simulation involves the *what-if* analysis to improve the decision-making performed in an organization. The corresponding agent-based decision-support system can optimize key parameters in an agent-based business process simulation by applying, for example, heuristic search [2] or genetic algorithms [28, 29].
- *Agents and robotic process automation.* Robotic process automation (RPA) is a recent research area involving software agents that emulate humans in process-aware systems [31]. One of the purposes of agents in RPA is "to explore and manipulate a portion of their environment in order to find and collect information and data" [35].
- *Agent-oriented modeling and business process simulation.* As has already been mentioned above, agent-oriented approaches can be helpful for both modeling [26, 33, 41] and for simulating business processes [6, 19, 27], as well as for combining business process modeling and simulation [36].

- *Agents and process mining.* Event log data about utilizing resources by an organization can define the creation of agents in an ABM [15, 32]. For example, employees of an organization can be reflected by the corresponding number of agents in the model. Similarly, the arrival of new cases, such as patients in a healthcare service, can be represented by the creation of the corresponding agents in the model. PM has also recently been employed for identifying the goals by individual agents [21, 40].

7.2 Agents in the BPM Lifecycle

The business process analysis of an organization proposed in this chapter includes the selection, identification, and definition of which processes are relevant to consider, among the many existing business processes of the organization. As better detailed in Chap. 2, a typical BPM lifecycle includes five phases: analysis, modeling, implementation, execution, monitoring, and optimization of business processes. The initial steps of business process analysis and modeling render the process as a sequence of activities (*process discovery*) based on the goals of the organization. In addition to analyzing (*process analysis*) and modeling (*process modeling*) the business processes, the initial steps also include redesigning the business process model (*process redesign*). The next steps are the implementation of the business process involving a support for the execution (*implementation of the process*) and the evaluation of the resulting business process (*process monitoring and controlling*) [4, 13].

Figure 7.1 shows how the agent-oriented approach can be integrated with the BPM lifecycle. Specifically, Fig. 7.1 describes the individual steps of the integration: once the business process of interest has been selected (*process identification*), the agent-oriented modeling of the business process (*design*) addresses the construction of an agent-oriented business process model. At the next phase, the business process is implemented (*execution*), and the implementing information system records the corresponding data of interest generated from the execution of the process in the form of process event logs. The next stage allows the progress of the business process flow to be monitored (*monitor*). Thereafter, the performance of the business process can be examined through applying an appropriate set of process performance indicators in the *diagnosis* phase. In addition, the PM techniques of process discovery and compliance checking can be applied to the data recorded during the execution phase as the event logs.

The information derived from performing the real business process can also be examined analytically by means of historical data analysis to identify the values of the parameters needed for configuring the ABM. After that, a scenario analysis (*what-if*) can be conducted by means of ABM by utilizing the results of the data analysis reflecting the real business process. The usage of event logs can improve the model by defining more precisely the distribution of new instances arriving in the process, the duration of the activities, and the behavior of the agents involved

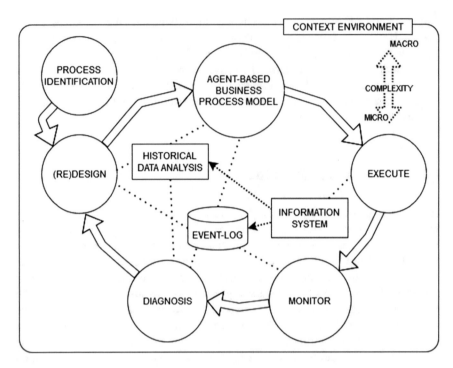

Fig. 7.1 Agent-based business process lifecycle. After identifying a business process to be analyzed, the event logs are recorded and are then used to define ABM. The mutual influence between variables of the micro and macro levels is also considered

in the process. One can also consider how the resulting system interacts with its external environment. Doing that involves the identification of the contextual variables that may impact the model. The analysis must also include micro-macro aspect of complex systems' analysis that was treated in Chap. 6. Finally, another reason why agent-oriented approaches are increasingly relevant is that traditional business processes within organizations are currently being supplanted by more dynamic ecosystems of organizations [20], which conceptually consist of many parts, such as institutional agents, human agents, and man-made agents—software agents and robots—acting on their behalf [39].

7.3   ABM and Business Process Modeling

Typically, ABM considers models in which agents operate in a considerably simplified space-time environment involving a few or no constraints. On the other hand, BPM has accumulated during several decades a lot of experience of modeling the real world, while PM techniques can further improve the models of the real world by focusing on automatic extraction of event data and process models [34]. To utilize the accumulated experience, this section investigates how to import models represented in standard business process languages into NetLogo and how to manage such models in NetLogo.

After defining or importing the business process model in terms of sequences of activities and main decision points, one can also explicitly define the agents required for performing the business process and their behaviors. In NetLogo, the programmer can add the behaviors of the agents and other typical elements of an ABM, beyond the imported standard business process model. For example, the starting point of conducting a scenario analysis (*what-if*) can be a BPMN diagram. However, as we have pointed out in Chap. 5, being an activity-oriented approach, the emphasis of BPMN is on what activities take place rather than on which agents perform them. Therefore, "swimlanes" of BPMN models should be represented as agents, which can be done by following the methodology described in Chap. 5. In particular, employees of an organization can be modeled as agents that have knowledge about their hours of work and skills or abilities. Similarly, for an ABM, one should also elaborate the representation of activities by including their different possible duration in the form of a fixed or uniform distribution. In addition, process performance indicators should be introduced, allowing one to track the process by, for example, calculating the wait time or resource utilization, as is described in Sect. 2.2.3.

As has been mentioned before, to investigate the adoption of NetLogo to BPM, it is worth noting that: "In all of the proposed tools for simulation in process mining, interaction with the user and user knowledge is an undeniable requirement for designing and running the simulation models" [22]. Considering that, the following two sections describe how to import a standard BPMN model and a Petri net model into NetLogo. These sections are reinforced by the resources available online.[1]

7.3.1 Importing a BPMN Model

As introduced in Sect. 2.1.5, Petri nets are a well-known business process modeling language in the specialized BPM literature. In the web repository, the *ABBPS_PN-Demo-example* model describes the functioning of simple PN models, which can be loaded by the program or created by the user.

In addition, this section presents a practical example of automatically importing a BPMN model into NetLogo to obtain the corresponding workflow diagram in NetLogo. The *ABBPS_Import-BPMN* model loads a BPMN file to reproduce in the display area the elements of the business process, such as tasks, events, and gateways. This program is illustrated by Fig. 7.2).

---

[1] Visit http://www.processmining.org/event_logs_and_models_used_in_book.

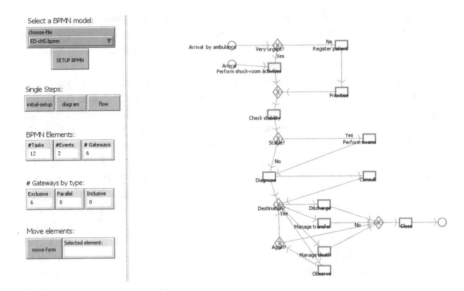

Fig. 7.2 Importing a BPMN diagram into NetLogo

The *ABBPS_Import-BPMN* model comes with some ready-to-load templates that are represented in the BPMN format. On the main screen, one can select the template of interest by means of the "choose-file" drop-down menu. To import one's own BPMN template, one should add it to the same path with the program by inserting the corresponding file name within the slider. For fine-tuning, one may need to work on the program code. In the program, the elements of BPMN are created as breeds called *bpmn-elements*, which are interconnected by links. Each element has a variable "kind" to distinguish between events (initial or final event), tasks, delays, sub-processes, and gateways (exclusive, inclusive, or parallel). Each element has a form that corresponds to the standard BPMN notation. One can describe by the corresponding label the content of the task, or the name of the gateway. The variable "name-link" may contain a text associated with the link, like in case of the "yes" or "no" branch within an exclusive gateway.

In this introductory program, a BPMN model created by means of standard tools, such as http://bpmn.io, can be imported into NetLogo. It is worthwhile to mention here that the examples provided with this program include a small number of tasks, as more complex models cannot be easily imported into NetLogo. Among the models included in the online repository associated with this book, the ED BPMN model has been adopted in Sect. 4.4.3. Therefore, Fig. 7.2 describes the ED model imported from the corresponding "ABBPS-ED.bpmn" file. Moreover, the button "Move-form button" in the main view of the program allows the user to re-locate the tasks on the screen to obtain a better visualization in case of overlapping elements and other similar cases. Finally, in the NetLogo desktop version, one can also benefit from the 3D view—a feature that can further improve the understanding of the model by the stakeholders. The 3D view is illustrated by Fig. 7.3.

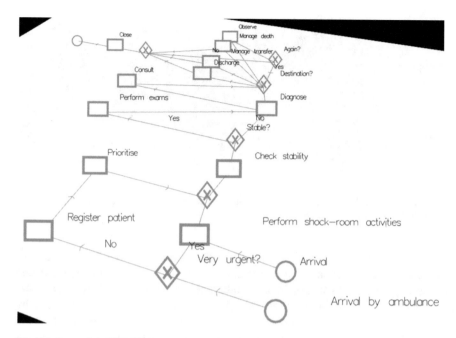

Fig. 7.3 Importing a BPMN diagram into NetLogo in the 3D view

7.3.2   *Importing a Petri Net*

The program *ABBPS_Import-PNML-CC* enables to automatically import a Petri net from the corresponding file into NetLogo as a workflow diagram. As an example, we describe in this section the Petri net model that has been obtained from a real-life event log that is based on the CCC-19 dataset [16] representing a medical training process. The NetLogo program reproduces in the view area the healthcare process model, with the corresponding places and transitions [11]. An overview of Petri nets is presented in Sect. 2.1.5.

Figure 7.4 represents the output of the CCC-19 Petri net in NetLogo. In the figure, the frequencies of places, transitions, and links are visualized by the corresponding three monitors on the left. The "Setup" button executes the corresponding code to set up the initial variables used in the program. To further investigate the programming language, interested readers may explore the procedures under the "Code" area.

```
to setup
    clear-all   ; NetLogo command to clear all variables
    setup-initial-variables ; To initialize variables
    file-close-all   ; Close files eventually opened from last
    run reset-ticks   ; Initialize time counter
end
```

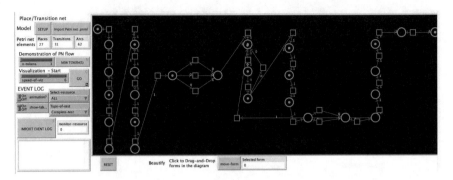

Fig. 7.4 Interface of the CCC-19 example with the Petri net of the model automatically created from the PNML file in NetLogo

The demonstration models presented in this section, for both BPMN and Petri net cases, are very simple and introductory examples for managing, opening, and importing business processes in the standard notation language. They allow to get an idea of how a business process simulation of an organization could work by using an agent modeling platform. Furthermore, reading parameters via file could allow characterization of both operators and simulation parameters, as in the case of activities duration. The models presented in the next chapter allow to deepen these aspects by examining multiple possible applications.

References

1. Amantea, I.A., Sulis, E., Boella, G., Marinello, R., Bianca, D., Brunetti, E., Bo, M., Fernandez-Llatas, C.: A process mining application for the analysis of hospital-at-home admissions. Stud. Health Technol. Inform. **270**, 522–526 (2020). https://doi.org/10.3233/shti200215
2. Ben Othman, S., Zgaya, H., Dotoli, M., Hammadi, S.: An agent-based decision support system for resources' scheduling in emergency supply chains. Control Eng. Practice **59**, 27–43 (2017). https://doi.org/10.1016/j.conengprac.2016.11.014
3. Di Francescomarino, C., Ghidini, C., Maggi, F.M., Milani, F.: Predictive process monitoring methods: Which one suits me best? In: International Conference on Business Process Management, pp. 462–479. Springer, Berlin (2018). https://doi.org/10.1007/978-3-319-98648-7_27
4. Dumas, M., La Rosa, M., Mendling, J., Reijers, H.: Fundamentals of Business Process Management, vol. 1, 2nd edn. Springer, Berlin (2018). https://doi.org/10.1007/978-3-662-56509-4
5. Foerster, J., Assael, I.A., De Freitas, N., Whiteson, S.: Learning to communicate with deep multi-agent reinforcement learning. In: Advances in Neural Information Processing Systems, pp. 2137–2145 (2016)
6. Gómez-Cruz, N.A., Saa, I.L., Hurtado, F.F.O.: Agent-based simulation in management and organizational studies: a survey. Eur. J. Manag. Bus. Econ. (2017). https://doi.org/10.1108/EJMBE-10-2017-018
7. Io, H., Lee, C.: Chatbots and conversational agents: A bibliometric analysis. In: 2017 IEEE International Conference on Industrial Engineering and Engineering Management (IEEM), pp. 215–219. IEEE, Piscataway (2017). https://doi.org/10.1109/IEEM.2017.8289883

8. Janiesch, C., Koschmider, A., Mecella, M., Weber, B., Burattin, A., Di Ciccio, C., Fortino, G., Gal, A., Kannengiesser, U., Leotta, F., et al.: The internet of things meets business process management: a manifesto. IEEE Syst. Man Cybern. Mag. **6**(4), 34–44 (2020). https://doi.org/10.1109/MSMC.2020.3003135

9. Jones, H., Saunier, J., Lourdeaux, D.: Personality, emotions and physiology in a bdi agent architecture: The pep-bdi model. In: 2009 IEEE/WIC/ACM International Joint Conference on Web Intelligence and Intelligent Agent Technology, vol. 2, pp. 263–266. IEEE, Piscataway (2009). https://doi.org/10.1109/WI-IAT.2009.160

10. Kir, H., Erdogan, N.: A knowledge-intensive adaptive business process management framework. Inform. Syst. **95**, 101639 (2021). https://doi.org/10.1016/j.is.2020.101639

11. Lira, R., Salas-Morales, J., de la Fuente, R., Fuentes, R., Sepúlveda, M., Arias, M., Herskovic, V., Munoz-Gama, J.: Tailored process feedback through process mining for surgical procedures in medical training: the central venous catheter case. In: International Conference on Business Process Management, pp. 163–174. Springer, Berlin (2018). https://doi.org/10.1007/978-3-030-11641-5_13

12. Maggi, F.M., Di Ciccio, C., Di Francescomarino, C., Kala, T.: Parallel algorithms for the automated discovery of declarative process models. Inf. Syst. **74**(P2), 136–152 (2018). https://doi.org/10.1016/j.is.2017.12.002

13. Maggi, F.M., Di Francescomarino, C., Dumas, M., Ghidini, C.: Predictive monitoring of business processes. In: Jarke, M., Mylopoulos, J., Quix, C., Rolland, C., Manolopoulos, Y., Mouratidis, H., Horkoff, J. (eds.) Advanced Information Systems Engineering, pp. 457–472. Springer, Cham (2014)

14. Marrella, A., Mecella, M.: Cognitive business process management for adaptive cyber-physical processes. In: International Conference on Business Process Management, pp. 429–439. Springer (2017)

15. Martin, N., Depaire, B., Caris, A.: The use of process mining in business process simulation model construction. Bus. Inform. Syst. Eng. **58**(1), 73–87 (2016). https://doi.org/10.1007/s12599-015-0410-4

16. Munoz-Gama, J., de la Fuente, R., Sepúlveda, M., Fuentes, R.: Conformance checking challenge 2019; 4tu. Centre for Research Data: Delft, The Netherlands (2019). https://doi.org/10.4121/uuid:c923af09-ce93-44c3-ace0-c5508cf103ad

17. Munoz-Gama, J., et al.: Conformance Checking and Diagnosis in Process Mining. Springer (2016). https://doi.org/10.1007/978-3-319-49451-7

18. Nguyen, T., Nguyen, N., Nahavandi, S.: Deep reinforcement learning for multiagent systems: a review of challenges, solutions, and applications. IEEE Trans. Cybern. **50**(9), 3826–3839 (2020). https://doi.org/10.1109/TCYB.2020.2977374

19. North, M., Macal, C.: Managing Business Complexity: Discovering Strategic Solutions With Agent-Based Modeling and Simulation. Oxford University Press (2007). https://doi.org/10.1093/acprof:oso/9780195172119.001.0001

20. Pasmore, W., Winby, S., Mohrman, S.A., Vanasse, R.: Reflections: sociotechnical systems design and organization change. J. Change Manag. **19**(2), 67–85 (2019). https://doi.org/10.1080/14697017.2018.1553761

21. Polyvyanyy, A., Su, Z., Lipovetzky, N., Sardina, S.: Goal recognition using off-the-shelf process mining techniques. In: Proceedings of the 19th International Conference on Autonomous Agents and MultiAgent Systems, pp. 1072–1080 (2020)

22. Pourbafrani, M., Vasudevan, S., Zafar, F., Xingran, Y., Singh, R., van der Aalst, W.: A python extension to simulate petri nets in process mining (2021). arXiv preprint arXiv:2102.08774

23. Rizk, Y., Bhandwalder, A., Boag, S., Chakraborti, T., Isahagian, V., Khazaeni, Y., Pollock, F., Unuvar, M.: A unified conversational assistant framework for business process automation (2020). arXiv preprint arXiv:2001.03543

24. Salvit, J., Sklar, E.: Toward a myers-briggs type indicator model of agent behavior in multiagent teams. In: International Workshop on Multi-Agent Systems and Agent-Based Simulation, pp. 28–43. Springer, Berlin (2010). https://doi.org/10.1007/978-3-642-18345-4_3

25. Santos, R., Marreiros, G., Ramos, C., Neves, J., Bulas-Cruz, J.: Personality, emotion, and mood in agent-based group decision making. IEEE Intell. Syst. **26**(6), 58–66 (2011). https://doi.org/10.1109/MIS.2011.92

26. Sterling, L., Taveter, K.: The Art of Agent-Oriented Modeling. The MIT Press (2009). https://doi.org/10.7551/mitpress/7682.001.0001

27. Sulis, E., Di Leva, A.: An agent-based model of a business process: the use case of a hospital emergency department. In: Teniente, E., Weidlich, M. (eds.) Business Process Management Workshops—BPM 2017 International Workshops, Barcelona, Spain, September 10–11, 2017, Revised Papers, Lecture Notes in Business Information Processing, vol. 308, pp. 124–132. Springer, Berlin (2017). https://doi.org/10.1007/978-3-319-74030-0_8

28. Sulis, E., Terna, P.: An agent-based decision support for a vaccination campaign. J. Med. Syst. **45**(11), 1–7 (2021). https://doi.org/10.1007/s10916-021-01772-1

29. Sulis, E., Terna, P., Di Leva, A., Boella, G., Boccuzzi, A.: Agent-oriented decision support system for business processes management with genetic algorithm optimization: an application in healthcare. J. Med. Syst. **44**(9), 1–7 (2020). https://doi.org/10.1007/s10916-020-01608-4

30. Sutton, R.S., Barto, A.G.: Reinforcement Learning: An Introduction. MIT Press (2018)

31. Syed, R., Suriadi, S., Adams, M., Bandara, W., Leemans, S.J., Ouyang, C., ter Hofstede, A.H., van de Weerd, I., Wynn, M.T., Reijers, H.A.: Robotic process automation: contemporary themes and challenges. Comput. Ind. **115**, 103162 (2020). https://doi.org/10.1016/j.compind.2019.103162

32. Szimanski, F., Ralha, C.G., Wagner, G., Ferreira, D.R.: Improving business process models with agent-based simulation and process mining. In: Enterprise, Business-Process and Information Systems Modeling, pp. 124–138. Springer, Berlin (2013)

33. Taveter, K., Wagner, G.: A multi-perspective methodology for modelling inter-enterprise business processes. In: Arisawa, H., Kambayashi, Y., Kumar, V., Mayr, H.C., Hunt, I. (eds.) ER 2001 Workshops, HUMACS, DASWIS, ECOMO, and DAMA, Yokohama Japan, November 27–30, 2001, Revised Papers, Lecture Notes in Computer Science, vol. 2465, pp. 403–416. Springer, Berlin (2001). https://doi.org/10.1007/3-540-46140-X_31

34. van der Aalst,W.: Process Mining—Data Science in Action, 2nd edn. Springer (2016). https://doi.org/10.1007/978-3-662-49851-4

35. Vidoni, R., García-Sánchez, F., Gasparetto, A., Martínez-Béjar, R.: An intelligent framework to manage robotic autonomous agents. Expert Syst. Appl. **38**(6), 7430–7439 (2011). https://doi.org/10.1016/j.eswa.2010.12.080

36. Wagner, G., Taveter, K.: Towards radical agent-oriented software engineering processes based on AOR modeling. In: Proceedings. IEEE/WIC/ACM International Conference on Intelligent Agent Technology, 2004.(IAT 2004)., pp. 509–512. IEEE, Piscataway (2004). https://doi.org/10.1109/IAT.2004.1343007

37. Wang, H., Chen, X., Wu, Q., Yu, Q., Hu, X., Zheng, Z., Bouguettaya, A.: Integrating reinforcement learning with multi-agent techniques for adaptive service composition. ACM Trans. Auton. Adapt. Syst. **12**(2), 1–42 (2017). https://doi.org/10.1145/3058592

38. Wautelet, Y., Kolp, M.: Business and model-driven development of bdi multi-agent systems. Neurocomputing **182**, 304–321 (2016). https://doi.org/10.1016/j.neucom.2015.12.022

39. Winby, S., Mohrman, S.A.: Digital sociotechnical system design. J. Appl. Behav. Sci. **54**(4), 399–423 (2018). https://doi.org/10.1177/0021886318781581

40. Yan, J., Hu, D., Liao, S.S., Wang, H.: Mining agents' goals in agent-oriented business processes. ACM Trans. Manag. Inform. Syst. **5**(4), 1–22 (2014). https://doi.org/10.1145/2629448

41. Zacarias, M., Pinto, H.S., Magalhães, R., Tribolet, J.: A 'context-aware' and agent-centric perspective for the alignment between individuals and organizations. Inform. Syst. **35**(4), 441–466 (2010). https://doi.org/10.1016/j.is.2009.03.014

42. Zimmer, N.: Socio-technical modeling and simulation of airline operations control. Doctoral Thesis, Technische Universität Braunschweig, Germany (2020)

Chapter 8
Practical Applications

Abstract This chapter describes several practical examples of applying ABM to BPM. The example models address different aspects of managing an organization, such as strategic thinking, decision-making, problem solving, optimization, and scenario analysis. The goal is to bring the reader closer to concrete problems and at the same time introduce key concepts and elements of programming in NetLogo to facilitate the construction of new models for different applications.

8.1 Strategic Thinking: Ford-Mazda Case Study

8.1.1 Business Process Re-engineering

This first example describes re-engineering of the purchasing business process of the merged Ford-Mazda company, after the acquisition of Mazda by Ford in 1979 [7]. This is a well-known example of business process re-engineering. To summarize the *Ford-Mazda case study*, Ford started reviewing its purchasing business process at the end of the 1970s in order to improve the throughput. At that time, the acquisition of Mazda enabled Ford to compare the execution of the same type of business process in the two companies. The differences were really striking: while Ford employed about 500 employees for performing the whole purchasing process, the size of the staff at Mazda working on the same purchasing process was about 100 workers. Consequently, the same back office in Mazda was a lot cheaper than the Ford one. Moreover, the purchasing process in Mazda was faster because of a reduced turnaround time [5].

The decision support concerned with the re-engineering case study of Ford and Mazda was explored in a generalized manner in Sect. 5.2. In the *Ford-Mazda case study*, the main organizational units involved in the organization of Ford are the following ones:

- Purchasing Office (PO)—the department with the function of procuring supplies or services; each request to a Vendor is accompanied by a Purchase Order.

© Springer Nature Switzerland AG 2022
E. Sulis, K. Taveter, *Agent-Based Business Process Simulation*,
https://doi.org/10.1007/978-3-030-98816-6_8

- Receiving Office (R)—the department receiving a product from a Vendor, which is a manufacturer or supplier.
- Accounts Payable (AP)—the department responsible for making payments to suppliers and other creditors.

The purchasing business process also involves Vendors (V) as external entities receiving orders from PO. Figures in Sect. 5.2 describe in BPMN the purchasing business processes in Ford and Mazda. The purchasing business process of Ford is modelled in Fig. 5.11, while the corresponding Mazda business process is represented in Fig. 5.12.

We next point out the most important differences in the purchasing business processes before re-engineering, in Ford, and after re-engineering, in Mazda. The purchasing process in Ford is represented in Fig. 5.11 and the process in Mazda in Fig. 5.12. In Ford, PO sends both a purchase order to V and a copy of the purchase order to AP. A vendor ships the goods to R and sends the corresponding invoice to AP. After that, AP collects the three documents—a confirmation message from R, a copy of the purchase order, and the invoice—before it makes the payment to V. At Mazda, the most important differences in the purchasing business process are concerned with the adoption of the Purchasing Information System (IS) capable of storing a copy of the purchase order received from PO, as well as the information about receiving goods from R and making the payment from AP. In Sect. 5.2, we described in detail how the two business processes can be rendered by the AOM methodology and in BPMN. Below we describe in more detail how the resulting business processes can be simulated in NetLogo.

In the *ABBPS_Ford-Mazda* model included in the web repository, we present a NetLogo simulation of the two different types of purchasing business processes, based on the agent-oriented problem domain analysis described in Sect. 5.2. In the NetLogo simulation, the organizational units Vendor, Purchasing Office, Receiving Office, and Accounts Payable are represented as the respective NetLogo "patches." The "patches" standing for organizational units are visually represented in different positions of the main NetLogo window of the simulation. Figure 8.1 shows the visualizations of both the organizational units of Ford on the left and the organizational units of Mazda on the right. The visualization of each organizational unit is distinguished by a different color as well as by the variable name of the corresponding patch, which can be PO, V, R, AP, or IS.

In the following sections, we describe in more detail the main execution flows of this model. The main NetLogo window of the simulation represented in Fig. 5.13 describes the simulation scenario with the relevant buttons and output areas. First, the user can choose between the cases of Ford and Mazda. Second, a "switch button" allows to change configuration parameters, such as the number of workers and the number of payment orders. Two graphs on the right distinguish between the working-time, waiting-time, and not-working-time of employees, as well as the state of the current order in the system, which can be "waiting," "served," or "delayed." The three monitors, respectively, indicate the states of orders, the states of workers, and performance.

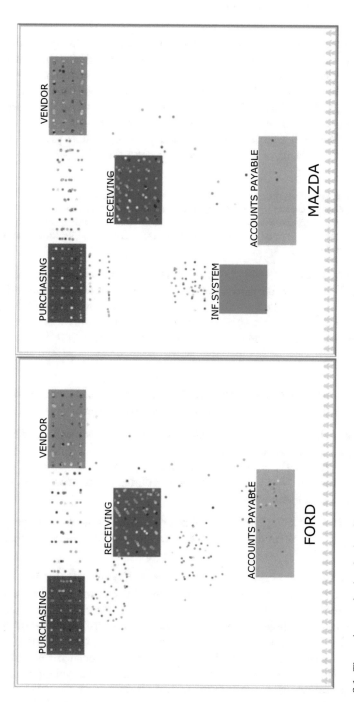

Fig. 8.1 The main organizational units of Ford (on the left) and Mazda (on the right) represented in the *ABBPS_Ford-Mazda* model

8.1.2 Agents and Variables

To perform agent-based simulations of the Ford-Mazda purchasing business processes in NetLogo, we have chosen to model workers as active agents and orders
as passive—reactive—agents. In NetLogo, the corresponding agent types—*workers*
and *orders*—have been modeled as particular "turtle breeds." We have also chosen to
model the copy of an order sent by PO to AP, *copy_orders*, as well as the *invoice* sent
by V as passive agents generalized by the respective "turtle breeds" of NetLogo. The
rationale of different design decisions of modeling real-life entities as agent types—
"turtle breeds"—or parts of the environment, "patches," of NetLogo is provided in
Chap. 5.

```
breed[workers worker] ; staff - active agents
breed[orders order] ; orders sent by PO to Vendors
breed[copy_orders copy_order] ; a copy of an order sent to AP
breed[invoices invoice] ; invoices generated by Vendors and
  sent to AP
```

Orders are visualized in NetLogo as small, randomly colored dots that first
arrive in PO. From PO, the flow of the business process continues into different
organizational units. Workers are visualized as circles in the lower area of the screen.
The color of a worker represents its state: it is gray when the worker is not working,
green when the worker is ready to start, and red when the worker is working on an
order.

Workers
Each worker in the ABM is characterized by the state variable *state-worker*, the
values of which represent one of the following three conditions:

- "waiting"—the state of the worker during working hours when the worker is not
  working but is waiting for an order
- "service"—the worker is working on an order
- "not-working-time"—the state of the worker during out-of-office time, such as
  lunch time, nights, and weekends.

Workers in the "waiting" state look for an order in the "waiting-for-worker" state
by committing to work for the period of time recorded in their "duration" variable.

Orders
An order is a passive agent implemented as a NetLogo *turtle* that has its own
variables, such as the one representing its state ("state-order"). In the course of
performing different activities of the business process, the state of the order can
change between "waiting-for-worker," "service," "moving," and "delay." Other
variables of an order define the movements of the order in the NetLogo visualization
(*destination, moving?*) and the worker that the order is associated with (*working-
with*). In the business process model of Ford, two additional variables represent the
arrival of the corresponding invoice from the vendor (*my_invoice_arrived?*) and the
copy of the order issued by the PO (*my_copy_order_arrived?*). Finally, two global

variables register the KPI values of the average cycle time and the average service time, respectively.

8.1.3 Time and Activity Flow Aspects of Business Process Modeling

In business process modeling, two other relevant aspects are concerned with the choices of rendering the passage of time and the flow of activities.

Time

In the *Ford-Mazda case study*, one time unit is represented by 1 *tick*, which corresponds to 1 minute. The arrival of the orders depends on two values: the frequency of arrival of new bunches of orders and the number of orders in a bunch. The frequency value is set to 15, meaning that every 15 min a new bunch of orders arrives. The number of orders in a bunch is set to 80, but it can be changed by a slider in the interface (*n-of-orders*) in the range from 10 to 100. To change this initial setting, you can have a look at the model *ABBPS_Interarrival-times.nlogo* in the companion website, which describes how different uniform and triangular distributions of order arrival times can be defined in NetLogo.

The working time depends on the number of *ticks*, whereby 60 *ticks* represent 1 hour and 3600 ticks 1 day. The corresponding global variable *working-time* specifies four different "working times" every day. In addition to the "night" time, they include three slots representing different periods of the 9 hours' working time between 9 and 18: the morning working time ("wt-morning"), the break for lunch ("lunch-time"), and the afternoon working time ("wt-afternoon").

In the *go* procedure, the sub-procedure "pass-time" modifies the four "working-time" values, depending on the values of the *ticks* variable. Similarly, the sub-procedure *check-time* modifies also the *state-worker* variable in accordance with the simulated time of the day. To avoid unnecessary cycles, the sub-procedure "pass-time" moves the simulation time forward during non-working time: at night and during lunch breaks.

Sequence of Activities

The purchasing business process model of Ford begins with passing an order from PO to V, which is accompanied by sending a copy of the order to AP. Within the final activity of the purchasing business process, the workers at AP check the following three conditions: whether they have a copy of the order from PO and the invoice from V and whether the goods have arrived in R. As soon as all the three conditions have been satisfied, the payment is made to V.

In the following NetLogo code, the flow of activities is defined by the *compute-next-state* procedure, while the *send-order-to-destination* procedure sends an order to the next organizational unit. Finally, the *compute-next-state* procedure updates

Table 8.1 Simulation output for ten runs of the Ford and Mazda cases, with 500 workers and 100 workers, respectively. Average values and standard deviations of the number of completed orders (Avg. Completed), process cycle time (Avg. Cycle Time), and service time by workers (Avg. Service Time)

Case	Avg. completed	Avg. cycle time	Avg. service time
Ford-500	11,434 (17.1)	633.7 (1.81)	78.5 (0.22)
Mazda-100	11,554 (24.7)	522.3 (6.45)	81.5 (0.04)

the variables used to indicate that the order is ready to move by setting the value of the variable *moving?* to *true* and the value of the variable *state-order* to "moving":

```
to send-order-to-destination [ d ]
  let dest one-of patches with [pname = d]
  set heading towards dest
  set destination-patch dest
  set moving? true
  set state-order "moving"
end
```

To reflect more adequately real life, performing each activity instance of the business process takes a different amount of time. The duration of the corresponding type of activity is represented as a uniform distribution between minimum and maximum values.

The purchasing business process of Mazda also includes as a resource the Purchasing Information System (IS) for recording (i) orders sent by PO; (ii) arrival of products in R; and (iii) making payments by AP.

Simulation Scenario

In accordance with the numbers provided in the research literature [1, 3, 12], the business process simulation of Ford was initiated with 500 workers, while the business process simulation of Mazda was initiated with 100 workers. We assume that workers are interchangeable in the NetLogo model of the purchasing business processes. Table 8.1 summarizes the simulation results. According to the table, the case of Mazda seems to be performing better than the case of Ford by having a shorter average cycle time (522 min instead of 633 min), while the shares of average working times of workers are very similar (78.5 % and 81.5 %). Table 8.1 also clearly shows that about 11,500 orders are completed in both cases, despite the different numbers of the workers involved.

8.2 Queuing System

A typical application in simulation models is concerned with queue management. The *ABBPS_Serpentine-queue* model in the online repository describes the arrival of customers at service counters. Customers are arranged in a queue for waiting to reach a counter with an available operator. Queue modeling is a kind of process case

Fig. 8.2 The serpentine queue system of the *ABBPS_Serpentine-queues* model

study largely explored by means of discrete event simulation or system dynamics. Many existing simulation tools already handle this topic in their introductory tutorials. For example, an example of arriving at a banking office is represented in both AnyLogic.[1] and SimPy.[2]

We describe here a NetLogo 3D application for investigating the arrival of customers in a service to reach the registration counters. This application can be useful for educational purposes, as well as for analyzing relatively simple practical cases. The serpentine queue example also demonstrates the capabilities of a 3D visualization to improve the readability of the process.

Serpentine queue can be defined as a line where all customers are tunneled into a single queue and then dispatched to the first available counter. This is usually the case with airport check-in, bank office, and the entrance to a stadium or concert. Customers arrive in the area of the service at certain times, entering individually into the serpentine queue. Finally, they move to reach the counter of an available operator. From a business process perspective, the start event corresponds to the arrival of a customer in the queue, to start waiting for working with an operator. The final event is the exit from the service area, after completing the activity with the operator. Another possible final event is leaving the queue during the waiting, as in the ticket vending machine (*ABBPS_TVM-queues*) and emergency department (*ABBPS_ED-3D*) models. The process performance metrics relevant for the serpentine queue are concerned with the time distribution of the arrival of customers and the working and waiting times of operators. The *serpentine queue* model is represented in Fig. 8.2.

---

[1] See the Bank Office Model https://help.anylogic.com/index.jsp?topic=%2Fcom.anylogic.help %2Fhtml%2F_ELT%2FBank+Model.html.

[2] https://pythonhosted.org/SimPy/Tutorials/TheBank.html.

8.2.1 Key Elements

The *serpentine queue* model includes two types of agents: operators as active agents who work at the counter and customers as passive agents who enter the queue and move to the counter. Operators are modelled as active agents because they call customers to work on their cases. In addition, operators may decide to perform back-office work instead of providing front-office services.

In the NetLogo simulation, customers arrive at certain times at the top left of the serpentine queue illustrated by Fig. 8.2. New customers can arrive according to a uniform time distribution, in the range from *min-value* to *max-value* as defined through the NetLogo interface. Different types of distributions can be considered, such as a triangular distribution, or a normal distribution defined by the *ABBPS_Interarrival-times.nlogo* model in the web repository of this book.

The current state of each agent of the simulation is represented by the agent's *state* variable. In the main loop, the procedures are called that involve different agents depending on their corresponding states modelled in Fig. 8.3. The procedures of the main loop are described in more detail in the next section. In the NetLogo model, other options include setting a short or long serpentine queue or tracking paths by customers. The simulation stops when there are no more agents in the queue. Finally, the values of performance indicators are calculated to evaluate the entire process and the workloads by individual agents involved. The performance indicators include time-related indicators for measuring the duration of the main steps, such as the time spent in the queue or at the desk, and the cycle time. Systematic variations of the model's configuration settings can be obtained by BehaviorSpace, as described in Sect. 4.2.6.

8.2.2 Initial Setting

The view in the interface represented in Fig. 8.4 maintains the original dimension; we have just reduced the *zcor* value—the maximum *z* coordinate of the patches—

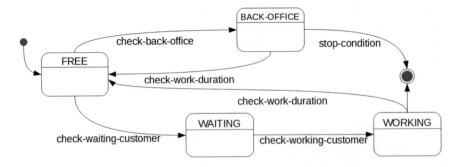

Fig. 8.3 UML state diagram of the serpentine queue model

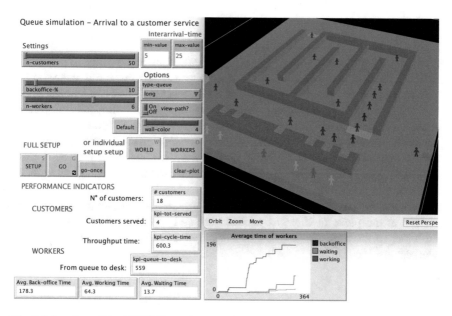

Fig. 8.4 Interface of the *ABBPS_Serpentine-queue* model

to better manage the rotation of the screen. The initial setting modifies the 3D environment, which is included at the beginning of the program by means of the command:

```
__includes [''environment.nls'']
```

The source code of the procedure *Build-walls* is an external file (*environment.nls*) included during the setup of the program. The color of the patches defines the world. A flat gray floor is defined by setting the z-coordinates of the patches to the gray color:

```
if pzcor = -1 or pzcor = 0 [set pcolor gray ]
```

The user can customize the display through the user interface by changing the color of the barriers in the serpentine queue. In fact, a variable in the *Interface* can be set to a different color.

The following *setup* procedure initializes the general variables of interest (*setup-variables*), as well as the worker variables (worker-variables):

```
to setup
  ca
  build-walls      ;; create the environment
  setup-variables  ;; initialize the variables
  setup-workers    ;; initialize the operators
  reset-ticks
end
```

8.2.3 Main Cycle

The simulation is carried out by repeating for each time unit a series of procedures until the end condition becomes true, like reaching a certain time limit or the absence of customers in the queue. A time unit is a *tick*, whereas a tick corresponds to one second, as a rule. An example of a procedure is a set of commands concerning a customer or worker. The main cycle procedures are as follows: *check-arrival* (to set the arrival of a new customer); *check-moving* (manages the movement of agents while their state is "moving"); *check-workers-backoffice* ("free" workers may start back-office operations according to the probability defined through the interface with the slider *backoffice-%*); *check-workers-waiting-cust* ("free" workers may check for the waiting customers); *check-workers-working-cust* (workers have arrived at the place of the next task but are still "waiting" for the arrival of a customer to start the service); *check-working-time* (when a task is finished, the workers involved become "free").

```
to go
  tick
  if ticks = 28880
    or (kpi-tot-served > 0 and not any? customers) [ stop ]
  ; the stop condition: 1 day or no more customers
  check-arrival ; start (new) agents to move
  check-moving ; move agents with state "moving"
  check-workers-backoffice ; workers check back-office
  check-workers-waiting-cust ; workers wait for customers
  check-workers-working-cust ; workers work with customers
  check-working-time ; check if the working time is finished
end
```

If there are workers available to start their service (`any? workers with [state = "free"]`) with a customer, they select the first customer ready on the waiting line (`one-of customers with [...]`) and call it by applying the corresponding procedure (`call a customer`). Finally, they commit to work with the agent by setting `state` and `working-with` variables accordingly. To provide the reader with an idea of the NetLogo program code, we present here the corresponding procedure:

```
to check-workers-waiting-cust
if any? workers with [state = "free"]
[ ask one-of workers with [state = "free"]
   [ if any? customers with [state = "waiting"
       and [pname] of patch-here = "waiting-line"]
     [
       let cust one-of customers with [state = "waiting"
           and [pname] of patch-here = "waiting-line"]
       set state "waiting"
       set working-with cust

       call-a-customer self cust
     ]
```

```
    ]
  ]
```

The *call-a-customer* procedure includes the code for calling a customer based on the following two parameters: the worker (w) and the customer (c). Specifically, the NetLogo agent—*turtle*—representing the client is asked to engage with the worker (set working-with w), turn its face toward the desk of the corresponding worker ([worker-desk] of w), set its variable destination, and start moving:

```
to call-a-customer [w c]
  ask c [
    set working-with w
    face [worker-desk] of w
    set destination "worker-desk"
    set state "moving"
  ]
end
```

Finally, we comment here on one of the most relevant procedures of the main loop, i.e., the check-workers-working-cust procedure. This procedure addresses the situation where workers, who are sitting at their desks, check if a customer has arrived and is ready to be served by them. The procedure therefore requires the worker to check whether the desk in front of her is free or occupied by a customer who is ready to be serviced. This situation occurs when the customer has the variable *pname* set to "worker-desk," as can be seen in the following procedure:

```
if any? customers with
  [state = ''waiting'' and patch-here = [worker-desk] of myself]
```

If the customer is ready to be serviced, the workers start working with the customer (set state "working"). It is worth noting that the duration of a task (*work-duration*) can be improved by considering workers' skills (experienced or novice) and average task duration. In the code presented below, the task duration is between 60 and 120 ticks.

```
to check-workers-working-cust
  if any? workers with [state = "waiting"] [
    ask one-of workers with [state = "waiting"] [
      if any? customers with [state = "waiting"
      and patch-here = [worker-desk] of myself ] [
        set state "working"
        set work-duration ticks + 60 + random 60

        set kpi-worker-time-waiting kpi-worker-time-waiting
        + (ticks - kpi-time-start-waiting)
        set kpi-time-start-working ticks

        ask one-of customers with [ state = "waiting"
        and patch-here = [worker-desk] of myself ] [
          set state "working"
          set kpi-time-starting-served-at-desk ticks
```

```
              compute-kpi-queue-to-desk
               (kpi-time-starting-served-at-desk    -
               kpi-time-arrival-at-serpentine-start )
          ]
        ]
      ]
    ]
  end
```

KPIs are updated accordingly (`kpi-worker-time-waiting`) also by means of specific procedure (`compute-kpi-queue-to-desk`), as better detailed in the next section.

8.2.4   Performance Indicators

To study performance indicators, some special-purpose variables have been added to the agents—the NetLogo *turtles*. These variables are set during the simulation. We have adopted the following time-related performance metrics, tracking the movements of a customer from the start (*kpi-time-start*) to the arrival at the counter (*kpi-time-starting-served-at-desk*):

```
customers-own [ ; variables of "customers" agents
  destination  ; the "patch" customers have to reach

  kpi-time-start ; customer's KPI: the moment an operator
    arrives in the serpentine queue area
  kpi-time-arrival-at-serpentine-start ; enter the serpentine
  kpi-time-arrival-at-waiting-line ; the end of the queue
  kpi-time-starting-served-at-desk ; at the operator desk
]
```

Process performance indicators may include measuring the passage of simulated time as well as individual metrics about the process (see Sect. 2.2.3). In the *serpentine queue* model, we are interested in both the cycle time and the time between the arrival of a customer in the serpentine queue and the arrival of the customer in front of the counter desk:

```
to compute-kpi-cycle-time[t]   ; update KPI (and monitors)
  ifelse kpi-tot-served = 0 [ set kpi-cycle-time t ]
  [
    set kpi-cycle-time
      ((kpi-cycle-time * kpi-tot-served) + t) / kpi-tot-served
  ]
  set kpi-tot-served kpi-tot-served + 1
end
```

Another relevant performance indicator is the total amount of time worked by the operators involved in the business process. In order to track the amount of time worked by operators, particular local variables have been added to the

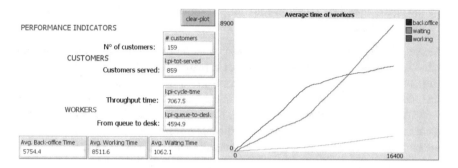

Fig. 8.5 Monitors and plots of the serpentine model process performance indicators

NetLogo *turtles* representing workers to indicate when the worker starts working with a customer (*kpi-time-start-working*), starts back-office work (*kpi-time-start-backoffice*), or starts waiting for a customer (*kpi-time-start-waiting*).

There are also global variables monitoring the process trends by computing the average values of the total waiting time (*kpi-worker-time-waiting*), the total working time (*kpi-worker-time-working*), and the total back-office time (*kpi-backoffice-time-working*) of the operators. Finally, the interface includes a plot visualizing the performance indicators in the interface (Fig. 8.5).

8.3 Reinforcement Learning

Self-learning systems are applications of growing interest in many fields, such as robotics, banking, and autonomous vehicles. One of the most widely applied AI strategies is reinforcement learning, which consists of automatic learning by an agent based on a series of random explorations of the solution space. Reinforcement learning is described in detail in Sect. 6.4.3. The purpose of this section is to describe the learning process by an agent based on introductory examples of the corresponding agent-based simulation in NetLogo. An organization involved in the production of this kind of artifact can be interested in demonstrating to its stakeholders how the self-learning agent works. In the next section, we will introduce and explain a case study where this kind of agent is a self-driving car (SmartCab). In this example, the following paragraphs describe the corresponding basic notions of RL, introduced in Sect. 6.4.3. *State space*. An agent can perform different actions according to its state. The set of all possible states in which an agent can be is called its state space. Each state contains information useful for the agent for performing its next action. *Action space*. The set of all the actions that an agent can perform in its given state is called its *action space*. In the SmartCab example, the action space consists of the following four movements and two actions by the agent with their respective identifiers: moving south (0), north (1), east (2), or west (3) or pick up (4) or drop off a passenger (5).

Reward Table When the environment is created for the SmartCab, an initial reward table is created. We can think of it as of a matrix with the numbers of states as rows and the numbers of actions as columns. In a more elaborate version, we can include for each action the corresponding probability to perform this action, as well as the next state where performing the action would take the system. Other elements attached to the action are the expected reward, and a variable for checking the completion of the task, such as the completion of a trip by SmartCab.

Q Table The Q table is a matrix where we have a row for each state and a column for each action. The values in the Q table are first initialized to 0 and are updated after training. Note that the Q table has the same dimensions as the reward table.

8.3.1   Case Study of a Self-Driving Car

A typical self-learning system is a self-driving vehicle that needs to learn the path between the starting and ending points of its route. In the NetLogo simulation of a self-driving car (*ABBPS_RL-demo-8-directions* model), we considered the movements of an agent within a grid of 8 × 8 cells. The environment of the agent contains obstacles like trees and houses. The NetLogo simulation developed by us is based on the Maze program of Reinforcement Learning (RL), which originates in the NetLogo User Community Models.[3] Our implementation improves the basic model in the following three ways. First, the car can move in eight directions— horizontally, vertically, and even diagonally—rather than just in four directions. Second, the learning process records a sequence of actions each time and saves only the shortest path that is displayed at the end of the program by means of the "View best route" button. A third improvement is concerned with the final choice of the shortest path instead of paths of the same length but with more curves, by executing the `count-diagonal` procedure. Finally, the *3D View* of the NetLogo model improves the visualization of the path learned by the self-driving car. This is reflected by Fig. 8.7.

Figure 8.6 describes the self-driving car model user interface with sliders and buttons for setting up the main variables. Once the modeler has decided how many obstacles should be randomly added to the map, the learning process will be performed. The learning process ends when the car collides with an obstacle or moves outside the simulation area, as well as when the goal of the simulation is reached, i.e., the car reaches its destination (Fig. 8.7).

---

[3] See the RL Maze model at the following url: http://ccl.northwestern.edu/netlogo/models/community/Reinforcement%20Learning%20Maze.

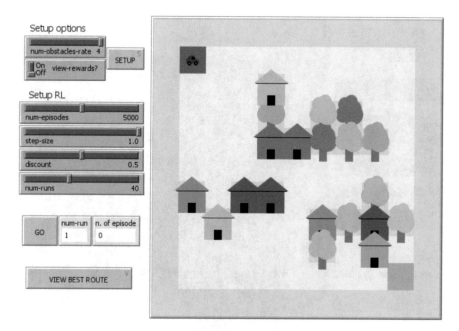

Fig. 8.6 The interface of the self-driving car model

Fig. 8.7 A particular view from the self-driving car model

8.3.2   Case Study of a Self-Driving Car with GIS

As we already learned in Sect. 6.4.3 subsection, a self-driving car is an autonomous agent that learns the path to be taken from its start point to the end point. The locations to be reached can be processed by the agent as a sequence of actions to be performed. In the initial phase, the agent consults a GIS file that contains for each task of the agent the relevant location(s) of the self-driving car. The GIS file also includes location information about streets, rivers, buildings, and other objects of the environment. The *ABBPS_RL-GIS-self-driving-car* model describes how to exploit

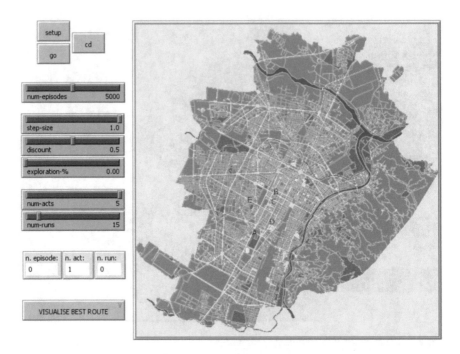

Fig. 8.8 A program to import a GIS map of the city of Turin, Italy

Fig. 8.9 An agent (robot) on a GIS map of the city of Turin, Italy

RL in an agent-based GIS environment. Utilizing different information originating in GIS data layers of ABM is discussed in Sect. 6.4.1.

Configuring this type of RL program is quite easy in NetLogo. Figure 8.8 describes the interface of the application.

The map can be explored with higher or lower granularity. Zooming into or out of the streets is illustrated by Fig. 8.9.

8.3.3   Case Study of a GIS-Based Medicine-Carrying Robot

Another example of an autonomous vehicle is an intelligent self-driving robot delivering medicines to patients in a hospital. This kind of robot should be able to learn how to reach a sequence of different locations while avoiding obstacles. This kind of robot moving in its environment can be simulated by the NetLogo *ABBPS_RL-GIS-medicine-carrying-robot* model. In this program, a robot must learn a path enabling it to reach different points on a map. The program utilizes an RL algorithm for teaching the robot how to learn moving around in a georeferenced environment. Moreover, NetLogo allows the robot to manage the interactions between the GIS layer and the agent layer. The import of the GIS data into the program is based on the corresponding NetLogo extension, which is presented in Sect. 6.4.1.

8.4   Using Genetic Algorithms in a Decision-Making Process

A decision-making task that may have a complex solution can benefit from genetic algorithms (GA), which is a technique for solving an optimization problem by exploring a large search space. This section describes a simple agent-based business process model for demonstrating the application of GA that is described in Sect. 6.4.2. This example represents a typical decision-making process about allocating human workers to different activities. A manager can estimate the output of the whole process based on the settings of initial parameters.

The purpose of the model (*ABBPS_GA-example*) is to investigate a simple business process in an organization where workers perform a consequence of activities of the three types A, B, and C. These three types of activities may correspond to three types of production facilities, three types of medical units, or three functional areas of a company. Activities of the types A, B, and C are followed by the final activity of the type D. The example is illustrated by Fig. 8.10. Two sliders on the NetLogo interface enable defining the total number of workers in the organization, as well as allocating the corresponding percentages of workers to the activities of the types A, B, and C. In addition, the user interface of the NetLogo program includes sliders that enable modifying the duration of activities of each type.

The three types of activities can be easily distinguished by their different positions in the main view of the NetLogo user interface. Accordingly, new cases enter the business process at the position with the coordinates 0 (*xcor*) and 0 (*ycor*), while activities of the type A have the coordinates (8, 0), activities of the type B the coordinates (16, 0), activities of the type C the coordinates (24, 0), and activities of the type D the coordinates (32, 0).

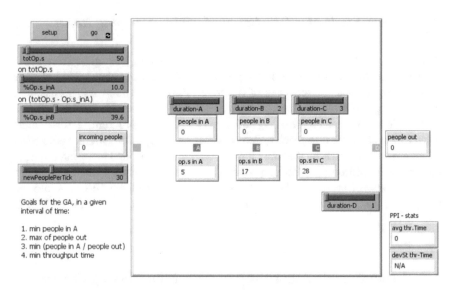

Fig. 8.10 Interface of GA_BPM example to apply GA to a simple business process consisting of activities of the types A,B, and C, and including different numbers of workers as defined by the corresponding slider buttons

In the following, we will briefly explore the program code. First, the "operators" variable of patches, standing for workers, is initially declared with the following statement:

```
patches-own [operators]
```

The *setup* procedure initializes the workers (operators) for activities of all three types as follows:

```
ask patch 8 0  [set operators int(totOp.s * Op.s_inA / 100)]
ask patch 16 0 [
 set operators
  int((totOp.s - [operators] of patch 8 0) * Op.s_inB / 100)
]
ask patch 24 0 [
 set operators
  totOp.s - [operators] of patch 8 0 - [operators] of patch 16
]
```

Activities of a different type are created at each iteration of the main loop by the instructions shown for the activities of type A here:

```
set actions A [operators] of patch 8 0
```

At each iteration, for every NetLogo *turtles* that arrives in a patch representing activity of a certain type, the value of the variable representing the action to be performed is decreased by the command *set steps steps - 1*. The final activity of the type D of the business process includes the sub-procedure `go-out` for computing the throughput time and updating the corresponding monitor before disappearing (`die`), as follows:

```
if xcor = 8
    [
        if actionsA > 0
            [
                set steps steps - 1
                set actionsA actionsA - 1
            ]
    ] (...)
if xcor = 32
    [
        set steps steps - 1
        if steps = 0  [ go-out die ]
    ]
```

In addition, we will explore in this section the BehaviorSearch tool described in Sect. 4.2.6. The purpose of applying the BehaviorSearch tool is to meet the following four research objectives, by means of incorporating the corresponding configuration files:

- Minimize the number of workers allocated to activities of the type A. The corresponding code is as follows:
  `count turtles with [xcor = 8 and ycor = 0]`
  The online repository includes the file: *1ABBPS_GA.bsearch*.
- Maximize the number of customers served by the business process. The code to maximize "people-out" is as follows:
  `count turtles with [xcor = 32 and ycor = 0])`
  The online repository includes the file: *2ABBPS_GA.bsearch*.
- Minimize the ratio between workers allocated to activities of the type A and the number of customers served.
  The online repository includes the file: *3ABBPS_GA.bsearch*.
- Minimize the throughput time, e.g.,
  The online repository includes the file: *4ABBPS_GA.bsearch*.

The search space of all feasible solutions depends on both the percentage values of the workers allocated to activities of the type A (from 20 to 70 in increments of 0.1) and activities of the type B (from 20 to 80 in increments of 0.1). This constitutes a set of possible 300,000 (500 × 600) combinations, from among which the desired solution can be found.

The BehaviorSearch tool greatly facilitates finding a solution because searching through the solution space by "brute force" would be computationally expensive. Figure 8.11 represents the main configuration windows of the *4.bsearch* example provided in the repository that aims to minimize throughput time.

The interested reader can find an introduction to GA in Sect. 6.4.2. In this example, the initial settings of the GA include an initial population of 50 candidate solutions, with a mutation rate of 0.03 (*offspring*). The *crossover rate* of this

Fig. 8.11 BehaviorSearch settings for the GA_BPM model to optimize the fitness score of throughput time, with the level of granularity 0.1, the initial population of 50 solutions, the crossover rate 0.7, and the mutation rate 0.03

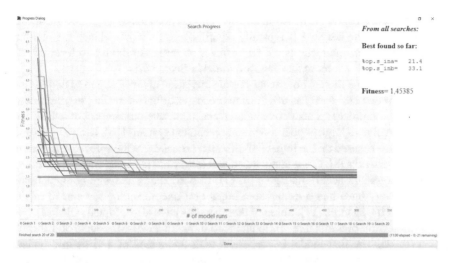

Fig. 8.12 GA search trends by the BehaviorSearch tool

"tournament selection" is 0.7, while the tournament size is 3. This means that three solutions are randomly retrieved from the previous generation, and the best one among them is selected to be reproduced. The initial settings of the BehaviorSearch tool are illustrated by Fig. 8.11.

The simulation allows one to define how many times the search should be repeated to improve confidence; for example, 20 or 30 times may be enough to find the best configuration of parameters. Moreover, several files contain different previous results of the algorithm in order to provide basis for further analysis.

The output of the BehaviorSearch algorithm consists of the values of the parameters of interest to obtain from all searches the best performance or fitness score. The trend of each individual search is represented by the plot like the one shown in Fig. 8.12.

For example, the optimal solution to minimize the throughput time can be 1.4 workers for activities of the type A and 33.1 workers for activities of the type B. These parameters are obtained by 20 searches with 500 steps in each search. Consequently, this example of applying the BehaviorSearch tool describes how decision-making can be reliably improved within a reasonable time using a standard medium-capacity computer.

8.5 Diffusion Processes

Diffusion processes are concerned with relationships in complex systems between the level of individual agents and the aggregate level of the system. In BPM, diffusion processes have considerable impact on an organization. Studies of diffusion processes focus on both the level of an organization by investigating its internal processes and the micro-macro interactions between the organization and its environment. The last case is typically regarded as a macro-level analysis that has consequences for interactions within business processes at the micro level. Micro and macro levels are more thoroughly defined in Sect. 6.3.1).

We already mentioned how agent-based simulation are well suited to understand diffusion processes. Analysis of diffusion processes offers interesting suggestions as to when these processes occur over a large space, or when the impact of a diffusion process involves a large population in sociotechnical systems [16]. Recently, several studies have focused on the impact of diffusion processes in the spread of viruses in complex networks [8]. Computational epidemiology has achieved authority to direct policymakers and health managers [6, 11]. In particular, studies in computational epidemiology have had a remarkable impact on understanding the spread of the 2020 COVID-19 virus [17]. Some of these studies have also adopted ABM [2].

This section presents three introductory and practical ABM models of diffusion phenomena. The first model is concerned with the spread of a virus in a typical epidemic process that considers agents of the types susceptible, infected, and recovered (SIR). In particular, we describe the recent S.I.s.a.R simulation model [15]. The second example introduces the diffusion of entities in an environment, such as new products, ideas, or technologies spreading to a specific market or population. Our example is about studying a model of information diffusion by means of ABM. We conclude this section by exploring an introductory framework for utilizing both GIS and SNA extensions, the tool described in Sect. 4.3, for modeling supply chains. Indeed, the network of customers, subcontractors, and suppliers can be modelled by positioning them as nodes on a map. The resulting model can be applied for further simulation-based analysis.

8.5.1   Contagion Processes and Decision-Making

Simulations of real diffusion processes can help decision-makers define appropriate public policies. The recent COVID-19 pandemic has identified an urgent need to improve understanding of spread processes. In this context, agent-based models of the SARS-CoV-2 outbreak are useful because they allow for the analysis of the sequences of contagions in simulated outbreaks and enable the identification of the locations where the outbreaks occur.

For studying the spread of the COVID-19 virus, we introduce here the S.I.s.a.R. model [10] that significantly distinguishes between symptomatic and asymptomatic infected agents representing patients. This model also represents the locations where the infections occur. In addition, the model reproduces a realistic public policy schedule consisting of decisions by the national or local government in an Italian region of Piedmont with 4 million inhabitants. This model can be easily calibrated for other areas. We emphasize here the capability of this kind of ABM to offer decision support in the manner described in Chap. 5.

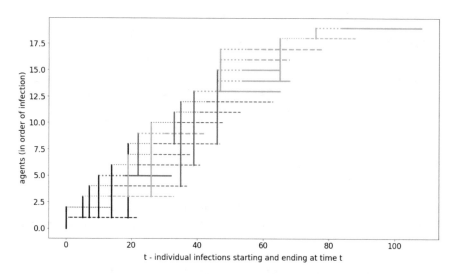

Fig. 8.13 The initial contagion cases in the S.I.s.a.R. model

The graphical representation of the infections in the S.I.s.a.R. model describes each infecting agent as a horizontal segment with a vertical connection to another agent receiving the infection [9]. As an example, Fig. 8.13 describes two infected agents at time 0, represented by different colors; the first agent models a regular patient, as is conveyed by the thickness of the segment, starting at day 0 and finishing at day 22, who is asymptomatic, as is represented by a dashed line, and has infected five agents; the second agent models a young patient, as is conveyed by the thickness of the segment, starting at day 0 and finishing at day 15, who is asymptomatic, as is represented by a dashed line, and has infected no other patients; the first one of the five infected agents received the infection at home, as is represented by the cyan color, and that patient turns out to be asymptomatic after a few days of incubation, as is represented by a dotted line. Solid lines denote symptomatic infected agents, and dashed lines refer to asymptomatic infected agents. The brown color stands for workplaces, orange color for nursing homes, yellow for schools, pink for hospitals, and gray for open spaces. Thick or extra-thick lines, respectively, refer to fragile or particularly fragile agents. Lines with regular thickness and thin lines represent regular individuals and young individuals, respectively. Recent work exploit the model with the AI technique to suggest the best vaccination campaign strategy. [14].

8.5.2   A Dissemination Process Model

ABM also facilitates the studying of spread phenomena and their dynamic interactions among large collection of individuals. For example, an information dissemination model can describe the diffusion between people initially connected to

Fig. 8.14 The network of agents in the diffusion process model

each other according to a particular network topology. The purpose of this kind of
model is to investigate the dissemination processes corresponding to the network
topology [13].

The *ABBPS_Dissemination-process* model in the web repository relies on the
values of several parameters that can be configured by means of the NetLogo
user interface, while the output area of the user interface displays the network
of agents as nodes connected by curved gray edges. A 3D view of the model is
shown in Fig. 8.14. In the Interface, buttons control the simulation setup, while
monitors display the simulation results. The *setup* procedure initializes the patches
and variables of agents, while the main loop *go* includes the following procedures
corresponding to the functions for changing the internal state of each agent:
spreading, *forgetting*, and *verifying*. At the beginning of the simulation, each agent
is in a particular state according to a set of initial probabilities defined through the
user interface. The *state* variable records one of the following three states of a person
modelled by the agent: susceptible ("S"), believer ("B"), or fact checker ("F").
During the simulation, an agent can change its state according to the probabilities
defined by the model.

In this model, the agent network is generated with the help of the *nw* library
(see Sect. 4.3.1). The *type-of-network* drop-down menu button enables the user
to select simulating the dynamics of the diffusion processes according to either
the "Barabasi-Albert" algorithm (by default) or the "Erdos-Renyi" algorithm. The
initial settings of the model always lead to creating a network in which agents are
mostly susceptible (90%) rather than believers (10%). The topology of the network
is visualized in Fig. 8.15. The visualization of the graph shown in the figure can
be further improved by adopting a spring layout [4], as well as by expanding the
distances between the nodes. The output of the simulation focuses on counting
the three different types of agent states, describing the evolution of the diffusion
process.

From the perspective of BPM, the diffusion process may be about a particular
innovation in a network of companies. For example, there may be companies
that are able to diffuse a certain innovative practice, such as the adoption of
RFID technologies in warehouse management, while some other companies may
not be yet ready to accept the innovation. Studying phenomena of this kind
can take advantage of the NetLogo implementation of the dissemination process

Fig. 8.15 Network analysis in NetLogo: A representation of the network of customers, suppliers, and subcontractors of an Italian company

model described in this section, as well as of the following model concerning the distribution and supply of products.

8.5.3 Network Analysis of a Supply Chain Model

This section concerns an introductory example (*ABBPS_Supply-chain*) of representing a supply chain network between a particular company and its stakeholders—suppliers, customers, and subcontractors. Such network addresses the supply chain of materials and products consumed or produced by the given company.

The data used by the network analysis is recorded in four different CSV files, in which each row stores information about a purchase order. In particular, each purchase order includes arrival data, latitude and longitude coordinates, the number of items in the order, and the number of days between this order and the next one. The NetLogo program developed for network analysis of a supply chain creates a node for each company involved. The program also creates links between the node representing a particular company and the nodes representing its customers, suppliers, and subcontractors.

The program has the following three main types of functionalities:

- *Setup and create a company* allows the creation of the NetLogo world where a central node corresponds to the main company to be analyzed, which is rendered by the green color. The NetLogo world is created by means of importing the CSV file.
- *Create nodes and edges* allows to represent on the geographical map (GIS) the following kinds of links between the company being analyzed and its stakeholders:

- – i. links to the customers standing for shipping orders of products by the given company;
- – ii. links from the suppliers standing for purchasing orders by the given company;
- – iii. links from and to the subcontractors of the given company

For the three kinds of links, the weight of a link represents the number of items in the particular order.

The user interface of the NetLogo program of network analysis offers the following types of analyses:

- *Computing network metrics.* Visualizes in the output area of the program additional information on the network. Typical metrics concern the number of connections (network degree) or the properties of individual nodes in the network (e.g., centrality).[4]
- *Data analysis.* Counts the number of companies linked to the company being analyzed.
- *Temporal network analysis.* Represents for each order its location and time. Enables to describe the temporal dynamics of the network between the company being analyzed and its stakeholders.
- *Network visualization.* Represents the *star* type of network between the company being analyzed and other companies with the appropriate weights of the links, standing for numbers of items in the corresponding orders.

8.6 Registration Process

This section describes agent-oriented modeling and simulation of the business process for accessing to a service, e.g., registering in a healthcare service (*ABBPS_Registration_process* model in the web repository). In the registration process, workers provide a service to the customers (i.e., the patients), who go through different activities. This type of business process starts with the arrival of a new customer, in accordance with a realistic distribution of cases. All customers wait in different queues before performing activities such as registering, paying the ticket at the machine, and receiving service. Activities can be automated or performed by humans. Each activity has a name and duration, which is determined by exploiting some typical distributions, such as the standard random distribution or triangular distribution. In the following subsections, we will first describe the business process model of the registration process, which is followed by the description of the NetLogo implementation of the corresponding business process.

---

[4] https://ccl.northwestern.edu/netlogo/docs/nw.html.

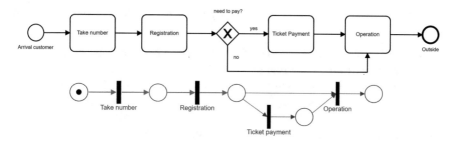

Fig. 8.16 The business process of registration to a service in BPMN (above) and the corresponding Petri net (below)

Business Process Model The business process model of registering for a service consists of the following major parts, which are specified by the business process diagram in BPMN, represented in Fig. 8.16:

- The start event ("Incoming Patients") and end event of the process.
- Two activities that involve human labor ("Registration" and "Operation") and can be performed if the following two conditions hold: a patient is waiting in the corresponding queue, and a worker is available to start performing the activity. If this is the case, both the worker and the patient commit to working on the corresponding activity.
- Two automated tasks ("Take the number" and "Paying the ticket"), in which a patient starts performing an activity when an activity of the corresponding type becomes available. Otherwise, the patient continues waiting in the queue.
- A gateway dividing the flow of the business process after the registration between the "Ticket Payment" and "Operation," standing for service provision.

In NetLogo, the business process model of registering for a service is rendered as explained below, where the activities of a business process model are mapped to the corresponding tasks of NetLogo.

Agents In the model, agents are patients and operators which act accordingly to their "states." In particular, both types of agents [*ag_op* and *ag_pat*], respectively, standing for workers and patients, can be in one of the following states:

- Moving. Agent is moving in order to reach the next task.
- Waiting. Agent is waiting for the next task and is ready to start the task.
- Service. Agent is performing a particular task and is engaged in the service.

In addition, an agent can be in a fourth state—*Looking*. In that state, the agent is looking for a "free" task, while customers are waiting to receive the corresponding service.

Actions The process includes both tasks performed by humans and automated tasks:

- Regarding the tasks performed by the workers, the program behaves as follows: if an agent performing the role of worker has no service to perform, it will start looking for a patient ready for receiving the service. A patient is ready to start being served if the following three conditions occur: (i) the variable representing the patient's next task to be performed does not have a value; (ii) the patient is the first agent to be served in the corresponding queue; and (iii) a worker is free and available to start performing the service. If these three conditions occur, the worker will engage with the patient by sending a message that will prompt the patient to move on to the next task, and at the same time the worker will also move on to the same task. When both have arrived and are waiting to start, they engage in the intended service by staying on that task for a certain period of time. If they have finished their scheduled time on that service, the patient will move on to the next task, while the worker will resume looking for a new patient to work with.
- In automated tasks, such as receiving a ticket from a ticket machine, patients wait in the corresponding queue until the task becomes available. If this happens, the patient on the top of the queue will move to the task and will start the corresponding service for the scheduled time, after which it will move to the next task in the flow of the business process.

Duration of Tasks All the tasks include a "duration" variable to identify the number that is randomly assigned, based on realistic values. There is a table describing the duration and types of assets required by each task. For example, the duration of the automated task "Take number" is 5 seconds on average with a standard deviation of 0.5 seconds. As another example, the duration of the task "Record" is defined by a triangular distribution of 2.5 (minimal value), 5 (mean), and 9.5 min (maximum value).

Flow Representation In the NetLogo user interface, tasks as well as the start and end event of the process are represented by NetLogo patches, which are visually rendered as small squared pieces of pavement on the screen. Using colors helps distinguish between different types of tasks. The arrangement of tasks in the final representation can be similar to the flow that is depicted in Fig. 8.17.

A Glance at the Code

Declaration of Variables The initial part of the program includes the declaration of variables of various types. First, the *breeds*—types of agents or *turtles* according to the NetLogo terminology—should be defined. The types of agents in the given NetLogo program are *worker* and *patient*. Second, local variables should be defined for each agent type, which are declared as *own-variables* according to the NetLogo terminology:

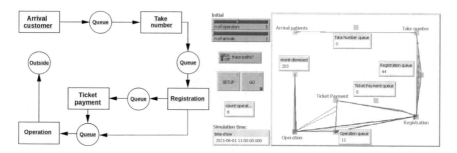

Fig. 8.17 The flow of the tasks in the registration process and its NetLogo representation (*ABBPS_Registration_process* model)

```
tokens-own [
   state     ;; ''M'': Moving (to the next task or queue)
             ;; ''W'': Waiting (for the task)
             ;; ''S'': Service (performing the service)
   next-task         ;; name of the next task
   destination ;; ''patch'' where the agent is supposed to move
   arrival-time ;; the time at the arrival in NetLogo ticks
   work-durat-task ;; the duration of the task
]
```

In addition to local variables relevant for agents of particular types, "global" variables should be defined. They contain values of interest for the entire NetLogo program, such as variables that present results in the interface monitors of the program.

Setup and Go Procedures Setup initializes the program and the main global variables in the corresponding procedures *setup-world*, *setup-labels*, *setup-operators*, and *setup-monitors*. The final command in the Setup procedure initializes the simulation "clock" by resetting the ticks. Each procedure contains specific commands, for which the *n-of-operators* slider in the interface helps define the number of cases that arrive at each simulation step:

```
to setup-operators
   create-operators n-of-operators [
      setxy 0 3
      set shape ''person''
      set state ''F''
      set work-durat-task 0
   ]
end
```

The Go procedure begins with the time increment command (*tick*), as well as the "stop condition." They are followed by other procedures of the process. Their traversal by the agents depends mainly on the states of the corresponding agents. The final procedure checks if the agents have finished working on the task:

```
to go
  tick                              ; increasing time
  if ticks = 10000 [ stop ]; stop condition
  arrival-tokens                    ; create new tokens
  move-agents                       ; move agents in the screen
  check-agent-in-queue              ; ask agent in queue
  start-automatic-tasks             ; check if both operator and token
  ;; are waiting for an automated task: if yes, start service
  "S" start-human-tasks             ; check if both operator and token
  ;; are waiting for a human task: if yes, start service "S"
  operators-looking                 ; look for operators
  check-time                        ; check the duration for agents
end
```

Flow Representation The patients move toward different tasks, which are represented by patches, depending on their properties declared in the *patches-own* procedures. Each patch has been defined as being located in the desired position by setting its coordinates (*pxcor* and *pycor*), as well as the other variables such as the color (*[set pcolor gray]*) and the name (set name "Take number").

The next task in the flow is computed by the following dedicated procedure which starts from the actual task at hand:

```
to-report compute-next-task [ actual-task ]
  let nt nobody
  if actual-task = "Arrival customer" [set nt "Take number"]
  if actual-task = "Take number" [set nt "Registration" ]
  if actual-task = "Registration" [
    ifelse random 100 < 70 [ set nt "Ticket payment" ]
    [ set nt "Operation" ]
  ]
  if actual-task = "Ticket payment" [ set nt "Operation" ]
  if actual-task = "Operation" [ set nt "end" ]
  report one-of patches with [name = nt]
end
```

Arrival Generation To create a new token. The command create-tokens 1 can be used. New patients arrive with a certain frequency, such as a number of patients x arriving randomly every 60 seconds. We can define x by using a "slider" in the interface enabling to easily change the arrival frequency.

The arrival of customers typically follows specific pattern derived from real data, shaped by particular distribution functions, as described by the *ABBPS_Interarrival-times* model in the web repository.

The procedure *crea-token* creates a token as follows by setting the *arrival-time* corresponding to the *tick* in the moment of the creation:

```
to crea-token
  create-tokens n-of-arrivals [
    set shape "dot"             ;; initialize variables
    set work-durat-task 0       ;;
    set arrival-time ticks      ;;

    move-to one-of patches with [ name = "Arrival customer"]
```

```
    ;; the new patient starts in the Arrival

    set next-task one-of patches with [ name = "Take number" ]
    ;; compute-next-task [name] of patch-here

    insert-in-queue self next-task
    ;; add 'token' into the corresponding list (queue variable)

    set destination one-of patches with [
      name = [name-queue] of [next-task] of myself
    ] ;; set the variable destination

    set heading towards destination ;; turn the head

    set state "M" ;; set state to move

    if trace-paths? [pd] ;; trace the paths of tokens
    ]
  end
```

Queues The patch corresponding to a particular activity includes a list where patients can be inserted waiting for the activity. The following command adds an element (e.g., newValue) to a list (e.g., myList):

```
set myList fput newValue myList
```

The new element can be added by means of the lput (meaning "last put") command to the end of the list:

```
set myList lput newValue myList
```

To remove the first or the last element of a list, the corresponding item can be stored in a temporary variable (e.g., "el") as follows:

```
let el first myList
```

Thereafter, the list can be stored by removing the first item—the one located by the index 0:

```
set myList remove-item 0 myList
```

Another way to perform the same operation is to use for that purpose dedicated built-in commands, as follows:

```
set myList but-first myList
set myList but-last myList
```

Each task has a queue represented as a patch variable:

```
ask patches with [name != ""] [set queue []]
```

This example allowed us to address and perform a first practical example of queue management.

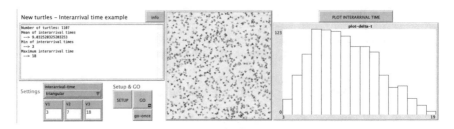

Fig. 8.18 A view of the *ABBS_Interarrival-times* model to explore the distribution of the arrivals of entities

8.7   Inter-arrival Times

To conclude this section of practical applications, we briefly describe a model that can be useful for describing possible distributions of incoming entities, which can be used in many models involving the arrival of products, customers, orders, and patients with some frequency.

The *ABBS_Interarrival-times* model (Fig. 8.18) allows the reader to explore different methods to perform the arrival of new entities with different inter-arrival times: (i) At fixed time (i.e., one new turtle every n ticks); (ii) uniform distribution (from a minimum value up to a maximum value); (iii) triangular distribution (minimum, mean, maximum values); and (iv) normal distribution.

Such diverse examples shown in this chapter have provided an overview of the possibilities of applying an agent-oriented paradigm in the context of simulations of business processes. Next section introduces the reader to a more advanced topic, the process mining perspective involving the analysis or real data concerning the sequences of events and their timestamps, typically collected by log files in the information system of an organization.

References

1. Alameemi, A.: Business process reengineering. Ford's accounts payable study. https://bprford. wordpress.com/2014/03/12/business-processreengineering-fords-accounts-payable-case-study. Accessed 1 Sept 2021
2. Aleta, A., Martin-Corral, D., y Piontti, A.P., Ajelli, M., Litvinova, M., Chinazzi, M., Dean, N.E., Halloran, M.E., Longini Jr, I.M., Merler, S., et al.: Modelling the impact of testing, contact tracing and household quarantine on second waves of covid-19. Nat. Hum. Behav. **4**(9), 964–971 (2020). https://doi.org/10.1038/s41562-020-0931-9
3. Davenport, T.H.: Process Innovation: Reengineering Work Through Information Technology. Harvard Business Press (1993)
4. Eades, P.: A heuristic for graph drawing. Congressus numerantium **42**, 149–160 (1984)
5. Hammer, M.: Reengineering work: don't automate, obliterate. Harvard Bus. Rev. **68**(4), 104–112 (1990)

6. Liu, J., Xia, S.: Computational Epidemiology: From Disease Transmission Modeling to Vaccination Decision Making. Springer, Berlin (2020). https://doi.org/10.1007/978-3-030-52109-7

7. O'Neill, P., Sohal, A.S.: Business process reengineering a review of recent literature. Technovation **19**(9), 571–581 (1999). https://doi.org/10.1016/S0166-4972(99)00059-0

8. Pastor-Satorras, R., Castellano, C., Mieghem, P., Vespignani, A.: Epidemic processes in complex networks. Rev. Mod. Phys. **87**, 925–979 (2015). https://doi.org/10.1103/RevModPhys.87.925

9. Pescarmona, G., Terna, P., Acquadro, A., Pescarmona, P., Russo, G., Sulis, E., Terna, S.: An agent-based model of COVID-19 diffusion to plan and evaluate intervention policies (2021). https://arxiv.org/abs/2108.08885

10. Pescarmona, G., Terna, P., Acquadro, A., Pescarmona, P., Russo, G., Terna, S.: How can abm models become part of the policy-making process in times of emergencies-the sisar epidemic model (2020)

11. Salathe, M., Bengtsson, L., Bodnar, T.J., Brewer, D.D., Brownstein, J.S., Buckee, C., Campbell, E.M., Cattuto, C., Khandelwal, S., Mabry, P.L., et al.: Digital epidemiology. PLoS Comput. Biol. **8**(7), e1002616 (2012). https://doi.org/10.1371/journal.pcbi.1002616

12. Schäl, T.: Workflow Management Systems for Process Organisations, vol. 1096. Springer, Berlin (1998)

13. Sulis, E., Tambuscio, M.: Simulation of misinformation spreading processes in social networks: an application with netlogo. In: Webb, G.I., Zhang, Z., Tseng, V.S., Williams, G., Vlachos, M., Cao, L. (eds.) 7th IEEE International Conference on Data Science and Advanced Analytics, DSAA 2020, Sydney, Australia, October 6–9, 2020, pp. 614–618. IEEE, Piscataway (2020). https://doi.org/10.1109/DSAA49011.2020.00086

14. Sulis, E., Terna, P.: An agent-based decision support for a vaccination campaign. J. Med. Syst. **45**(11), 1–7 (2021). https://doi.org/10.1007/s10916-021-01772-1

15. Terna, P., Pescarmona, G., Acquadro, A., Pescarmona, P., Russo, G., Terna, S.: An agent-based model of the diffusion of covid-19 using NetLogo. https://terna.to.it/simul/SIsaR.html (2021)

16. Vespignani, A.: Predicting the behavior of techno-social systems. Science **325**(5939), 425–428 (2009). https://doi.org/10.1126/science.1171990

17. Vespignani, A., Tian, H., Dye, C., Lloyd-Smith, J.O., Eggo, R.M., Shrestha, M., Scarpino, S.V., Gutierrez, B., Kraemer, M.U., Wu, J., et al.: Modelling covid-19. Nat. Rev. Phys. **2**(6), 279–281 (2020). https://doi.org/10.1038/s42254-020-0178-4

Chapter 9
Beyond Process Simulation

Abstract This section introduces the perspective of agent-oriented modeling and simulation to the recent BPM research area of business process mining. These days, most business process analysis starts from the analysis of real data. A typical application of business process mining is concerned with the discovery of activity sequences based on the information extracted from event logs. A few researches have already explored agent-based modeling in this context. This section suggests some introductory NetLogo programs for dealing with event logs and agent-based modeling based on business process data. First, a process discovery example demonstrates the steps of the Alpha algorithm, with the purpose of automatically setting up an agent-based simulation environment. The second example concerned with the "conformance checking" approach for comparing the real behavior of a business process with the expected behavior. Finally, it is described how to handle the XES format to import data into the NetLogo agent modeling platform.

9.1 Process Discovery

This section is concerned with business process discovery [9]. In particular, it discusses the Alpha algorithm and its implementation in NetLogo. As has been mentioned in Sect. 2.3.2, the Alpha algorithm is one of the first ever process mining algorithms capable of recreating the workflow from traces of executing a business process. The proposed practical application discovers Workflow Nets in the form of Petri nets from digital traces in the form of event logs. In particular, the NetLogo model *ABBPS_Process-discovery-alpha-algorithm.nlogo* allows to focus on a set of activities denoted below with letters (A, B, C, D, E), as follows:

- (i) *Direct succession* from A to B (A > B), if the log includes traces where A is followed by B;
- (ii) *Causality* from A to B (A >> B) if there are traces with A > B and no traces with B > A;

© Springer Nature Switzerland AG 2022
E. Sulis, K. Taveter, *Agent-Based Business Process Simulation*,
https://doi.org/10.1007/978-3-030-98816-6_9

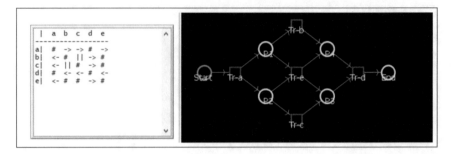

Fig. 9.1 The implementation of the Alpha algorithm in NetLogo with the footprint matrix on the left and the Petri net on the right

- (iii) *Parallel* (A || B) activities, if there are traces with both A >> B and B >> A;
- (iv) *Independence* between two activities is denoted as (A # B).

The set of all discovered existing relations can be represented by the *footprint matrix*. In the NetLogo program, the results of each step of the Alpha algorithm are presented in the output area, while the corresponding Petri net appears in the main window. The program interface has a set of buttons on the left for configuring the model. The output area visualizes textual results, such as the *footprint matrix* explained above. Finally, the view area is on the right. Figure 9.1 represents the output area in the standard desktop version of NetLogo. We already described in Sect. 7.3.1 how to simulate the arrival of tokens in a Petri net model.

The main interest here is to introduce the reader to a process discovery algorithm and its individual steps. From the "EventLog" drop-down menu, one can select a trace. The program comes with two main functionalities. The first functionality can be invoked by pushing the "Alpha Algorithm" button. This functionality entails performing all the individual procedures to print the results in the *output area*, as well as to display the graphical representation of the results in the view area. The second functionality is invoked by pushing the "Footprint Matrix" button. This functionality consists of printing in the output area the corresponding matrix. It also includes a number of dedicated buttons associated with the individual procedures. By pressing each button, one can more closely explore the execution of the individual procedures of the Alpha algorithm. To improve the readability, one can exploit the "3D view" by right-clicking in the view area, as is shown in Fig. 9.2.

Finally, the model is directly accessible online by means of NetLogoWeb introduced in Sect. 4.2.8. This helps improve the usability, as well as the dissemination of the model. The corresponding web page allows to execute the program in a web browser, as in the web repository.

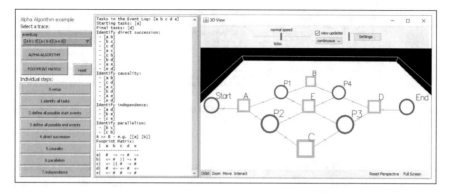

Fig. 9.2 The 3D version of the NetLogo program implementing the *Alpha algorithm*

9.2 Conformance Checking

This section describes an exploratory example which focuses on the adoption of the NetLogo tool to perform conformance checking [2] that was introduced in Sect. 2.3.3. We presented Petri net as a standard modeling language to describe a business process in Sect. 2.1.5. The (*ABBPS_Import-PNML-CC*) model has been already introduced to import a file in the PNML format in Sect. 7.3.2, by starting with the following command:

```
file-open "CCC19-PNmodel.pnml"
```

Here we explore the second part of the program for addressing the arrival of tokens in a Petri net model based on real data. In particular, we exploit the corresponding file proposed in a recent conformance checking competition,[1] included in the web repository of the book.

Our goal is to introduce the reader to how the conformance of the business process model with the process behavior manifested by the corresponding event log file can be checked. In the NetLogo implementation of the Petri net model, the "New Tokens" button introduces new arrivals in the starting place by creating one or more tokens. The "Go" button starts the execution of the model. The movement of the tokens can be slowed down either by means of the "normal speed" bar on the top of the NetLogo screen or with the "speed-of-viz" button in the NetLogo user interface.

From the conformance checking perspective, it is relevant to compare the expected behavior of the model with the real data about the events that have occurred. Therefore, in the NetLogo user interface, the "event log" area includes monitors and buttons to manage the real business process behavior. In this example,

---

[1] https://icpmconference.org/2019/icpm-2019/contests-challenges/1st-conformance-checking-challenge-2019-ccc19/.

```
CASEID,RESOURCE,ROUND,EVENTID,ACTIVITY,STAGE,START,END,VIDEOSTART,VIDEOEND
1,R_13_1C,Pre,1539301115461,Hand washing,Operator and Patient Preparation,10/11/2018 23:00:55,10/11/2018 23:01:07,55,67
1,R_13_1C,Pre,1539301145312,Ultrasound configuration,Ultrasound Preparation,10/11/2018 23:01:24,10/11/2018 23:02:17,84,137
1,R_13_1C,Pre,1539301204591,Anatomic identification,Locate Structures,10/11/2018 23:02:23,10/11/2018 23:02:23,143,143
1,R_13_1C,Pre,1539301214887,Compression identification,Locate Structures,10/11/2018 23:02:34,10/11/2018 23:02:34,154,154
1,R_13_1C,Pre,1539301252286,Gel in probe,Ultrasound Preparation,10/11/2018 23:03:11,10/11/2018 23:03:18,191,198
1,R_13_1C,Pre,1539301297253,Get in sterile clothes,Operator and Patient Preparation,10/11/2018 23:03:56,10/11/2018 23:04:04,236,244
1,R_13_1C,Pre,1539301310093,Hand washing,Operator and Patient Preparation,10/11/2018 23:04:09,10/11/2018 23:04:14,249,254
1,R_13_1C,Pre,1539301317097,Get in sterile clothes,Operator and Patient Preparation,10/11/2018 23:04:16,10/11/2018 23:07:06,256,426
1,R_13_1C,Pre,1539301466782,Clean puncture area,Operator and Patient Preparation,10/11/2018 23:07:25,10/11/2018 23:08:06,445,486
1,R_13_1C,Pre,1539301504204,Drap puncture area,Operator and Patient Preparation,10/11/2018 23:08:14,10/11/2018 23:09:12,494,552
```

Fig. 9.3 First ten rows of the CCC-19 healthcare process event log, from the CSV file imported by the *ABBPS_Import-PNML-CC* model

NetLogo opens a CSV file containing the logs of real events and visualizes them in the form of the corresponding animation. In particular, Fig. 9.3) describes a small example of the CSV file, containing the event log.

In the NetLogo user interface, the "Import event log" button starts the execution of the corresponding procedure for visualizing in the main output area of NetLogo the real behavior extracted from the file. In addition, some sliders allow the selection of specific assets and other configuration settings for the emulation of the business process extracted from event logs. This way, we can perform the *replay* step which is a PM technique for replaying real events from event logs. The visualization immediately conveys how the real behavioral patterns of agents executing the business process do not correspond to the expected workflow. In fact, the real traces of events highlight the tasks to be executed in the order they appear, allowing for an immediate understanding of discrepancies between the event log representing the observed behavior and the model representing the expected behavior. Such discrepancies can then be further investigated and quantified by means of the NetLogo program (Fig. 9.4).

9.3   A XES Extension to NetLogo

The XES standard format [1] defines a grammar of a tag-based language, the purpose of which is to capture system behaviors in terms of event logs and event streams, represented as was explained in Sect. 2.3.1. In this section, we describe a NetLogo program that enables parsing and writing XES files to demonstrate how to generate, write, and read objects according to the XES standard. This model is based on an open-source NetLogo extension written in Scala. The program consists of the library complying with the GNU General Public License v3.0, which is hosted in a freely available Git-repository.[2] The extension implements the following four classes: XeScalaClassManager, XeScalaExtension, XesReader, and XesWriter. It also utilizes OpyenXES[3][8].

---

[2] See XeScala ReadMe file here: https://gitlab.com/amarino/xescala.

[3] http://www.xes-standard.org/openxes/start.

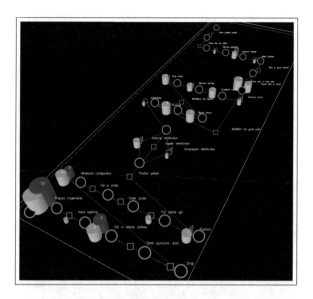

Fig. 9.4 A comparative analysis of two different cases from a compliance control perspective

A practical example of the NetLogo extension is provided in the *samples* folder, which also includes some XES files. Finally, to manage logs of the extension plugin, the NetLogoLogging[4] application can be adopted.

A General Example in XES

The *ABBPS_Manage-XES.nlogo* program makes use of the main features of a XES file. It is worth mentioning that this kind of model is based on the XES extension, which should be properly installed following the instructions in the corresponding *GitLab* repository. Once the extension has been properly installed, one can import the extension by adding the following statement to the top of the code area: `extensions [ xes ]`

Figure 9.5 describes the user interface of the NetLogo program. First of all, one needs to press the "Read XES file" button to import a "general example" XES file and display the different features of the corresponding business process, e.g., the names of the assets, the names of the activities, and so on. The initial exploration of the imported dataset leads to displaying the features of interest in the output area depicted in the right part of the figure.

The *general_example.XES* file contains a well-known XES example in the PM community, which includes information about staff, activities, and costs. The program imports information about activities, which are represented as circles in the main NetLogo output area. Several buttons in the output area of the right side of the user interface enable exploring task and asset information, which can be rendered

---

[4] https://ccl.northwestern.edu/netlogo/docs/logging.html.

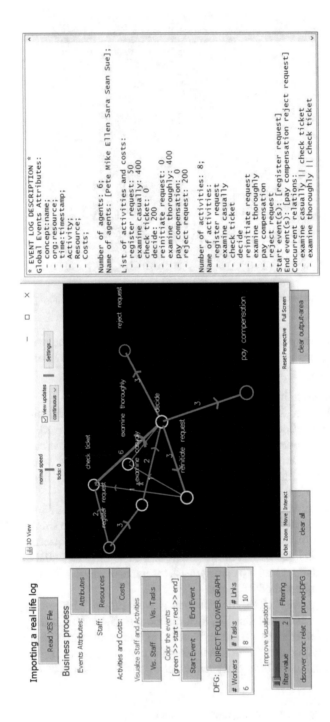

Fig. 9.5 Interface of the CCC-19 example with a DFG automatically created from a PNML file

in the simulation as agents or patches of the environment. For example, the "Vis. Staff" button creates a number of agents corresponding to the assets represented in the XES file, including their local variables. Similarly, the "Vis. Tasks" button creates the NetLogo patches corresponding to the tasks represented in the event log. Finally, the XES extension enables creating a Direct Follower Graph (DFG), which is a graphical representation of business processes widely used in the BPM community. Pushing the "Direct Follower Graph" button performs all the steps toward creating the corresponding DFG, which can be filtered to discover competing relationships and finally pruned to enhance the view as depicted in the main output area of NetLogo. To enhance the visualization, the "3D view" option can be selected by right-clicking on the view area to enhance the visualization.

9.4 Perspectives of Agent-Based Modeling

This exploratory chapter described some directions for investigating the relationship between agent simulation and business process analysis based on real data. This is an interdisciplinary perspective between agent-oriented studies and the PM research area, which aims to extract knowledge about an organization's business processes based on event data recorded in business information systems. In particular, modeling and simulation based on real data such as the log data collected by an ERP is one of the most recent challenges with wide repercussions on both research and industry. We focused on the subject through some exploratory models that allow to introduce aspects of the PM discipline. Recent works have already addressed the use of agent-based perspective within the new scenario [6, 7]. As a matter of fact, some of the main problems to be faced are those of data availability and data quality [4]. The challenges for process mining in organizations include the reliability and the transparency of the adoption of computational and mathematical tools to predict future trends [5], as well as integrating different forms of knowledge from different disciplines [3]. This is the current situation of the integration of business studies, with computer science and its algorithms or applications, from machine learning to computational simulations, of which this work intends to be part, with its didactic examples and multiple practical cases. The examples and models described in the book once again demonstrate that one can start using an ABM platform (NetLogo) as a versatile tool for various applications, providing an educational tool for both parties: ABM and BPM and Industry and Research. The business process management applications tested in the platform, with the practical examples described throughout the book, pave the way for further exploration to apply agent-oriented modeling and simulation based on real-world process analysis.

References

1. Acampora, G., Vitiello, A., Stefano, B.N.D., van der Aalst, W., Günther, C.W., Verbeek, E.: IEEE 1849: The XES standard: the second IEEE standard sponsored by IEEE computational intelligence society [society briefs]. IEEE Comput. Intell. Mag. **12**(2), 4–8 (2017). https://doi.org/10.1109/MCI.2017.2670420
2. Carmona, J., van Dongen, B.F., Solti, A., Weidlich, M.: Conformance Checking—Relating Processes and Models. Springer, Berlin (2018). https://doi.org/10.1007/978-3-319-99414-7
3. Martin, N., Fischer, D.A., Kerpedzhiev, G.D., Goel, K., Leemans, S.J.J., Röglinger, M., van der Aalst, W., Dumas, M., Rosa, M.L., Wynn, M.T.: Opportunities and challenges for process mining in organizations: Results of a Delphi study. Bus. Inf. Syst. Eng. **63**(5), 511–527 (2021). https://doi.org/10.1007/s12599-021-00720-0
4. Martin, N., Van Houdt, G., Janssenswillen, G.: Daqapo: Supporting flexible and fine-grained event log quality assessment. Expert Syst. Appl. **191**, 116274 (2022). https://doi.org/10.1016/j.eswa.2021.116274
5. Rizzi, W., Francescomarino, C.D., Maggi, F.M.: Explainability in predictive process monitoring: When understanding helps improving. In: Fahland, D., Ghidini, C., Becker, J., Dumas, M. (eds.) Business Process Management Forum - BPM Forum 2020, Seville, Spain, September 13–18, 2020, Proceedings, Lecture Notes in Business Information Processing, vol. 392, pp. 141–158. Springer, Berlin (2020). https://doi.org/10.1007/978-3-030-58638-6_9
6. Sulis, E., Di Leva, A.: An agent-based model of a business process: the use case of a hospital emergency department. In: Teniente, E., Weidlich, M. (eds.) Business Process Management Workshops—BPM 2017 International Workshops, Barcelona, Spain, September 10–11, 2017, Revised Papers. Lecture Notes in Business Information Processing, vol. 308, pp. 124–132. Springer, Berlin (2017). https://doi.org/10.1007/978-3-319-74030-0_8
7. Tour, A., Polyvyanyy, A., Kalenkova, A.A.: Agent system mining: vision, benefits, and challenges. IEEE Access **9**, 99480–99494 (2021). https://doi.org/10.1109/ACCESS.2021.3095464
8. Valdivieso, H., Lee, W.L.J., Munoz-Gama, J., Sepúlveda, M.: Opyenxes: a complete python library for the extensible event stream standard. In: van der Aalst, W., Casati, F., Conforti, R., de Leoni, M., Dumas, M., Kumar, A., Mendling, J., Nepal, S., Pentland, B.T., Weber, B. (eds.) Proceedings of the Dissertation Award, Demonstration, and Industrial Track at BPM 2018 co-located with 16th International Conference on Business Process Management (BPM 2018), Sydney, Australia, September 9–14, 2018, CEUR Workshop Proceedings, vol. 2196, pp. 71–75. CEUR-WS.org (2018)
9. van der Aalst, W.: Process discovery from event data: Relating models and logs through abstractions. Wiley Interdiscip. Rev. Data Min. Knowl. Discov. **8**(3) (2018). https://doi.org/10.1002/widm.1244

Printed in the United States
by Baker & Taylor Publisher Services